William John Knox Little

Sketches And Studies In South Africa

William John Knox Little

Sketches And Studies In South Africa

ISBN/EAN: 9783744753012

Printed in Europe, USA, Canada, Australia, Japan

Cover: Foto ©ninafisch / pixelio.de

More available books at **www.hansebooks.com**

SKETCHES AND STUDIES

IN

SOUTH AFRICA

BY

W. J. KNOX LITTLE M.A.

CANON RESIDENTIARY OF WORCESTER
VICAR OF HOAR CROSS

LONDON
ISBISTER AND COMPANY Limited
15 & 16 TAVISTOCK STREET COVENT GARDEN
1899

I DEDICATE THIS VOLUME

BY PERMISSION

TO

THE RIGHT HON. CECIL J. RHODES

A FAR-SEEING STATESMAN

AND

A FAITHFUL FRIEND

PREFACE

SOME whose judgment I value are of opinion that the following "Sketches and Studies" may be of general interest. If so, it will be chiefly because the views and opinions expressed in them have been formed, not by reading books—although I have read everything on the subject which has come in my way for many years—but because I have had opportunities of conversing freely with men who know, on all sides of the questions involved.

South Africa is, for many reasons, one of the most interesting parts of the Empire; and it has before it—one cannot doubt—a great future. It affords examples of some of our gravest mistakes, and gives us, therefore, lessons for the time to come. It is encouraging, as being the theatre of some of the most energetic efforts of Englishmen. I am unable to recount any striking or sensational journeys in waggons, or any hairbreadth escapes in pursuit of "big game"; but to many it may be interesting to realise what rapid strides civilisation has made in a land scarcely known until recent years, and what a wealth of interest and beauty belongs to a region still—as a part of the Empire—young.

W. J. KNOX LITTLE.

CONTENTS

PART I. NARRATIVE AND DESCRIPTIVE

CHAP.   PAGE

I. CAPETOWN AND ITS NEIGHBOURHOOD   15
II. CAPETOWN TO JOHANNESBURG BY NATAL . . . 30
III. JOHANNESBURG, PRETORIA, BOKSBURG, TO MAFEKING   51
IV. MAFEKING TO BULUWAYO, THE MATOPPOS, KIMBERLEY   80

PART II. HISTORICAL

I. CAPE COLONY . . 107
II. THE ORANGE FREE STATE 147
III. THE TRANSVAAL ANNEXATION AND AFTERWARDS . 171
IV. THE TRANSVAAL—THE SURRENDER . . . 201
V. THE TRANSVAAL—THE RAID AND AFTERWARDS 244

PART III. GENERAL

I. CONFEDERATION—THE BARTLE FRERE POLICY . . 277
II. SOUTH AFRICA NOW 290
III. HOMEWARD BOUND . . 310

INDEX . . 323

PART I

NARRATIVE AND DESCRIPTIVE

CHAPTER I

CAPETOWN AND ITS NEIGHBOURHOOD

WE left England, driven out in search of health, in the late summer of 1898. Our voyage to the Cape, like many other voyages, was uneventful and pleasant. Not many hours before reaching our destination, we first sighted land. The Table Mountain and the wild rocky ridge of its attendant peaks rose more and more above the horizon. We passed Robbin Island, entered the beautiful harbour, saw the beetling crags towering above us, and the city lying outspread below, and so, just eighteen days from London, found ourselves one glorious evening of a southern spring safe, after a prosperous voyage, on the long looked for shores of South Africa.

Capetown and its neighbourhood are of immense interest. The town itself is in no way striking, but it is an improving town and compares very favourably with the new towns of America. There are some fine streets, and, gradually, the low houses are being replaced by more lofty ones. The Houses of Assembly, the General Post Office, and the Standard Bank are really fine buildings; "the Avenue," as it is called, is a pleasant promenade, and affords refreshing shade on a burning day. The buildings of the South African College and the Good Hope Hall are well adapted for their respective purposes. The Cathedral, an ugly erection of the Georgian stamp, built in imitation of St. Pancras Church, is spacious and well suited for congregational purposes; the harbour is one of the finest in the world; and in the Docks there is the usual scene of bustle and seafaring energy which speaks of commercial vigour. Adderley Street is a busy and lively street and contains excellent shops; and the whole city, though possessing no buildings of any special interest or beauty, is a town of respectable proportions and capacities.

What is really striking in Capetown is its situation, the actual view from its thoroughfares, and its surrounding neighbourhood.

When the traveller walks in the streets of Innsbrück, he has indeed the venerable houses and the quaint and picturesque alleys of the ancient town; but these are set off by the ring of majestic mountains rising around in the Bavarian highlands and the Tyrol. In Capetown, indeed, there are no quaint streets nor picturesque monuments of the past, but there is a view of majestic mountains. Raising one's eyes when walking in some of the streets, they rest on the rugged cliffs above the town. Directly above it rise to the height of three to four thousand feet the bold and beetling crags of Table Mountain. First there is a slope, in parts clothed with green underbrush and mountain grass, and above this are rugged and threatening precipices. The top, though really broken into gullies and depressions, appears flat, and hence it has its name—a name perhaps too *bourgeois* and domestic for the dignified mountain it denotes. At either end are separate and bold pinnacles of crag, and onward, one after another, continue what may be called the lines of the related mountains, while away before it stretch the beautiful blue waters of the Bay.

To the north-west of Capetown the scenery is very striking. Here is the pretty suburb of Sea Point, a favourite resort of many of the inhabitants of the town. Bay after bay cuts into the coast-land with wild boulders of rock and mountain landward, and seaward the constant heavy swell and fierce breakers of the Atlantic. There is a fine drive here, "the Victoria Road," round the peninsula, which reminds one of the roads winding along the coast to the North and North-west of Ireland, and which commands entrancing views towards mountain, valley, and sea.

Eastward and south-eastward the environs appeared to us even more beautiful. A series of pretty villages or towns are scattered along the bays which on either side open out into the Atlantic or the Indian Oceans, or stud the line across the peninsula—Woodstock, Mowbray, Rondebosch, Newlands, Wynberg, Muizenberg, St. James, and so on. All of these, and—away from Wynberg — Constantia, are of indescribable beauty. Woodstock, a station on the Capetown-Wynberg Railway, is in itself no way remarkable; but behind it up the slopes of its mountain—an offshoot of the Table Mountain range—the views are of wonderful loveliness. Between the railway and the mountain runs the main road for tramcars and general traffic between Capetown and Wynberg. At Woodstock this road is not striking—pretty enough with its fine fringes of eucalyptus-trees tossing their soft sad leaves in the wind, but certainly the least pretty part of the route;

B

but above this, on the rough slope of the mountain, there stands a large Anglo-Catholic establishment for mission work, under the care of the All Saints' Sisters, and a little lower down to the left a small hospital under the charge of an excellent English Sister and some good nurses. To this admirable little hospital we owe a debt of gratitude for the good nursing which, with the kind and skilful medical treatment of Dr. Fuller — an eminent physician in Capetown — restored to health, after severe illness, one in whom we had the deepest interest. It is, however, the beauty of the scene from and around Woodstock Hospital with which we are now concerned. Immediately behind are dotted solemn woods of stone pines, and above them rises the jagged mountain peak. Standing on the hospital *stoep* (or verandah), the eye ranges across the blue waters of the Bay. To the left is seen the shipping about the harbour of Capetown, to the right a part of the flats of the peninsula, until the eye rests on the rugged line of giant mountains which guard it towards the north-east.

It is impossible to exaggerate the beauty of form and outline of this bold range, the outlying sentinels of the Quathlamba. Seen in the evening from Woodstock, and still better a little farther on in the direction of Mowbray, they " gather lights of opal," and recall to one's mind, in the exquisite effect of atmosphere upon them, the beauty of the mountains of Attica. There, the rugged ranges are, like these, greatly denuded of wood, but, like these also, they never suggest to the eye that they are bare, being *clothed* with an exquisite garment of atmospheric colour. Here, and indeed throughout South Africa, the marvellous hues of the mountains and the tender clearness of the opalescent air often reminded us of similar effects in Attica and the Peloponnese, where the Ancient Greeks were

"Ever delicately marching
Through most pellucid air—" *

Farther to the east on the same line of road is Mowbray. The little town has less of the "ragged" appearance of small houses, squatted about anyhow, which belongs to the nearer environs of Capetown. It is the entrance into the well-wooded neighbourhood near Wynberg and Constantia. It has, too, a *character* of its own, and suggests something of the "home" feeling of an English village, with still the fine solemn mountain peaks above it, and the brilliant colouring of South African flora everywhere.

It is here that one is first struck with the splendid avenues of pine which form such a feature in the peninsula. Leading up from Mowbray village to Mr. T. E. Fuller's pretty place—Bollihope—is one of these fine avenues. The pines are of vast height, and on a breezy night there is something weird and ghastly in the sound these giant trees make in striking against one another—where they seem to ache and groan under the lashes of the wind. From this, eastward, the road becomes more and more beautiful. There are dense woods and overhanging mountains. Fine old places are to be found embedded in these woods, and of these the most interesting and striking is Groote Schuur, the seat of the Rt. Hon. Cecil J. Rhodes.

This remarkable man was the younger son of a

* ἀεὶ διὰ λαμπροτάτου
βαίνοντες ἀβρῶς αἰθέρος.—Euıip. *Med.* 829, 30.

clergyman in Hertfordshire. He first came to South
Africa in 1871 on account of the then delicate state of
his health. He entered at Oriel College, Oxford, in
1874; but, having suffered from a chill caught in
rowing, returned to South Africa owing to the consequently injured condition of his lungs. His fortune,
as is well known, was made by persevering effort and
ability in the diamond fields of Colesberg Kopje
in Griqualand, now known as Kimberley. Men soon
discovered that, unlike the ordinary run of money-
getters and speculators—of whom South Africa has
had more than its share—Mr. Rhodes cared nothing
for money in itself, but only for what he deemed the
patriotic and unselfish uses to which it could be put.
The passion of his life became the expansion of
England's influence over the unappropriated regions
of Africa, and thereby the enlargement of that civilisation and liberty which Englishmen have some reason
to believe can be hoped for only—at least in their
completeness—under the English flag. No man has
suffered more from false friendship and bitter enmity.
No man has been more subjected to calumny and de-
traction from the heated partisanship of political
opponents.

His successes have aroused bitter envy in jealous
rivals; his one grave mistake has been condemned
with unsparing violence by detractors who have
seemed willing enough to compass, if possible, the ruin
of his patriotic schemes and the paralysis of his political life; but he still remains, one is forced to confess,
the greatest of Imperial statesmen, and carries on, in
spite of all difficulties and hindrances, the work which
he had undertaken as an Englishman convinced of

England's mission to advance enlightenment and progress and as an unflagging friend to South Africa. This by the way, as the details of the interesting events connected with his name fall rather under the head of history. We are concerned at present with the beautiful estate and house at Groote Schuur, which is to a great extent, in its present form, a characteristic creation of its owner.

The estate itself is formed from several farms which were purchased and thrown together. It includes a considerable part of the mountain range behind. Off the main road at Rondebosch the house is approached by one of those avenues of pine and oak so frequent in this neighbourhood. A short, straight, wide drive turning to the right out of the first avenue leads to the front of the house. The present house, though with all the appearance of antiquity, is really, in great part, quite modern. The old house was gutted by fire almost entirely in 1896. There is a characteristic story told of the owner at that time. He was absent in Rhodesia when the fire occurred; his old friend Dr. Jameson was laid up with severe illness. His friends felt that to tell Mr. Rhodes of the destruction of Groote Schuur was a thankless task, as the place was his home, and he loved it with a genuine affection. "I am sorry, I have very bad news for you, Rhodes," said one of them at last. "What?" he asked, with a look of horror. "Groote Schuur is burnt," was the answer. "Oh, thank God!" was the reply in a tone of relief. "I thought you were going to say that Jameson was dead. We can build up Groote Schuur again; we could not have built up Jameson."

The house is in the best old Dutch style. At the

head of the flight of steps by which it is entered is a *stoep*, and within, two spacious entrance-halls. The drawing-room, dining-room, library, and billiard-room are all lofty and striking, as is the main staircase. At the back is a long deep verandah (or *stoep*), where it is pleasant to rest in the heat of the day, or from which it is restful to gaze in the quiet evening at the changing lights and deepening shadows on the mountains above. The long front is terminated at either end by quaint gables, and the chimneys are extremely picturesque, with a twist like the chimneys of ancient manor houses in England, especially, for instance, Compton Winyates, of the date of Henry VII.

The house has one main characteristic. It is *distinguished* and unusual; the mark of *distinction* is unmistakably upon it, and, like its owner's character, it is the distinction of what has been called "massive simplicity." There is nothing about it gaudy or vulgar or petty. There is no display of wealth, but everything in it is beautiful, real, and in good taste. The furniture is well chosen and mostly antique. The spacious bedrooms and wide airy passages and staircases have a simple dignity about them which is almost monastic in its severity, and yet in no house in the world, probably, are guests made more thoroughly comfortable and "at home." It is difficult to compare it with any other house of its dimensions: like its owner, it falls into no common category. It is unusual; it is distinct.

The grounds around the house are as striking and as remarkable as the house itself. Passing out under the broad beautiful colonnaded *stoep* at the back, the eye rests first on low walls or balustrades marking off the gravelled court from the rising ground above.

On these low walls cluster bougainvilleas, of which the deep hues contrast strikingly with the clear white of the low balustrade and the rich brown of the gravel. Beyond the balustrades rise terraces with steps of old brickwork, and, on either side, flower beds rising up— height above height—to the green turf beyond. But there are no *tiny* flower beds cut out in trim arrangements, but huge masses of flowers—fuchsias, tall many-coloured kannas or Ceylon lilies. To the right, and stretching down past the right-hand gable of the house, are fascinating rose gardens. These are on a large, almost *wild* scale, and yet of the choicest and most exquisite roses. It is impossible to imagine anywhere in a comparatively small compass a greater profusion of magnificent flowers. Farther down, towards the avenue leading to the house, is a further extent of garden mixed and herbaceous with sweet-smelling herbs and flowers. But *the* feature of the flower gardens is higher up beyond the rose garden. Here is a wide far-reaching cavity in the stretch of turf which slopes towards the heights above. This has been treated in a masterly way. Anything small or pre-Raphaelite—so to speak—in detail, would be out of harmony with the stately background of the giant mountain. Instead of attempting to treat this perplexing reach of ground in the ordinary way by laying it out in garden beds, it has been made an extensive acreage of the most magnificent blue hydrangeas, so that there is a wide extent of glorious colour contrasting with the green forest scenery and rugged mountains close above. For when the eye is raised and rests upon the turf in the upper terrace, it meets long lines—like the aisles of a great cathedral—

of gigantic pines. Beyond these are the wilder plantations of oak and pine and silver-trees, and, as a background, the stately mountains.

The forms of the mountains here are singularly bold and picturesque. Nothing of its kind can be imagined more beautiful than the view from the *stoep* towards these gardens, forests, and hills. The exquisite atmosphere, the ever-varying lights and shadows in the crannies of the mountain precipices, the bold colours of the gardens, the deep green of the lofty pines with their gigantic blue-brown shafts, the wide wash of the soft violet-coloured hydrangeas, in every light—in the gold of an African morning, or the opal of the African sunset, or the dreamy wealth of basking colour of the South African afternoon, or the warmer clearer brilliance of the African moon and stars—create a scene which is a constant dream of beauty. As in and about the house itself, so in these grounds everything is on a large scale. There is nothing petty or finikin. Nature and art combine to make it all wide, generous, inspiring of great thoughts, like the character of its owner, as that character was sketched to us, not by mere flatterers, but by *good* men who know him well—a character whose wonderful width of sympathy and breadth of mental grasp and imagination the whole place reflects.

To the right of the spectator as he gazes from the *stoep* or the drawing-room or dining-room windows towards the mountains, stretches a long straight walk, rising up some quaint steps to " the Glen." Here in a cleft of the hillside, deep down, is a wealth of flowers—above all, more of the many coloured and magnificent hydrangeas; while above, under the deep shelter of the forest trees, are walks winding about, and rustic seats from which the eye can range through vistas of trees and flowers over a wide stretch of country to the glorious mountains terminating the peninsula towards the north-east, and where the grateful shelter protects the loiterer from the burning sun.

In England we have a wealth of noble parks and mansions, and some of them are made available from time to time for the amusement of the people; but we are by nature an exclusive and retiring and reserved, if not selfish, race, and among us great landowners, as well as small, are too often addicted—though perhaps not now so much as formerly—to locking and barring and fencing themselves up from all intruders, and to considering themselves aggrieved if others enjoy their beautiful grounds or gardens, unless under the strictest limitations, and in some cases not even then. What strikes an Englishman and a stranger is the large generosity with which Mr. Rhodes shares the delights of his beautiful place with his humblest neighbours. There is scarcely a gate of any kind in the place, and never a lock and key, except in the enclosures up the mountain-side where native birds and animals of Africa wander freely in a kind of wild and beautiful "Zoo," or in the large building appropriated, also higher up on the mountain slope, for some African lions. The whole place literally serves as a great "People's Park." There is never a Sunday afternoon, scarcely any week day, when "all sorts and conditions of men" are not to be found with their wives and children enjoying the beauty of the place after the heat and dust of the town. On great holidays such as Christmas and New

Year's Day—which of course occur in the African midsummer—it is a sight to see half Capetown and its neighbourhood trooping about the grounds of Groote Schuur, picnicking, having games of all sorts, and carrying away armfuls and even cartloads of splendid flowers from "the Glen," and not seldom some of them invading the verandah and peeping into or entering the house itself! When some have ventured to suggest that he was "too kind," and that occasionally the people were over-greedy about his flowers, he only smiled and answered, "Well they enjoy it: why should I keep it all to myself?" Whatever real faults may be his, or whatever invented faults enemies may have placed to his account, one thing cannot but strike a dispassionate onlooker—there is nothing narrow, self-seeking, or small about this remarkable man. Having visited the place, one can well understand the saying of a London newspaper at the time Groote Schuur was partly burned, when it remarked, with perhaps a considerable but pardonable exaggeration, that "the feeling in South Africa on hearing of this lamentable event has been much what the feeling in England would be were Windsor Castle destroyed by fire." The kindness shown in regard to the grounds and gardens is only matched—such is the universal testimony—by the generous hospitality indoors. The welcome given is the simplest and most sincere. The house is a positive *home* for all who may need it, or who may be convenienced by such a welcome. There is not a touch of the *display* of wealth too common among those who have "made their money," but there is open-hearted kindness. All is simple, generous, and interesting. A lady of some social distinction in South Africa observed to the present writer, "To stay at Groote Schuur is to be reminded of 'ships that pass in the night'—you meet and know all sorts of interesting people, and then they are gone." It is a *central* place, and with a world-wide hospitality.

Farther along the road which goes eastward the traveller reaches Claremont and Wynberg—pretty little towns nestling among the perpetual avenues of stately trees. Farther on, also, is Bishop's Court, the residence of the Archbishop. Among these glorious avenues also are the celebrated fruit farms and vineyards of Constantia. Groot Constantia is an interesting old Dutch farmhouse, and here there is the same striking combination of soft and bold scenery—fine vineyards, lofty mountains, and, towards False Bay, the exquisite colouring of the outstretched sea.

Vitteboomen, the fruit farm of an excellent Dutch gentleman, Mr. Van der Byl, is excessively picturesque. Not far from the house, in a corner of the woods, is the weird old burying-ground of the family, after the fashion of the early Dutch settlers. Behind the house and across some of the fruit gardens rises a precipitous and rocky crag, clothed below with the pine and the silver-trees and shooting up above into jagged cliffs—a glimpse of Devon or Cornish scenery with South African foliage, and bright with a South African sun. The Van der Byl family came from the better class of farmer settlers, and is said to have been connected with the great House of Orange. Many of these old Dutch families on the peninsula preserve much of the rugged force and character of their ancestors, and would appear to be among the most staunch subjects of the British Crown, carrying on the better traditions of the past and being superior to a large number of the rude and untrustworthy Transvaal Boers, who are sprung from a much lower class of the first immigrants.

It is impossible to exaggerate the beauty and the unusual character of the scenery in this neighbourhood. Nowhere probably is there anything of the kind so fine. The pine woods compare well in their height and dignity, although not perhaps in extent and density, with the *pinetas* of Viareggio and Ravenna. The red earth is as red as that of Devon, and the underbrush as green as our English greensward. The mountains are more jagged and picturesque in form, if possible, than those of the Abruzzi, and here and there are glimpses or perfect views of a blue and beautiful sea. "There is a thorn in every rose," however. Here, too, as everywhere apparently in South Africa, clouds of dust abate the pleasure of living, if any excuse for flying dust is given by a rising breeze. Much in the scenery and climate recalls the charm of Italy, although one misses the profusion of grey-green olive with its "shimmer of silver" and "twinkling lights," notwithstanding the fact that in many parts of the mountains the silver-trees which are really more beautiful, if not so weird and sad, take the place of the olive with a more brilliant effect.

The railway from Capetown by Mowbray and Rondebosch leads to Muizenberg, St. James's, and Simon's Bay. These are favourite places of resort, for sea air and sea bathing, not only to the inhabitants of Capetown, but also to many from the hotter climate of the north. Here there is always a splendid sea, in some places a pleasant and extensive stretch of sand, and always fine mountain views. The air is ever strong and bracing, and the difference between this vigorous atmosphere and that of Capetown and the more wooded parts of the peninsula is very marked.

Simon's Bay forms a fine roadstead in which large ships can lie with excellent shelter, and here is the appointed anchorage for any of the British fleet serving on the South African station. In the summer months these sea-coast places are full, and in the hot afternoons of Saturdays, or other days when work in Capetown makes less demand, busy men and their families often seek the pleasant change of this invigorating coast.

On the whole, it is impossible to exaggerate the charm of the country near Capetown. Few busy places have such easy access to some of the fairest and most delightful natural haunts in any part of the world. The most striking effects of light and shade over mountains and sea are, perhaps, in the early morning or late evening. The brilliance and delicacy of colouring then must give constant delight to an eye used to the less clear atmosphere of our own latitudes. The loss of twilight and the absence of the gradual coming of the spring are indeed felt to leave the peninsula widowed of some of the most characteristic delights of home; but there are compensations in colour, lights, and woods and flowers, which endow the homes of the Cape with a fascination all their own.

CHAPTER II

CAPETOWN TO JOHANNESBURG BY NATAL

WE decided to go "up country" in the first instance by the coast route in one of the liners. The sea on leaving the Cape and turning towards the Indian Ocean was at first rougher than anything we had experienced in our voyage from home. This, we were told, was not uncommonly the case. At the same time, as far as our experience goes, we had always less troubled seas in these latitudes than are very common in crossing the North Atlantic from Liverpool to New York.

There is nothing striking, so far as we could see, in the eastern coast. It is, for the most part, low-lying. The land gradually rises inland until it attains the heights of the rugged mountains—the Quathlamba (or Katlamba) range—the backbone of South Africa.

It is not more than seventy or eighty years ago since the first European settlers fixed their abodes in this part of Cape Colony. In 1820 a British settlement was formed at Albany. In the April of that year a body of British immigrants arrived. The Government had voted £50,000 for purposes of colonisation, and those who came out showed astonishing perseverance and daring in the face of almost insuperable difficulties. Natural hindrances were in the way of their crops;

Kaffir raids had always to be resisted ; but still they struggled on. In that year, 1820, in the interior, at the sources of the Kowie, there were but few small houses where now Grahamstown is a flourishing and picturesque city. Other places sprang up, Queenstown, King William's Town, and East London. We stayed some hours at East London. It is a flourishing and energetic port, and the coast here begins to be pretty, with undulating land, and woods in some places coming down near the sea.

The boldest scenery near the coast is at the mouth of St. John's River (called by the natives the Umzimvoobu). The mouth of the river is plainly seen from the sea. The mountain here is cleft asunder and through the gorge flows the river. The height of the cliffs at a short distance up the stream is about 1200 feet. In parts they are clothed with forests, and are always bold and precipitous. The boldest part, where the opening narrows in, as it makes seaward, has the name of the Gates of Umzimvoobu, or the Gates of St. John.

We stopped for two days at Port Elizabeth, which is a very interesting town. It was by the settlers of 1820 that the foundations of this thriving port were laid. The policy of the British Government at that time, as so often since, was to avoid expansion in South Africa. The object of the effort to settle a large number of colonists on Algoa Bay was to place a shield of white inhabitants between Cape Colony and the Kaffir tribes. The plan adopted, however, did not, and indeed could not, forward the object of the home authorities. It was soon found that these colonists needed protection and assistance, and so step by step our colonies advanced in South Africa in spite of the opposition of the Government at home. The country must have seemed sufficiently forbidding to the original settlers. In front are sloping hills, far behind is seen the range of the Quathlamba. Strong winds from the sea swept across the dreary hills, and the sea itself did not seem to supply the best possible roadstead. Energy and persistence, however, as usual, achieved wonders. When the immigrants came they had to land by means of boats hauled through the surf. Only a very few inhabitants were there already, and a mere small knot of insignificant dwellings. The first encampment of the new comers was behind some sandhills, the site of which is now marked by the principal street of Port Elizabeth. They numbered over 1000 men, about 1000 children, and about 600 women. The town gradually grew, so that in 1846 the number of inhabitants had mounted to about 4000. Sir Rufane Shaw Donkin had been Acting Governor. The name of his late wife—to whom he was tenderly attached, and whose virtues are recorded on an obelisk which stands near the lighthouse—was given to the town, which has been known ever since as Port Elizabeth.

It is a bright busy place with all the appearance of activity and stir about it. There is a fine town-hall, drill-hall, Athenæum, opera-house, custom-house, and railway station. The electric tramway carries passengers up some very heavy gradients, and from the hilltop above are views of the sea, and, inland, of the mountain range. Immediately beyond the town, too, is a large and interesting collection of kraals of the native settlement. There are also pretty public gardens. There is a fine church, St. Mary's, lately destroyed in great part by fire, but handsomely restored under the auspices of Dr. Wirgman, the learned Vice-Provost (for St. Mary's is a collegiate church), and a nice Roman Catholic Church, named under the invocation of St. Augustine. There is nothing specially beautiful or striking, as far as we could see, in the neighbourhood, but Port Elizabeth has all the appearance of a busy, thriving, active place, and gives a visitor the impression of brightness and vigour. It carries on a brisk trade.

In visiting some of these South African towns, it struck one that the artisan class is the most likely to furnish successful colonists. At present, at least in the more recently settled parts of the country, there is abundance of land for agricultural purposes, and no doubt, as time goes on, there will probably be vast agricultural and grazing farms. But the clearing of the land is expensive, much capital is needed, and though the kindly soil does a great deal of itself to repay man's efforts, there are terrible enemies with which to contend—rinderpest, locusts, storms. But the carpenter and bricklayer and builder and blacksmith and saddler—these are always needed, and, like the prudent and able storekeeper, are sure to find return for their skill. However, in this part of the colony and in the neighbouring Natal, there is plenty of successful farming, and exports as well as imports make the port a busy one. The roadstead is a fine one, sheltered on all sides except the south-east, and much has been done, and further extensive works are projected, for the perfecting of an excellent harbour.

Our steamer then carried us northward along the coast of Natal. There is nothing striking in this coast, but it is pretty and sometimes homelike. It is an undulating country, sometimes grassy, sometimes wooded, especially with low underbrush, often bright with flowers. Every now and again, after a stretch of what appears untroubled solitude, are pretty houses—always with the *stoep* or verandah as a shelter from the heat—and homesteads and gardens, and in the cultivated parts are groves of pines or mangoes or bananas, and fields of coffee or tea or sugarcane. Gradually from this coast the land ascends. There are higher terraces and consequent changes in vegetation; and so with deep valleys, and then still higher terraces, the land mounts towards the great central range.

The highest point of this part of the Quathlamba is close to the junction of the boundaries of Natal, of the Orange Free State, and of Basutoland. From Natal these peaks are very splendid. They rise in crenelated lines of rock—a threatening rampart defending, apparently, the land beyond. Those known as the Giant and Champagne Castle attain the height of 11,000 and 12,000 feet. Beyond the crest, however, there is no great fall. Central South Africa is really a vast plateau: though there are parallel lines of peaks, the country in fact only gradually subsides by depressions widely extended towards the westward. The Quathlamba is really the gigantic rocky wall of a wide-reaching plateau.

From Port Elizabeth our liner made her way to Durban. No town in South Africa made a more pleasant impression upon us than this. For some miles it stretches along the coast-land round the Bay, and then climbs the heights and spreads along the quarter known as the Berea. The situation is beautiful; but also from a commercial point of view the port is of considerable importance. A promontory called the Bluff runs out to the north-east, and this is almost met by the Point, as it is called—a stretch of land running out from the north. Thus there is an almost landlocked harbour. The Bluff Channel forms an entrance to this from the open roadstead. Unfortunately the force of the ocean, when the wind is in certain quarters, has created a sandy bar at the mouth of this channel. Every effort has been made, and works are still in progress, to prevent this bar from interfering with the coming and going of large vessels. These efforts have been crowned with considerable success. The great mail boats still lie beyond the bar, but large numbers of vessels of no small draught cross to the inner harbour. The consequences to ourselves, as to other visitors here, were amusing. It is necessary to land by means of a small tug boat. To be transhipped to this from the mail boat is not always an easy matter. A very heavy swell sometimes rolls in from the Indian Ocean, and it has been found necessary to lower passengers by means of baskets, worked by a crane or windlass, from the larger to the smaller craft. These baskets are large round crates of the height of a tall man, with a door in the side, and capable of accommodating, if we may use such a word, some four or five or six persons as a tight fit. We were fortunate in coming among the last to land, and were committed to the crate only our two selves together. The basket had the door bolted upon us, and was then swung off and lowered to the deck of the attendant tug. As the little vessel rises and falls on the waves, the crate when lowered, sometimes, in spite of the great care that is taken, touches the deck with a bump, more amusing to onlookers than to the caged prisoners.

We landed in Durban on a lovely summer, or perhaps we should say spring, afternoon towards the end of October. The work of getting through the Customhouse was not rapid, but the officials were most polite and obliging. Never have we been struck with the appearance of contentment and brightness anywhere more than in Durban. There are, of course, well-to-do persons and even rich men among the citizens, but the general impression is of the absence of overwhelming wealth and the total absence of poverty. There is a brightness, happiness, and general contentment about the air of the whole place, both amongst the coloured men and the white men, which is extremely striking. Doubtless, as in other assemblies of human beings, there are here sin and immorality to be found when men penetrate beneath the crust, but there is a free, bright look about the place and the people which leads one to hope that these sad attendants on the life of fallen man are less powerful than elsewhere. The consciousness of the presence of these is more thrust upon the visitor—so one felt—in the Transvaal; it is strikingly withdrawn in Durban. The stranger cannot but feel the healthy atmosphere of a free, diligent, contented people enjoying the blessing of a good government and unshackled public opinion—in vivid contrast with the feeling of which it is impossible to rid himself in the neighbouring State, where liberty, both for white man and coloured man, is under narrow restrictions.

In Durban there are a large number of rickshaws drawn by Zulus. These strange little vehicles—new to us—were imported from Japan. There are some in use in Maritzburg, but they seem to have "taken root" in Durban. They are singularly picturesque. From the verandah of our hotel we were amused by watching a "stand" of them. The Zulus who draw the little vehicles are fine-looking men. They have not learnt to vulgarise their appearance by tawdry European dress as "Cape Boys" do, and they delight in wearing the most characteristic and startling headgear. It is amusing to see their little antics, pawing and curvetting in imitation of restive horses, and trying by various fascinating arts to induce foot-passengers to drive in their rickshaws. They are men splendidly built, and seem to draw the light carriage with the greatest ease. It is curious to notice how very often, as far as physique is concerned, the passenger looks a very inferior specimen of humanity as contrasted with the man in the shafts. They go with a quiet swinging trot. For the most part they are used on the level roads and streets. To climb hills with passengers, or even a single passenger, or certainly to climb hills of any steepness, would evidently entail a degree of fatigue that could not but be detrimental to health. They gave one the idea of a light-hearted, merry, contented set of fellows. Their leisure time when waiting to be engaged was spent in all sorts of harmless fun and chaff and frolic. Nothing could be more amusing than the way in which these fine-looking fellows scrambled with energy, dexterity, and good-humour for stray coins thrown to them,—like a pack of schoolboys.

We received, as everywhere in South Africa, great kindness in Durban. Hospitality and kindness, indeed, seem prominent marks of colonial life. There is much kindness in the world, with all its sorrow, if we open our hearts to it; but, in our older civilisation, and in the more reserved ways of England, perhaps it is less fully realised than in newer and fresher lands. Certain it is that in the colonies hearts seem to open with wonderful warmth and readiness—as, I must say, they also do in America—to kin from across the sea. Kind thoughts, kind words, kind deeds, are often heaven-sent messengers, more able and eloquent than many more formally accredited; and it is a happiness to Englishmen to know and feel that the harshness or mistakes of diplomacy are often rubbed off by the kindness felt in human contact, and that the ties between the colonies and the mother country, and, indeed, between our great Empire and the great Republic founded across the ocean by our own kin, are drawn constantly closer, not only by common interests, but by kindly intercourse.

The lower town, as we have seen, is chiefly made up of handsome streets, with shops and public buildings. There are all the usual accompaniments of a busy modern place,—churches, clubs, shops, warehouses, banks. The streets are broad and good; the town-hall is a very fine building. The population is somewhere about thirty thousand. There are a considerable number of native servants, and now a great number of coolies. These make excellent servants, but the influx from India for one reason or another is at present, I believe, causing some uneasiness in the colony. Natal has, as we know, gone through its anxieties, like other places in South Africa, from native wars and especially from the Zulus, but the natives now seem wisely and kindly managed. They are, of course, not allowed to possess arms or ammunition, and they are wisely, and indeed necessarily, forbidden the use of intoxicating drinks.

The Berea is a beautiful district. It rises above the lower town, and is the quarter in which the more well-to-do reside. It presents the appearance of a handsome park, running along the crests of the hills, thickly interspersed with pretty houses. The whole place has a healthy English air about it, and the views from some of the homes in the Berea are of singular beauty. Around the houses are the usual shrubs and flowers of South Africa, and green carpets of grass like English lawns, and from the *stoeps* and the windows are glorious views across the harbour and away to the Indian Ocean. In an evening drive, and then again during a drive on a sunny afternoon for which we were indebted to the kindness of one of the leading citizens in the place, we had opportunities of enjoying the beautiful Berea and the exquisite views towards the sea, and certainly among some of our most pleasant and sunny recollections of South Africa are our memories of Durban.

From Durban we went on by rail to Maritzburg. After leaving the comparatively low-lying lands along the coast, the country gradually ascends in almost regular terraces. These are marked by climate and produce. At first everything is semi-tropical. Here will grow fruits—pineapple, banana and mango, lemons and oranges, and such produce as arrowroot, tea, coffee, sugar, and abundance of Indian corn. Then comes a rougher, wilder country of rock and pine wood, and as we near Maritzburg, a terrace of lands good for growing, and rich in, ordinary crops—potatoes, corn, and vegetables. The railway gradually rises by sharp gradients until an altitude of, I suppose, 3000 to 4000 feet is reached. Through the greater part of Natal up to the border of the Transvaal the whole line is singularly beautiful. Except in the Alps or the Alleghanies, there can be few railways which pass through wilder and more striking country—bold hills up which the engine strains and struggles, rapid descents down which the train rushes, gorges passed by bridges at giddy heights, sharp curves and even zigzags in ascending the hills, and all the while the most glorious views of distant mountains, with peeps of opening plains between the traveller and the great ranges.

Between fifty and sixty miles from Durban we reach Maritzburg. It takes its name from two Dutch farmer emigrants, Peter Retief and Gert Maritz, just as Durban takes its names from Sir Benjamin D'Urban, one of those able governors at the Cape who have had, in proportion to their knowledge, wisdom, and statesmanship, to struggle against the mistakes of the Colonial Office. Maritzburg dates from 1839. It is a pretty town and prettily situated, but we did not find it so pleasant as Durban. The climate, when we were there, seemed to be more oppressive and relaxing, although it stands at a much higher elevation; but then Durban has the advantage of the breezes from the sea, and altogether gives the impression of greater movement and life. At the same time Maritzburg is finely situated. Towards the east is seen a noble mountain, with the flat or "table" top not unusual in South Africa, and in the same direction stretches the valley where flows the river Umsindusi, and round the city northwards are protecting hills. The streets are broad and have a bright boulevard appearance from the rows of trees planted on either sides. The park is exceedingly pretty, both from the undulating character of the ground, and the vivid green of the grass and underwood, and the fine trees. Never anywhere can one see such abundance of weeping willows as in South Africa. This is especially true in Natal, and in the neighbourhood of Pretoria in the Transvaal. Wherever there is water—and in this respect Natal is not badly off—these willows grow to an amazing size, and with a wealth of rich and graceful foliage quite surpassing anything of the kind elsewhere. Maritzburg, like Durban, is essentially English, and is bright and clean, and has an air of prosperity and civilisation. It has a population, I believe, of about 18,000 or 19,000, and far the larger moiety of this is composed of Europeans. It is a pretty, bright place, and has some excellent shops —especially a strikingly good bookshop — and some handsome buildings, though it has not the feature which, in Durban, is so attractive—the glorious views of the sea.

We travelled on again by train to Estcourt. It was still the same wonderful ascent, and the train climbed through a country wild and picturesque. High as it was the heat was very great during the day, but, as ever in Southern countries, there was the sudden chill at sunset, against which the traveller in South Africa has to be on his guard just as he has in Middle and Southern Italy. Indeed in South Africa, though in many respects the climate is most delightful, it is, quite apart from the malarious districts, exceedingly treacherous. It is impossible, with safety, to put definitely aside winter clothing. For though the heat is often, of course, excessive, the changes are sudden, and the quickness of the sunset chills after a burning day is not without danger, as the traveller sometimes learns to his cost. The day's journey from Maritzburg had been very hot, but walking up at night, in the beautiful moonlight, a short distance from the station at Estcourt to the home of our friends, it was in no way oppressive to wear even fur coats or cloaks.

Estcourt was very interesting. The situation is fine. It is a mere village—if village it can be called—and gives one more idea of the country life of the colony as distinct from what we had hitherto seen of the life of the towns. The vicarage was very pretty, and, *mutatis mutandis*, with all allowance for the difference between South Africa and England, gave us a good idea of the life of home. The garden around the house where we stayed was nicely cared for and there were beautiful flowers. There was the usual *stoep* with its clustering creeping plants and refreshing shade in the burning heat of the day. There were one or two well-groomed horses in the little stables, an absolutely necessary adjunct to clerical life in such a place, where the parishes extend some ninety miles in one direction by eighty in another. The servants were, of course, natives, with all their faults and all their virtues, needing, and in this case having, a strong hand but a kind hand over them. There was in the household a boy—the inevitable "Tony"—who interested us much. He was an able little servant, but requiring, as most native servants do, *constant* supervision and guidance. He seemed to me to live in a chronic state of inquiring wonder at all things. He preferred to sleep, I think, for the most part on the mat outside our bedroom door, but appeared to be moved by no more than his normal condition of curiosity and wonder, when I tumbled over him unexpectedly to both of us one morning. A mistress of a house in South Africa appeared to me to have no light task. Though native servants, pleasant in many ways, can do the work well, they require help or guidance, and the fact that they have done anything neatly and exactly as they have been taught one day, is no sort of guarantee that they will do so the next!

The neighbourhood round Estcourt is very striking. A walk up the rugged pathway or track towards the rising ground of the rocky hills gave us opportunities for views down below towards the farms and cultivated country and beyond to the great range of the Quathlamba (or Drakenberg, or Berg as the Dutch called it), where the evening lights and shadows show examples of that unspeakable beauty of atmospheric effect and colour which constitute the main part of the loveliness of a South African landscape. There are many central spots now in the colony, like Estcourt, round which clusters population. There is, in such places, sheep-farming, I believe, for the most part, and the export of wool is a staple commodity in South African trade with the home markets. The vessel in which we made our voyage back to England carried a large cargo of wool from the eastern ports. Stock-farming, too, has been a chief resource on these farms; but farmers have suffered heavily, especially in recent years, from rinderpest and horse-sickness. Indeed, the farmers in South Africa, if they have much to help them in a rich and responsive soil, and, in many ways, delightful climate, have also to be prepared to face heartbreaking hindrances.

In this colony the rainy season is in the summer, exactly the reverse of what obtains in the Cape Colony; and when we were at Estcourt, though the summer was advancing the rains had not come, the consequence of which was much anxiety among the farmers. One of the most terrible scourges are the hailstorms. These are frequent in this neighbourhood and the other upland districts of Natal. They come with such irregularity that, so far, no way of foretelling their approach or in any way guarding against them—even if that were possible—has been discovered. They often pass over a narrow area, but wherever they pass they destroy. Flourishing crops, fruit, flowers, which have seemed to be promising good returns, will perish utterly in an incredibly short time under this scourge. The size of the hailstones is enormous, sometimes three or four inches in diameter, and of very considerable weight. Unless windows are protected by wire defences they will sometimes break every pane of glass in a house; and though in some places there may be a respite from them for years, they may, none the less, appear several times in a single season.

Of course there is also the scourge of locusts, which is common to all regions of South Africa, and not specially, or perhaps in so great a degree as elsewhere, limited to Natal. Another drawback, not to agriculture but to life in Natal, is the abundance of snakes. These are, of course, also common to all South Africa, as well as poisonous spiders and suchlike creatures, but they are less common in Cape Colony than here. A few days before our arrival at Estcourt a gloom had been cast over the community by the death of a prosperous young farmer from a wound received from a black mambra. There are cases in which life is saved and wounds are healed both among animals and men if taken properly and in time, and further scientific discoveries may make cures more common, but at present there is probability of their proving fatal. We noticed that all natives carried in their hands pliable sticks, which are useful for killing snakes with a blow. However common they may be, and certainly are, these venomous creatures are seen much less frequently than might be imagined. Ordinarily they are more afraid of man than man of them, and, usually speaking, will rather try to hide or fly than to attack. When suddenly startled or exasperated, they will, however—especially the puff adder and mambra—"go for" their enemy with dangerous swiftness and vigour.

At Estcourt there appeared to be a united and happy community. Certainly they had an excellent clergyman, and all his efforts for the good of his flock were well seconded by his wife, who, though not really strong in health, was untiring in work. Near the vicarage was a very nice church with well-ordered and hearty services. Not far from this was a clubroom with an excellent and increasing library. While we were there we witnessed the vigorous play of a cricket club, in which the parson took an energetic interest. On a Sunday he had, after his two morning services, a ride of fifty miles to conduct another service in a distant part of his parish, and we were, at Estcourt, strongly impressed with the healthy English vigour of the place both in Church and State.

We left Estcourt—with warm feelings of gratitude towards our hospitable friends, and the pleasantest possible impressions of the place—on a beautiful early afternoon of late October. The railway journey to Ladismith was exceedingly interesting. Natal has been no way backward in making necessary railways. It was the first colony to lay down rails at all, and about 1880 the line from Durban to Maritzburg was opened. Since then it has been carried on to the frontier of the Transvaal. The Natal coal fields, which are very valuable for the colony, have now railways to them, and the engineering of all the railway system in the colony has been a work showing very high ability. The gradual rise in elevation of the country from Durban is, as we have seen, very great. We were informed that every train from Durban, before it reaches Charlestown on the Transvaal border, has risen a height equivalent to a vertical rise of two and a half or three miles. The railway over which we travelled to Charlestown was completed in 1891, and is a wonderful piece of engineering: sharp curves, very great rises, gradients of 1 in 30, and what may be called zigzags over a broken and wild country, are salient features in the character of the line. Close to Durban is the beautiful Manda Valley, and all the way, there is the wildest and most striking scenery right on at either side of the tunnel at Laing's Nek, up to the Majuba heights in the Quathlamba—two names, alas! associated with England's defeat and, still worse—as it seemed to many in South Africa—disgraceful surrender.

We reached Ladismith in the evening. Not far from the railway station we stayed at a very comfortable hotel. It was not very large, and was in some respects primitive. We found the place clean, the food good if plain, and the mistress of the establishment and her servants kindly and attentive. After our evening meal I went out to inspect the town. It appeared, like all such places, straggling and growing, and scarcely yet fully formed. In coming back to the hotel I had to traverse some very "unfinished" roads, and, endeavouring to follow the directions of some of our soldiers whom I met in the street, I completely lost my way. Above, the heavens were bright with stars, but below there was impenetrable gloom. My director, by his tongue, had revealed himself an Irishman, and had characteristically endeavoured to ease my mind as to the absence of all difficulty in my return journey, rather than to give me accurate information as to my route. Before long I found that the track was beginning to climb the wild hills above the town and to say good-bye to the habitations of man. Tumbling and tripping over broken ground, with cheering visions of wild beasts and venomous snakes, I began to retrace my steps. At length a glimmer of hope came as I made out through the growing gloom a native making his way home. I paused to ask him the way. He stopped for an instant, and then rushed past me with a piercing shriek. The sudden emergence of a black figure like myself, blacker than the surrounding gloom, and in such a desolate spot, was too much for his nerves. I must have presented to his excited imagination the figure of the ghost of some departed ancestor travelling from the mountains to work him ill. However, I was fortunate soon afterwards in meeting some wayfarers who were less nervously superstitious, and who directed me to my hotel, which, if late, I reached at last in safety.

We left Ladismith very early in the morning for the Transvaal. The character of the line and the scenery was the same—strange and beautiful. We stopped for a considerable time at Charlestown. Here we were struck by the immense number of natives flying from the Transvaal. There were numbers of open trucks on the incoming train perfectly crammed with them. We had some conversation with a very bright, pleasant fellow—an officer in the Natal police force—who told us that there was a perfect rush of these natives into the colony of Natal. They are at all times treated with roughness, and even brutality, by the Boers, and are chiefly led to the Transvaal by the good wages on the mines. The Pretoria Government, amidst its many liberal pieces of legislation, compels them to work for a year on a farm before they are allowed to go to the mines. Just then, however, the Boers were engaged in their great campaign to subdue the Magato tribe under the unfortunate Mpefu, of the success of which they have been since so amusingly proud, and the natives seem, many of them, to have been seized with a panic lest they should be *commandeered* for service against men of their own race, and so they made their way to Natal.

We first realised fully that we had reached the Transvaal at Heidelberg. Everything marked the fact that this country, which our Government had, in misguided benevolence, presented to a people as unfit to govern anything or anybody as the Boers are by nature, was different in many ways from the colony we had left. Hollander officials were everywhere on the railways. Mr. Krüger—who is said to hate Englishmen with a hatred of the sort said to be felt by those who, it is said, when they owe gratitude to others cannot endure the persons who have placed them under an obligation—and who is too acute a person to trust his own Boers—has placed Hollander officials in every possible post of importance. The Boers, it is affirmed, greatly dislike them, and are jealous of their advance; but they suit the policy of the President and are his docile creatures, and against the word of the autocrat of Pretoria even the law-hating Boer is practically powerless. At Heidelberg, too, we became conscious of the sway of a paternal Government. Everything was doubled in price. The idea of a penny for a newspaper was absurd! Three-pence in silver was the lowest coin accepted in exchange. As for copper, "it was nothing accounted of" in those parts!

As the line approaches Johannesburg the traveller becomes more and more conscious of the proximity of "the Golden City." The railway runs along the outside edge of the Main Reef. From the first sight of the Rand there are all the marks of the usual transformation of nature into an industrial mining district.

"The Black Country" itself cannot be more dreary by day, and more Dantesque and picturesque in its fiery display by night, than the Witwatersrand. There are the great chimneys of the engine works, the huge sheds for the batteries where the crushing, cleaning, amalgamating works go on day and night. There are the cyanide works and reservoirs, and machinery at the top of the mine-shafts—for miles and miles—a strange, weird scene! What was once the wild, dreamy, open veldt has become the place of man's

D

fierce emulation and unflagging activity in extracting the precious metal from the earth.

The train at length nears the town and soon we find ourselves in the Park Station, and a carriage ready to carry us to our destination in Johannesburg.

CHAPTER III

JOHANNESBURG, PRETORIA, BOKSBURG
TO MAFEKING

JOHANNESBURG wore the brightest and most fascinating appearance to us as we entered it. There are few pleasanter sensations than the arrival, after a hot and dusty journey, at a place long thought of and long looked for. Who ever forgets his first arrival in Florence, his first entry into Rome? Who can fail to remember the first view of Monte Pellegrino and the spires and towers of Palermo? Or the first glimpse of the Acropolis across the waves of the Ægean? And though it is a sad falling in poetry from such landmarks of history and centres of art and beauty to the more commonplace and new-born Johannesburg, yet we were conscious of something akin to those feelings of a nobler past when we entered for the first time "the Golden City."

The night was beautiful. The heavens were a mass of brilliant stars; there was little wind, and the air, though balmy, was bright and exhilarating, as it always is in the capital of the Rand, and we were looking forward, after long parting, to meet one dear to us again.

The kindly hospitality of South Africa has prevented us from being authorities, to any great extent, on

South African hotels, but we are able to speak of one of them. Nothing in the way of a hotel could have been more inviting than " Heath's Hotel " on the evening when we arrived. In was well lighted and clean and welcoming. From the pleasant verandah on which our bedroom window opened, the streets with the cabs and carriages and passers-by looked bright and lively. We enjoyed thoroughly the sensation of a new place, a bright, lively city, a brisk, healthy air, and the interest and wonder attached to a town so handsome and so young, which had sprung up chiefly from English energy, notwithstanding the hindrances placed in the way of all improvement and advance by obstinate and stupid misgovernment.

The drawback to Johannesburg is unquestionably the plethora of dust! Dust is always a trouble in South Africa, but dust in Johannesburg becomes a striking phenomenon. The slightest breeze sends the dust everywhere, searching into the crannies of the houses and making the very food gritty, and when a gale is blowing the dust-storms in the streets of " the Golden City " are a spectacle indeed !

On the other hand, the climate of Johannesburg has much in it that is delightful. It stands very high— some seven thousand feet or so—and the air is consequently light and exhilarating. It seemed to us to have all the reviving power of the climate of the Ober Engadine, though, of course, with none of the beauty of its scenery. But for actual *sensation* of vitality and lightness I have felt nothing like it except in St. Moritz or Pontresina.

It is one of those climates in which one feels that vigour and activity are necessities. One *must* be doing.

The consequence is probably, as it is often said by residents there, that people are likely to be worked out and worn out sooner than elsewhere ; and women, so it is said, suffer from the over-stimulation of the climate more than men. In the summer months—January and February—the heat is said to be excessively trying; but when we were there, although the weather was undoubtedly hot, and the middle hours of the day very hot indeed, yet the brisk, exhilarating air and the pleasant fresh nights made up for any extra excess of heat. In winter it is said to be at times very cold ; and ice, and even snow, are not unknown on the Rand.

The town itself is a fine town and well laid out. It is full of all the life and bustle of a great commercial place. There are fine buildings—Eckstein's Chambers, Farrar's Buildings, the Standard Bank, and so on. By the kindness of a gentleman who called upon us, and took pains to show us much of the place, I went carefully over the post and telegraph office. The telegraph office is one of the best arranged and most interesting places of the kind I have ever seen. The managers and clerks are, of course, for the most part Hollanders. The printing office of the *Star* newspaper is also extremely interesting, and I have to thank the officials there for the kindness with which they laboured to show me the marvellous newly invented printing machines, which were of extraordinary interest. The ingenious inventions for *making*, arranging, and setting up the types by machinery with the least possible human intervention are truly astonishing. The Rand Club is a fine building, and there are grounds for races and " the Wanderers' " ground for athletic exercises, as well as two fine theatres. There are churches of the various Christian bodies usually found in South Africa, besides the Anglo-Catholic church (St. Mary's) and the Roman Catholic church. There is also a Jewish synagogue.

Many parts of the neighbourhood of Johannesburg are extremely pretty. The drive round Hospital Hill is quite beautiful. Trees have been planted in large numbers and have flourished well. The views away far over the country, especially about sunset, are exquisite; and the pretty villa residences which have grown up give life to the scene.

The most interesting if not the most beautiful part of the neighbourhood of Johannesburg is, of course, the Witwatersrand. Other gold has been discovered in South Africa—some beds in the Transvaal itself, some in Rhodesia; but these are "reef" beds. The gold of the Rand is in *banket* beds, so called (it is said) from their resemblance to a Dutch sweetmeat, and these are supposed to be much more productive. Experts are of opinion that the output of these mines will continue for many years to come; some say even into the middle of next century. For there are not only "outcrop" properties which are said to be capable of lasting for another thirty years, but the "deep level" beds, which can be worked at great depths, are only beginning to be worked, and will probably yield an immense harvest in the future. From the Rand have come gigantic fortunes to individual capitalists. Companies, too, bring in handsome fortunes to many individuals. For at least eleven miles along the Main Reef of the Rand some thirty-six companies have claims pegged out of "deep level" workings some 1200 feet wide. Beyond the companies now at work, there are some three thousand claims here, which are believed to be certain to give a large "deep level" yield in the future.

The appearance of the Rand is dreary in the extreme, and it is impossible not to feel a certain sadness on reflecting on the life of Johannesburg. There are good people everywhere, but the sudden acquisition of great wealth is not conducive to goodness. The city—if one may be pardoned the expression—"*stinks*" of money! Here men have made vast fortunes; others have hoped and failed. The tendency has probably been, as in South Africa generally, to make men feverishly anxious to grow rich quickly, and to diminish the healthy sense of the duty and dignity of labour and of receiving honest wage for honest work. The madness of speculation has had its fever heat, and fortunes have been made which have proved a curse to those who have made them.

Things would be infinitely better under a good administration, but the tendency is to subsidise and help the lazy and "stationary" Boers, in whose hands England has placed the country, at the expense of Englishmen, Americans, Germans, and of "Uitlanders" generally. Wise and steady and diligent men employed by the leading companies will make their way in a modest and honest fashion—as character, honesty, and perseverance always tell; but it is impossible for any, under the present wretched Government, to take an interest in the country, as intelligent and good men should. To be "hewers of wood and drawers of water" for a less advancing race is not a condition which Englishmen can view with permanent satisfaction, and it is, therefore, not to be wondered at if either great capitalists, or far less moneyed men, should make what they can and then leave the country. This they have been blamed for. It is, however, the inevitable consequence of a corrupt and unjust Government. This temper has to some extent, no doubt, had an influence throughout South Africa. Mr. Cecil Rhodes, indeed, is one of the brilliant exceptions. In him—as, of course, in some few others—you find a man in whom an effort to accumulate wealth is subordinated to an enthusiasm for the advancement of the country where the wealth has been won, to a loyal desire to assist the best interests of his native land, and to an unflagging effort to promote the welfare of his fellow men. Mere money-getting has always its seamy side, and the history of later South Africa has supplied the world with some ghastly instances. The desire for gain anyhow, especially by the gambling of speculation, the love of gain for its own sake, and for the power of self-gratification which it gives to its owner, these create that superheated steam which drives men on in the race for wealth. But religion, refinement, culture, tend to check and restrain much that is dangerous and degrading in all this. The circumstances in which so many men in Johannesburg are placed tend to reduce these checks to a minimum. There are good men and true in Johannesburg. There are cultivated and cultured men. But no one can fail to feel in the place, with especial acuteness, that religion, refinement, culture, are very far from being the motive powers and governing forces. How things may work out in the end, to what the place may settle down in time, who can tell? Meantime the city and its surroundings, so young and yet so full of vigour, is a marvellous testimony to the energy of Englishmen and of Uitlanders generally, notwithstanding the difficulties with which they have had to contend.

Although the climate of Johannesburg and its neighbourhood is bright and bracing, the sanitary conditions are not good. The Transvaal Boer is by nature opposed to all progress and all improvement; and the city, notwithstanding its extent and wealth, is not permitted by the enlightened authorities to have a municipal government of its own. Sanitation and water supply are in a wretched condition, and the place is therefore a *locus classicus* of typhoid fever. No one there, who can avoid it, drinks water, unless boiled or very carefully filtered. Many, of course, are unable to take these precautions. Most people have made considerable use of mineral waters hitherto, but one of the last efforts in finance made by the Volksraad has been to tax these heavily, so that their use must be necessarily more restricted for the large number who are not wealthy. Heavy tariffs, monopolies, and concessions, together with high taxes upon food stuffs, have been hitherto the Government plan of finance. Concessions are now, it is said, less in vogue, and taxation on the Rand industry, which will, there is little doubt, steadily increase, is more likely in the future to be the means found for supporting an oppressive Government, and freeing the burgher Boers from all financial burdens, to which they have a decided objection.

We visited Pretoria. It is a pretty little place. It lies lower than Johannesburg, and is less fresh and breezy; in fact, it was extremely hot. Before the annexation, the square was overgrown with grass, and things looked in a poor condition from the Republic being somewhat "out at elbows;" but since then the money spent by England on the country while it governed it, and the improved condition of finances now that the Uitlanders can be utilised as wealth-producers, have caused things to "look up." There are now some fine buildings. Of these the most pretentious is the Raadzaal or Government buildings. Here are the Government offices and the chambers for the Volksraad. There are some other important buildings about the square, and in the centre a hideous Dutch Reformed church. This, I think I was informed, was to be removed.

The town itself is rather a pretty town. It is surrounded by hills. It has about it, and in it, abundant rose gardens and splendid weeping willows, like those we saw at Maritzburg, and lines and groves of eucalyptus.

A kindly acquaintance, who was intimate with the Government circles, insisted on introducing us to the President. I had no wish for it, as the study of the history of South Africa and many independent witnesses, as well as observation, for long, of the course of events, had not awakened in me any admiration for his actions or character. However, at last I consented and we went. The house in which he lives is a pretty Dutch house, with the usual *stoep* in front, and the railing or balustrade covered with creeping plants. Two somewhat primitive guards, dressed like policemen, were lounging at the gate. A word from our guide moved them to admit us. In another moment we were shown into a drawing-room furnished in an ordinary modern manner. On entering we found ourselves in "the presence." Mr. Krüger was seated in an armchair on our left as we entered.

He cannot be described by his greatest admirers as a prepossessing old man. He was dressed in a seedy, somewhat badly fitting suit of black. He wore his beard after the fashion usually known as a "Newgate fringe." His brow is rather low and his forehead narrow. The expression seemed heavy, and did not give the idea of any great intellectual capacity. His eyes are rather small, his eyelids thick and wrinkled, but these may have been specially so as the poor man was suffering from some affection there; the face is heavy and large, and the mouth wide when opened. His mode of receiving a visitor is not perhaps meant to be unkindly, but certainly seemed gruff and somewhat self-asserting. One was not struck certainly with that "noble simplicity" with which he is credited by his admirers in this country. He looks as if he possessed a temper (although perhaps that is not a defect, when it is well under control), and now that he has succeeded in establishing his autocracy, it is said that the Volksraad, as well as the judicial bench, have learnt to their cost that he will brook no opposition. There is a look of shrewdness, not to say cunning, about the face. The face, however, is less unpleasing when in repose. On the whole one cannot pretend at first sight to be impressed with anything exceptionally heroic.

Doubtless any man in such a position is liable to be surrounded by flatterers, who may be impelled from various motives to present a highly coloured portrait. John Bull is a kindly and credulous person, and the

"Oom Paul" who has been for long and sedulously presented to him has, not improbably, been somewhat idealised. He has been represented to us all *ad nauseam*, as a man of simple habits and deep piety, one fond of homely ways, who has dragged himself, Cincinnatus-like, from the plough to save his afflicted country; one whose indomitable courage and perseverence have succeeded against fearful odds in restoring liberty to an injured pastoral people; one who has upset the calculations of statesmen by a simple faith in God and love of rectitude, and who wrung not once, but twice, from unwilling opponents, conventions so framed as to place the fellow subjects of the statesmen who gave them at the feet of his faithful, simple, and injured burghers. This glorious character of homely virtue and unpretending uprightness, of courage and wisdom, and love of fair play, has done duty for long enough, thanks to the unfailing efforts of the President's admirers and the credulous, kindly English mind.*

To study Mr. Krüger's career and to see him face to face is to read the secret of his success. He is rough, astute, and gifted with immovable determination, not

* I had not the advantage of studying Mr. Bryce's delightful book on South Africa before writing, but my attention has just now been directed to a passage in it which somewhat astonishes me. It is this: "He is one of the most interesting figures of our time, this old President—shrewd, cool, dogged, wary, courageous, typifying the qualities of his people, and strong because he is in sympathy with them; adding to his trust in Providence no small measure of worldly craft; uneducated, *but able to foil the statesmen of Europe at their own weapons;* and perhaps all the more capable because his training has been wholly that of an eventful life, and not of books." Much of this is more or less true. The words which I have italicised, however, are rather, I think, wide of the mark. I cannot think of a single statesman whom Mr. Krüger has "been able to foil at their own weapons." It is true that he may have deluded Mr. Gladstone into a higher estimate of himself and his associates, at the time of the rebellion, than was just, but the action of the Liberal Government, unfortunate as it was, in 1881, was based upon mistaken notions of their own, and upon their political needs at home. Mr. Krüger has certainly had

to say doggedness. He is in fact the incarnation of Boerdom at its best. He therefore well represents the people over whom he has asserted his sway, chiefly, perhaps, because he thoroughly understands them.

They are a people, as those who know them best testify, who have some rugged virtues—the virtue of physical courage, and of easy good-nature if not aroused. There is, however, a dark side to them, and the rank and file are not attractive. They detest progress of any kind; are frequently regardless of truth, and unfaithful to promises when falsehood or betrayal of engagement will suit their purpose. They are subject to alternations of lethargic idleness and fierceness of courage which characterise many wild animals. Some of them are, of course, not bad fellows to get on with, if there is no reason for crossing them. They delight in isolation, detest work, dislike paying taxes, hate all progressive ways, cling to the most wretched stationary stage of semi-civilisation with unparalleled tenacity, and love what is called "independence"—that is, selfish self-seeking up to the verge and over the verge of licence. They are utterly uncultured—indeed have no conception of what culture means; their very language is incapable of expressing high philosophical ideas; and the pastoral home life so much insisted upon by their panegyrists thinly veils in many cases—such is

to do with one great statesman—Mr. Cecil Rhodes—and, fortunately, we may fairly say, for South Africa, was completely foiled by him in his efforts to extend Transvaal rule and all its consequences over other parts of the continent. The fact is Mr. Krüger has been a very fortunate man and has had sufficient craft to profit by the blunders of Englishmen. The unhappy mistakes of others have lifted him into a position for which it is by no means certain that he is eminently fitted, and which he retains probably more by astuteness than any profound statesmanship, and certainly in part owing to the long-suffering toleration of England.

the testimony of the many credible witnesses who have lived among them—the most odious vices. To this—as in any large body of people—there are, of course, brilliant exceptions, but the main characteristics of the Transvaal Boer seem to be these. The Dutch of the Cape Colony are, for the most part, vastly superior. Many of them are of a much better stamp and sprung from a much higher class of the original immigrants from Holland, and they have learnt some progress from their intercourse with the British, and have intermarried much more with the English, the Germans, and Huguenot French.

One secret of Mr. Krüger's success is, as I have said, to be found in his thorough knowledge of the Transvaal Boers, and his being himself a concentrated representation of their character on its tougher and its better side.

None the less the most ridiculous notions of his capacity and his simple rectitude have been palmed off by his interested supporters upon the ready good-nature and generosity of the English people. The simple method of the encomium-writers of the Transvaal Government is to deny flatly all adverse criticism. It is a simple Boer plan, and has its advantages. None the less, it is not, one need hardly say, consistent with facts.

That Government seems to have a consistent hatred of the British race, to whom the Boers owe everything. It has, when now in power, oppressed them and refused them their just rights. It—as they believe—plunders them for the sake of the Boers. The President himself has repeated *ad nauseam* his desire for the prosperity and peace of all over whom he rules. There have been the same canting phrases repeated again and again, and the same—let us call it—diplomacy and what look like broken pledges. But admirers still sing the praises of a simple government and of this "great" and humble-minded man. Cunning and faithlessness are, after all, often great forces.

Other things have helped the President. If he is a not really intellectual man, he is a singularly lucky man, and he has had sufficient astuteness to take advantage of his luck. He has had the good fortune to have had opportunities without end given him by the weakness, vacillation, and generosities of statesmen infinitely superior to himself in actual ability, and he has most certainly had the acuteness to make the most of those opportunities. There is something saddening in the notion that English statesmen should waste the courtesies of diplomacy on the Transvaal Government. These are misconstrued and, indeed, thrown away. It is to be regretted that outraged Uitlanders should continue to make appeals—hitherto certainly in vain —to a supposed respect for right where that respect is scarcely to be found. It is only necessary to consider the present state of things in order to feel that Transvaal Boers can hardly be blamed for their open contempt of the British, when it is remembered that the tactics of our politicians, or their mistaken though lofty sentiments, have made such a state of things possible. Englishmen will for ever waste their courtesies, appeals, diplomacies and sentiments on such people. An *ultimatum* with force behind it is the only thing that ever has or probably ever will move men of this sort to keeping pledges or making just reforms.

It has been the habit of Mr. Krüger's admirers in

literature and the press in England to dwell upon the respect felt by him and the Boers generally for Mr. Gladstone as contrasted with the opposite feeling among the British in South Africa. This I believe to be a thorough misrepresentation dressed up for the home consumption of the English people. It is unhappily true that generally throughout South Africa the name of the great statesman is received in a way painful to those who admired and loved him. This, however, is not unnatural, as South Africans consider that his serious though well-intended mistake as to the Transvaal was the source of all their sorrows. But the Boers seemed to me wholly indifferent or worse. On the occasion of our visit to Mr. Krüger I was entreated not to allude to certain persons or topics which, so it appeared, were likely to hurt his fine sensibilities, or, in other words, make him very angry. Accordingly, I turned the conversation to the subject of Mr. Gladstone, which I fully believed would be a pleasing topic. The way in which his name was received did not strike me as indicating admiration. After all, the Boers who have succeeded in great measure by craft are not likely to be capable of gratitude. They only feel contempt for nobler men whom they think they have succeeded in outwitting, and who have credited them with natures as high as their own. It is only fair to say that there is every reason to believe in the sincerity of Mr. Krüger's religious views. He would seem to be guided by his view of Old Testament teaching; and indeed it is not improbable that many of the Transvaal Boers consider coloured men and Uitlanders alike as Canaanites to be exterminated or kept under by the Elect People.

Mrs. Krüger appeared to be a homely *hausfrau*, kindly and human—particularly human at the time, as she was *crooning* over her youngest grandchild. She had had sixteen children, she told us, and her grandchildren she could not count. I am not sure whether to be glad that we saw the President. It was probably difficult to be fair to him and exactly balanced in one's judgments. I had been terribly dosed with his "greatness," his Bible reading, his piety, and so on, and human nature will revolt against "Aristides the Just"; but, perhaps, had one not seen him one might have had more belief in simple homely simplicity. I suppose the sort of liking which Englishmen have for the ideal "Oom Paul" is a covert admiration for one who has never betrayed his own people as we have ours, and who has succeeded by dogged determination in having his own way.

Thus in some ways I am not sorry to have seen him and spoken to him. Otherwise one might have gone on imagining him to be a "great" though not a cultivated man. When one visits prominent people of whose views or actions one cannot approve the poet Gray's advice to Nicholls sometimes comes over one's mind. It is thus described :

"When his young friend Nicholls was going abroad in 1771, just before Gray's death, he said to him : 'I have one thing to beg of you which you must not refuse.' Nicholls answered : 'You know you have only to command: What is it?' 'Do not go to see Voltaire,' said Gray, and then added : 'No one knows the mischief that man will do.' Nicholls promised compliance with Gray's injunction. 'But what,' he asked, 'could a visit from me signify?' '*Every tribute to such a man signifies*,' Gray answered."[*]

[*] Arnold's *Essays on Criticism*, vol. ii. p. 83.

Perhaps "*every tribute to such a man*" as we cannot really approve of—even from the most insignificant person—"*signifies*," even if he have none of Voltaire's brilliant faculties for mischief. However, it is better, perhaps, in such cases to judge for oneself, and certainly the main interest in our visit to South Africa was seeing and hearing men on all sides of the burning questions there. Certainly we were impressed with the fact that the acts of the Transvaal Government are singularly out of harmony with their constant assurances.

The contrast between the condition of the Dutch in Cape Colony and the English in the Transvaal brings into prominence the iniquity of the Pretoria Government. Indeed, it speaks for itself, and we found that it was acknowledged both by friends and foes. At the Cape the two races are treated as one. Both languages can be used in the Legislature, and in both the official documents are printed, and the members on entering the Legislative Assembly take the oath in either language according to preference. To quote what has been truly said on the subject :

"The equality of the two languages is carried out through all the branches of the Civil Service, and it is a *sine quâ non* that magistrates and all high officials should be as conversant with the one language as with the other. All Government Gazette notices, even in the smallest village or municipality, are published side by side in the English and Dutch languages. Educational grants are liberally made to schools, whether Dutch or English; in fact, in the minutest particulars England has placed her Dutch subjects on an absolute equality with her own."

Why should all this be reversed in the Transvaal? It is surely in the highest degree inequitable that

England should, by a large generosity—whether mistaken or not—create an Oligarchy which seizes every opportunity to treat the English inhabitants in a manner the very reverse of that accorded to the Dutch in Cape Colony.

" In the Transvaal "—to quote again—" the Government use every possible pretext to taboo and veto the use of the English language. Not a single legal document can be registered or deemed valid unless printed in Dutch, although both the contracting parties may not know a word of that language. Every official document and notice issued by the Government, even in Johannesburg itself, is printed solely in Dutch. British suitors in the Courts are forbidden the use of their own language, and are compelled to plead and defend their cases in the Dutch language through means of interpreters—a costly and dangerous method of procedure. In the Transvaal in actual practice no Government grants are made to schools where English is used as the medium of instruction; and this, too, although nine-tenths of the revenue of the country is contributed by the British population. The English language, written or spoken, is as severely checked and discouraged as are English goods and English manufactures." *

This is a state of things which, surely, on any principles of equity, ought not to be tolerated in a State of which our Queen is Suzerain, and which owes its existence to our clemency.

A visit to the Volksraad was interesting. The chamber in which the Assembly sits is a handsome chamber. Two large armchairs are placed on a raised platform side by side for the Chairman and the President, and round in front are a ring of semi-circular benches and desks. It gives to one more the feeling of an English court of justice than of a legislative chamber. We visited the English Residency,

* *Papers of the Imperial South African Association.*

were very kindly treated by Mr. Keith Frazer in the absence in England of Mr. Cunningham Green, felt better at having had our feet on the one spot in the Transvaal over which still floats the British flag, and finally returned to Johannesburg, feeling " sadder but wiser " after a very interesting day.

From Johannesburg, after a very pleasant visit, in which great kindness was shown to us by many hospitable and kind acquaintances and friends, circumstances led us to pay a short visit to Boksburg.

Boksburg is really on the Rand, and not far, therefore, from the mines. The little inn where we stayed for a night or two was of the most primitive description. The people, however, were very civil and attentive, and our sympathies were much touched by an Italian lady, fallen in fortunes, who was filling the post of housekeeper. It was strange to hear in that odd, somewhat desolate place, the sweet tongue of Tuscany, and to have talks with her of Florence and Rome. She had had sorrow after sorrow, as she had lost her husband and her daughter, and the little treasures which were mementos of both had been, I think, lost at sea. She spoke with a despairing self-restraint and resolution which were very touching. She was a religious woman, but so placed that to attend one of her churches (the nearest Roman Catholic church was in Johannesburg) was almost always impossible. Her hopes and thoughts were centred on her only son, who was partly crippled, but had employment in Johannesburg. She was full of a mother's anxiety as to the dangerous effects of the great wicked city on her child. She wrote to him daily and he to her, and fondly hoped that this bond would not be slackened as time went on. Her one hope (against hope) was to save enough to return with her son to her own people and her own land ; but doctor's bills and payment for his lodgings in a place so terribly expensive as Johannesburg had made a large hole in their united slender earnings. She did not complain. There was a quiet, settled sorrow about her which moved our hearts. Her surroundings were evidently uncongenial, and she was as evidently superior to some who had been her employers, and her heart was yearning and "watching through the stars for Italy." How we longed for the means to help her adequately ! How often, in this way, one is tempted in so sad a world to wish for wealth ! Perhaps if we had it we should be selfish ! There are many who have it and who are thoughtful and generous. Alas ! how many also who seem to have no idea of the needs of others, and of how little would ease off burdens and make others happy, and who have no idea of the supreme joy of giving ! *The* thing is, after all, to be faithful in such opportunities as one has, not to judge or criticise others as to the difficult question of charities, but oneself to do one's best. In this case an effort was made by a friend to help to a more lucrative employment, but from circumstances the arrangement unavoidably fell through.

Boksburg in itself seemed sufficiently dreary Thanks to kind friends we had some interesting drives, which gave us an idea of the Rand and of the open Veldt beyond, showing us by its strange loneliness what the Rand had once been. We recall also a walk one late afternoon, and the weird desolation of the track along which we went; but in spite of the unfinished and squalid appearance of things, again the marvellous atmosphere and gorgeous sunset lent to the desolation a mysterious beauty.

One Sunday afternoon, while staying with the manager of the East Rand, a drive was taken with his wife to see a native dance in one of the compounds. We drove straight into the compound and stayed in the carriage for some little time, until the horses began to get frightened with the sticks that were flourished so near them, when we promptly got out, and remained for about an hour and a half watching the dance, which fascinated us in its strangeness. There seemed to be several ways of beginning it, but the usual one is for one native to come out, or rather spring out with a huge leap and a jump from among the rest, and begin prancing up and down before them all, stamping his foot with such force on the ground that all his muscles fairly quiver, and chanting all the time something quite unintelligible of course to us, but which we were told was a story of a fight and of their chief's brave deeds and what they did to their prisoners. At regular intervals came the deep-toned chorus from all the others, and out came at the same time sixty or seventy black legs all stamping like the reciter. The way they keep time is perfectly marvellous, and their voices are strangely pathetic and almost musical. Then abandoning the prancing motion, the reciter grows more and more excited, and jumps and flings himself wildly about, stirring himself and his friends up to such a degree that they appear hardly to know what they are doing. Luckily they are not allowed arms of any kind, only sticks, and with one wild fling up, *that* reciter retires and another comes out. There were eighteen hundred of them in that compound, and all looking very contented and happy, otherwise we should probably have felt nervous, especially as, when they work themselves up into such states of excitement, the reciters do not seem to mind where they jump. Some of them were got up in regular war costume, others with any old uniforms they could find. Many were playing audience and applauding. But what they applauded most was one of the dancers suddenly bursting into the ring and doing the wheel trick on hands and feet like the London street boys, which to them seemed amazing and masterly, though to us, of course, it was anything but novel.

In the month of November I left Boksburg for Rhodesia. There was a certain sorrow and also a certain relief in preparing to leave the Transvaal. It is quite impossible for any healthy-minded Englishman not to feel a sense of depression in a country handed over by the faults or follies, or even virtues, of his own Government to a people behindhand in civilisation and devoid, apparently, of any idea of justice. On the other hand, many of the English and Americans in the Transvaal had been exceedingly kind to us, and a great deal that one had heard and seen was full of interest. One must have always a kindly feeling for this district of country, and wish it a happier future than at present seems probable.

I went by train to Krügersdorp. This place seemed to be a quiet commonplace Transvaal town, with nothing remarkable about it. There was a fairly good hotel and a few good shops. The day was windy, and the dust, as usual in South Africa, and especially in the Transvaal, was blinding, and the weather very hot.

It had been stated at the office in Johannesburg that the coach ran in connection with the train, and that it would start immediately on the train's arrival. Such, however, was not the case. There had been some confusion in a distant telegraph office, and the authorities in Pretoria had been obliged to send an official to take up the work in that place. A message was, therefore, telegraphed to Krügersdorp that the coach was to wait until the arrival of the official in question. All the passengers who had arrived by the special train, as well as the mails, had, therefore, to spend the day in the heat, dust, and dulness of Krügersdorp until the young man of the telegraph, accompanied by two detectives in disguise who were being sent to Mafeking, appeared in the evening. Such are the blessings attendant upon the paternal government of "Oom Paul"!

We left Krügersdorp about 6 P.M. It was a glorious evening. The coach inside was packed like a sardine-box, chiefly with Government officials and children. How they endured that night it is hard to imagine, but whenever they did emerge at any station in the course of the night they seemed kindly, genial, and good-tempered, if a little cramped in the limbs! On the roof of the coach was a fat, comfortable old Boer, who snored contentedly in sunshine or storm under shelter of a huge tarpaulin. I was on a seat behind the coachman, with a coloured "boy" who acted as a kind of guard. The coachman was a very fat, contented, and good-tempered-looking Boer, who wielded a mighty whip with astonishing dexterity; and, beside him, a "boy" who held the reins, and was one of the best drivers I have ever seen. We had a team of twelve horses, and very fine and well-kept horses they were. South Africa is a land of team-driving, whether in waggons, coaches, or large long carts. One constantly sees from eight to twelve horses or mules, and sometimes more.

It was a glorious evening as we left Krügersdorp. The sun was setting with a pageantry of splendour, but far away on the horizon were ominous banks of piled-up clouds.

The road for a time was a fairly good road, but it soon became little more than a track over the open Veldt, and at times was little else than a watercourse. Above, the sky was brilliant with stars, but below it appeared to me to be in complete shadow. We went through rolling country, down considerable hills and up equally steep rises, and all around right up to the horizon the mysterious distances of the open Veldt. We went at a swinging pace. The old coach, which sounded sufficiently creaky but was sound and strong, I was told, groaned and heaved and swung from side to side. At times we just grazed a mighty rock, at times travelled over a huge boulder, with every probability of an upset; but the horses seldom slackened, the driving seemed to me quite miraculously excellent, and we righted quickly after what at first appeared imminent peril, and on we went. Now and again the man with the whip played a rousing tune on his horn to warn those whom he descried in the distance. How he could see anything was a mystery to me, for on the road or track everything appeared of equal darkness. However, he *did* detect dangers ahead, for, soon after the blowing of the horn, we were sure to find some cart or waggon with a long team of donkeys, or more frequently mules or horses, drawn aside as far as possible from our course to avoid collision. Often we saw in the dim starlight waggons of wandering Boers drawn up for the night on the Veldt, or the fires burning at some Kaffir kraals, or stray watch-fires of some wanderers—like many a young Englishman after the Matabele rising was over, tramping it from Rhodesia to Johannesburg to seek his fortune.

Like the pampas in South, and the prairies in North, America, the wide open Veldt has a mysterious sentiment of its own. These vast spaces of apparently boundless rolling country, stretching away to the distant horizon of the starry heavens, with no sound but the sighing of the breeze for miles and miles, awaken those undefined longings and strange dreams which come so mysteriously to man when brought in contact, so to speak, with Silence, Solitude, Immensity. Men are given to smiling—almost sneering—at themselves for allowing such dreams; but there are few, except perhaps the coarsest and most blunted, to whom they do not come : the immortal spirit is conscious in such scenes and at such times of its kinship to infinity ; and the human heart pressed upon then, more than ever, by silence and distance, wakens to the tenderest touches of affection and sadness, and is most alive to the pathetic memories of Home, and "the sorrow's crown of sorrow" in "remembering happier things." In the wide weird sweep of the Veldt, even the creaking, swaying coach is forgotten, and is not powerful enough to hinder the play of dreams.

As we travelled on, however, dreams were disturbed by the low rumbling of thunder along the horizon, and soon began, in the distance, the pageantry of a splendid storm. For a *roar* of thunder, for vivid, varied, many-coloured, and scarcely intermitting forks and zigzags and *streams* of lightning, commend me to a South African storm! Nothing so magnificent have I ever seen before, either in the Alps or in America or on the open sea. We were still spectators without being sufferers. All round the horizon in front of us were ramparts of tremendous clouds, and the play of Nature's artillery, the splendid spectacle of Veldt, and cloud, and sky, as seen under the illumination of the lightning and the density of darkness between the frequent flashes contrasted with the dazzling brilliance, formed one of the most awful and glorious spectacles which it is possible to imagine. We were evidently driving at a rapid rate into the storm. A few heavy drops of rain had begun to fall just as we neared the first post-house. The horses were changed and on we went. We had not gone far, however, when we were aroused from any possible dreams by the stopping of the coach and the announcement of the coachman that we must camp out where we were, as it was perfectly impossible to see the track from the fierceness of the lightning, and the depth of the darkness which followed every flash, and that our journey could not, with safety, be pursued. How he had succeeded in distinguishing the track so far was to me perfectly marvellous, and in spite of the delay and discomfort, I think every one in or on the coach drew a sigh of relief on learning the decision of the driver; and afterwards when in the early dawn I saw something of the track we had to pursue, I felt surer than ever that that decision was wise.

Those inside the coach were safe enough. My Boer

friend under his tarpaulin seemed to be disturbed by nothing, the driver and the "boys" took to waterproofs and covers; various rugs were thrown over the horses. One of the travellers and myself preferred to descend and look for shelter elsewhere, for as for me, as I was travelling "in light marching order," no sort of protection could be had, unless I sheltered under the snoring Boer on the top of the coach! We accordingly elected to go, and having had a promise from the coachman that his horn should be sounded when ready to make a move, we ran for it. The rain had been coming and now it came. We were fortunate in finding refuge, almost immediately, in a little track-side store. Yes! the rain had been coming and now it came! Every one who has been in South Africa or in the tropics knows what rain is. Here one hardly knew which were the more incessant and indeed continuous, the sheets of water or the sheets of fire, and one could not resist a wondering fancy, Would the fire dry up the water, or the water extinguish the fire?

Fortunately for us, we were snug and safe in the kindly shelter of the store, and from that vantage ground we watched the splendid fury of the storm. How many hours we sheltered there I cannot tell. It seemed a long time. At last came the sound of the warning blast, and through what now was mud and slush and water we struggled back to our coach. The hollow where the coach stood was little else than a rushing stream, and when we started we soon became aware that our track lay through what seemed to be little else than a raving torrent, or over huge stones tumbled here and there by the rush of the rain. On we dashed in the dimmest grey light of morning, swinging and swaying and bouncing and rolling and splashing, over rough rocks, through deep mud, and across fierce *spruits* where water dashed along up to the wheel-axles; and so we descended and ascended until by a more or less steady rise we reached the highest and most open plateau of the Veldt. As daylight crept up, gradually objects became clearer. We made two stops and two changes of horses or (now rather of) mules, before we reached the highest watershed. The night sky was beautiful : there were splendid stars, and, after the tempest, fine, feathered, ragged clouds flung about the heavens, torn from the wings of the storm ; then the grey light came creeping up, then gradually there was a glorious sunrise ; but all that night and morning the cold on top of the coach was bitter. Never have I felt greater extremes of heat and cold than on my perch on that Krügersdorp coach. The night was almost icy, the following day grilling ! We paused at a little upland store at early sundawn. Then all the inhabitants of the coach assisted the "boys" at the store in lighting a fire and brewing some coffee. Never to a poor frozen mortal, with chattering teeth and aching bones, was coffee better than what we had that morning !

Along the Veldt we soon began to meet waggons, where the horses were being *inspanned*, and lines of Kaffirs marching out from their kraals to their work. Gradually the track descended, and we swept by many a rapid curve and down many a steep "brow" off the open Veldt into one of the prettiest "dips" of country possible to be imagined.

The name of the lovely little place at which we halted was not attractive. For some reason, not apparent, it called itself "Lead Mines"—if I remember rightly—but anything less like "Lead Mines" it is difficult to imagine.

The road descending an abrupt hill—reminding one of a Cornish or Devonshire lane—swept round a curve as abrupt. On the one side appeared to be hayfields, and by the road a deep and shadowy copse. On the other, a sparkling, rushing stream, bordered with willow, arum lilies, grass, and flowers; and before us, nestling in roses, bougainvilleas, and trailing shrubs bright with blossom, a cosy little wayside inn. It was all in striking contrast, in its bright and homelike beauty, to the bare and storm-swept Veldt.

Here we had the tidiest arrangements made for a refreshing wash and a comfortable breakfast, and—strange to say within the borders of this expensive Republic—at very reasonable charges.

The rest of the journey, all that day and into the late evening or early night, was through country most of which was extremely pretty. A part of the track ran for miles through wild but attractive and parklike scenery, so that, but for a difference in the *kind* of flowering shrubs, and some of the trees, and but for a greater wildness, a more tropical flora, an African sun of no gentle degree of warmth, and the absence of anything (except rarely) like a human habitation, much less like an English home, we might have been almost tramping through such places as Yoxall Lodge or Byrkley Lodge in Staffordshire. The day was splendid, the heat intense, the pace at which we travelled rapid, and the handling of the long team, either of mules or horses, masterly. The "boy" with the reins showed wonderful promptitude and dexterity, and we had, so it appeared to the uninitiated, thanks to that dexterity, many a hairbreadth escape from upset. He seemed to be prepared for all possible and impossible emergencies. The man with the whip used it seldom, but, when he did, with astonishing deftness; usually, however, he spoke to the individuals of the team, especially when we had horses, addressing them by name.

The last stage was done with a team of horses, and over a broad and excellent road, and that last fourteen or fifteen miles we travelled at a rattling pace. We had journeyed the route of the Raid, but this I tried to forget all night and all day, as an Englishman does not care to dwell upon that ill-starred expedition! Our drive in more peaceful times had been interesting, and through scenery often beautiful; but we were not sorry when, very late in the evening, and surrounded by a wondering crowd astonished at our delay, we stopped at last at Mafeking.

CHAPTER IV

MAFEKING TO BULUWAYO, THE MATOPPOS, KIMBERLEY

MAFEKING seemed a quiet little place with not very much going on. There were rows of trees to give shade in the heat round the principal open space or square, and some very fair shops. The hotel, for a place of that size, though in some respects primitive as many hotels in South Africa, was clean and comfortable, and my sleeping-room opened on to a verandah, or rather a sort of courtyard, which was cool and shaded, and grown over with creeping plants. In all the few hotels in which I happened to stay there was the comfort of excellent bathrooms. This was a real comfort, as the weather was very hot.

Talking of heat, I observed generally in South Africa —indeed, I had too much reason to observe it on the top of the Mafeking coach!—that however great the heat was during the day, the nights were fairly cool. If this is so, it seems to be a great improvement upon India, where one hears so many groans over the heat of the nights following the heat of the burning day.

I left Mafeking by train for Buluwayo. The journey was interesting if only for this, that it was over the new line which has been carried through with such astonishing energy and vigour. Few things bring home to one's mind the marvellous force and perseverance of our countrymen more than the fact that Buluwayo was, about four years ago, the seat of government—we should rather say, of massacre—of a bloodthirsty savage, and that now travellers can take return tickets by steamboat and railway from London to Buluwayo!

The railway carriages are well built and exceedingly comfortable. At present there is only a single line of rails, but land is reserved at either side for a second line when needed. The gauge is slightly narrower than that usually employed in England, but there is no sense of being cramped in the carriages. These are "corridor" carriages and very well ordered. The rate of travelling is, of course, very moderate, as some of the gradients are considerable, and the trains are very commonly composite—acting as passenger and goods trains in one; and in some parts of the line where water is not plentiful, tanks of water have to be carried with the train. The travelling is astonishingly smooth, and the *finish* of the line, considering its great extent and the rapidity of its construction, is very remarkable. The journey from Mafeking lasted for about—very nearly—two nights and two days. At many places where the train stopped there were opportunities for getting excellent coffee or milk or mineral waters, and at some places there were longer stoppages for regular meals. These, considering the remote part of the country, were fairly good, and fairly inexpensive—*very* inexpensive as contrasted with the exorbitant prices of the Transvaal. Here, however, the traveller finds himself no longer under an unenlightened and despotic but under a free Government.

The line passes through Bechuanaland from Vryburg, some short distance south of Mafeking, to the Shashi River, where it crosses into the Matabeleland part of Rhodesia. Bechuanaland, like Rhodesia, is British territory. A part of it—that which borders on the Cape Colony—is called British Bechuanaland, and the part north of this, which includes "Khama's Country," is known as "the British Protectorate." Through this British territory, and that north of it, pass the line and the telegraph—at present to Buluwayo, and before so very long, it is hoped, to Tanganyika by Salisbury, and so on to join our railway at Khartoum and our Egyptian possessions. Bechuanaland is interesting in its history as an example of English vigour and adventure, and the disasters only just averted thereby, which might well have happened through the hesitation of the English Government.

The inhabitants of Bechuanaland have been, ever since our explorers have first known them, a gentle and reasonable race as compared with some of the other native races with whom Europeans have had to do. Among these were the various tribes of the Bangwaketse, Bakmena, Baralong, Battaros, and Bataplin. The Bechuanas had stations for hunting in the Kalahari desert, which lies to the east of them and on the border, and here the natives subject to them, the Bakalahari and the Bushmen, acted as slaves to them or paid tribute. Missionary efforts have been made with steadiness and self-devotion among some of these for a long stretch of years. Dr. Livingstone, before he began his pioneering explorations, had worked among some of them. But the most important name among the missionary labourers in this part of Africa is, without question, that of Dr. Moffat. He and others worked here with ability and self-devotion for many years, and they have been followed by others in the same field of labour, and Dr. Moffat's son is one of the most energetic and excellent missionaries in more recent times.

The great achievement of these missionaries has been the conversion and education of Khama, the chief of the Bamargwato, which is the most important of the Bechuanas, and who is nominal King of this region. As of the missionaries' works, so of their chief converts in these parts, there are, of course, very conflicting opinions. Missionaries in South Africa have undoubtedly done a great deal of good as well as a great deal of harm. The extreme statements on both sides of the question have—as such statements usually have —to be discounted a good deal. There is probably truth *and* exaggeration on both sides. Khama is a case in point. Those who do not hold him in high esteem represent him as an ambitious and headstrong boy, making Christianity an excuse for rebellion against his father, and then acting in the most arbitrary way towards his own people, and governing by a system of *espionage* which destroys all confidence between man and man. They represent him as having behaved with gross ingratitude and high-handed injustice to his adviser and friend, the Rev. Mr. Hepburn. He had asked for our protection, and it is thought that, since it was extended to him, he has behaved like a spoilt child. It is probable that, with a touch of our kindly, sentimental folly, his being taken to London and " made a great man of" turned his head. Spasms of

this kind of false philanthropy come over us at times,
and usually do harm. Savages—even the best—are
not, and probably cannot be until generations have
passed, in a condition to understand or appreciate such
treatment. Like the semi-civilised Dutch Boer, they
think that kindness means fear.

Such is one view. There is another according to
which Khama is represented as "the wisest and most
enlightened of African chiefs," and one "to whose
splendid character traders, hunters, travellers, and the
highest officials unite in bearing testimony."* This is
a high encomium, but one cannot but suspect that it
is somewhat over-coloured and to be received with
reserves.

The history of our relation to Bechuanaland is also
interesting.

The Boers of the Transvaal, after they had first
obtained the recognition of their territory as an independent Republic, began to extend their borders.
Raids have always been familiar to them, and they
raided the natives, destroyed a part of the Zulu power,
having beaten Mozilekatze. But President Pretorius
determined to go further. He boldly issued a proclamation declaring the boundary of the South African
Republic to extend to Lake Ngami. This would
have absorbed the Hinterland and crossed the path
of all British — *i.e.*, of all civilising advance to the
north. At the same time, pretensions were put
forward to the possession of Delagoa Bay. This was
intolerable. "Consideration," as it has been well said,
"both of native rights and of Imperial responsibilities

---

* *Cf. The Illustrated Official Handbook*, chap. xxii.; *cf.*, *per contra*, Deele's *Three Years in Savage Africa*, pp. 36-38.

barred the way to the admission of such claims."*
The British Government at last woke up, and Pretorius,
through the firmness of Sir P. Wodehouse, then
Governor at the Cape, was obliged to withdraw the
proclamation. This is interesting as one of the first
clear indications of the schemes of the Pretoria
Government. This Government, at the time, was
indeed little else than confusion and anarchy, but the
spirit of licence and freebooting, of disregard for the
rights of others, and hatred and scorn for the native
races, was there. And the struggle was then, has been
ever since, and is now, whether a low state of civilisation, reactionary doctrines, stagnation, and tyranny
shall be paramount in South Africa under the guidance
of a Boer *régime*, or enlightened freedom and progress
under British rule.

As time went on there were troubles on the frontier
between Boer raiders and the Bataplin tribes. In
1882-83 a new and powerful figure in the political
life of South Africa had appeared in Mr. Cecil Rhodes.
When on the Commission for delimitation of frontier
in Griqualand, he found that, however filibustering
had been the attacks from the Transvaal, farms had
been taken up, and could not without some injustice
be reclaimed. For the protection of Mankaroane and
the resisting of Transvaal encroachments, a cession of
this part of Bechuanaland was by his instrumentality
obtained from Mankaroane. The Cape Colony, however, refused the cession. The Home Government
were then urged to accept it. This they decided to do
on condition that the Cape Government would be
responsible for half the cost of the administration.

* Egerton's *British Colonial Policy*, p. 412.

This, however, was again refused, but matters were brought to a head by the attitude of the Transvaal Government in 1884.

Mr. Mackenzie, a missionary stationed at Kureinam, was a man of force and character. The Transvaal delegates in London, under the inspiration of Mr. Krüger, were engaged in wringing from Lord Derby the unfortunate Convention of London. They had their eye on further expansion. Mr. Mackenzie, however, was too much for them. For once they were outwitted and "hoist with their own petard." They had gained their ends in 1881 by working upon the political bias and the mistaken philanthropic feelings of Mr. Gladstone and the men of "the Nonconformist Conscience." Mr. Mackenzie, however, was connected with the "Free Church Missionaries' Societies," and had himself, so to speak, the *entrée* to "the Nonconformist Conscience." Crowded public meetings were held throughout the country, the foremost Radicals urged upon the Government the need and duty of a forward policy, and, above all, the movement found support from Mr. Forster, whose influence, ability, and simple sincerity of purpose were of enormous value. The Transvaal tactics were made clear, and once and for all their "pretentions to unlimited expansion" were denied. Mr. Krüger's objects and methods were practically unmasked to those who had before been deluded on the subject, and it is probable that since then the Radical party have been too honest not to feel some unpleasant misgivings as to the "righteousness" of the course pursued, under, as is generally thought in South Africa, a considerable misapprehension in 1881.

Mr. Cecil Rhodes succeeded Mackenzie shortly

afterwards as Deputy-Commissioner in Bechuanaland. Sir Hercules Robinson and Mr. Rhodes have been blamed for their attitude towards Mackenzie as to the difficulties on the frontier; but, rightly or wrongly, they seemed to believe that they were acting with fairness to the Dutch who had acquired land, but that they could be firm towards the Transvaal Government. Offers made were refused by General Joubert, who tried to annex the territory, and was not content with the Dutch holding property under English rule. Krüger's enterprise, as conducted by Joubert, was of the usual Boer character. The Boers did not hesitate to slaughter numbers of natives under British protection and to seize their property. Commander Bethell was murdered by the Transvaal men, nor was any compensation ever paid by the Transvaal—a fact to be remembered in conjunction with the recollection of the way in which the Pretoria Government enriched itself, without any remonstrance from the English Government, at the time of Dr. Jameson's expedition.

Then came Sir Charles Warren's expedition. It was a conspicuous success. Mr. Krüger's effort to seize this central region—the key to South Africa—was defeated. In 1885 the proclamation was issued extending the Queen's sovereignty, up to the Malopo River, over British Bechuanaland, and shortly afterwards the Protectorate was declared. It was through this country that we travelled.

The country itself is undulating. In the distance, indeed, are lines of distant mountains. It was hot when I travelled through it, but the views of the mountains were most beautiful, and the sunset clouds and frequent thunderstorms were often very grand.

It appeared well wooded, and at times so thick are the woods that they often reach the dimensions of forests. There seemed to be plenty of pasturage, and it is said that the country if opened up would be excellent for ranching, and peculiarly suitable for cattle, but just now it had not recovered from the rinderpest. There are large and excellent native reserves. As far as one could judge from what appeared along the line and at the stations, the natives were poorly off from want of rain and from the results of the rinderpest. The country, however, was so fresh and green that it seemed evident that some day proper irrigation would be possible.

This district will probably be slowly developed. It seems a fine country, and is believed—as I have said—to afford splendid tracts for ranching purposes—finer than anything in America. What is needed for it, as well as for Rhodesia, is capital. To clear and to irrigate appear to be necessary, and these operations need money. It is to be hoped that, with our frightfully congested condition in England, every encouragement will be given to large immigration. What the mineral wealth may be of this region no man knows. Even in Rhodesia, —though something is known of the mineral resources of Matabeleland—Mashonaland has been very imperfectly if at all examined. Mines and mineral wealth are of enormous importance in helping to start a new country. In the Transvaal the mines and the energies and enterprise of the oppressed Uitlanders have been, as we know, invaluable for the support of a helpless government and lazy unprogressive farmers. Still the development of this fine region now open to British enterprise will be effected, probably, more gradually and in a healthy way by vigorous Englishmen, not all expecting to grow rich with feverish rapidity, but to earn the fruits of honest labour in regions which Nature has made to repay the efforts of energetic and patient workers. More colonists and more capital are needed for Rhodesia, and also for Bechuanaland. These, one can have little doubt, will come. Bechuanaland is invaluable as a road to the north, as the way which enables British enterprise to extend northward from the Cape, under the British flag; its fuller development, so it seemed to me, will probably follow upon that of Rhodesia.

But be it remembered that what is wanted here, to make this Bechuanaland as fine a country for ranching or for corn crops as some of the most flourishing parts of the American continent, is capital and labour, and not so very much capital either, I imagine. Nature is bountiful here, and readily takes a hint; what is needed is water, and no one in his senses can look at the abundant greenery without feeling pretty certain that water is not far to seek. The deep furrows of torrents show what vast volumes of water must go to waste every year. With such natural river-beds ready to hand, there would be no great difficulty in forming numberless reservoirs and *keeping* abundant streams. Wherever there is water to be had in such a region, there is sure to be plenty of yield. The more I looked at Bechuanaland and afterwards at Rhodesia, the more I felt that the labour of English colonists, showing just the same knowledge and energy here as elsewhere, would be richly rewarded. The money spent in North-West Canada, and the labour and the patience, would, I imagine, give a much larger return under a more genial climate. Mineral wealth may probably be in abundance *under* the soil, but many a colonist will make sure and lasting revenue by toil *upon* the land.

I thought the railway journey very interesting. The glorious climate—even though the heat was considerable —the lovely views, the mysterious far-stretching lands, where occasionally it looked almost like an endless English park—sometimes with wide sweeps of open country, sometimes with woods and thickets almost like forests close by the side of the line—the quaint little stations with their stores and refreshment-rooms and native locations; the extraordinary idea of steaming up in a comfortable railway carriage through what was not so long ago savage Africa;—all affected one's imagination and set one dreaming. It is enough to stir many musings to think of this fair region in so comparatively short a time placed under the sway of our Queen. One could not but be struck with the indomitable energy of our race, one could not forget the astonishing genius, devotion and activity, especially of one Englishman. One could not but wonder and think of what may be the happy future of such a region if Englishmen continue to show the higher qualities which belong to their race. τὸ ἥμισυ τοῦ παντὸς ἡ ἀρχη. "The beginning is the half of the whole." The beginning, one may say, has just been made, only just. Plenty of tough work has still to be done ere the work of development and civilisation is well begun, but with the telegraph already being made from the regions of the Nile down towards Rhodesia, with the railway ere long to follow, with our own people "far too thick upon the ground" at home, and with such opportunities for patient labour and enterprise in our new young colony, one cannot but hope that there lies in the womb of the Future a hopeful and happy prospect for South Africa under the guidance of those principles of fair play, honesty, honour to hard work, and freedom which are represented by the British flag.

We reached Buluwayo on the evening of the second day after leaving Mafeking.

It was dark—too dark to see anything of the town —when we arrived. That night I stayed at the Palace Hotel. Considering the age of the town— about four years old—the Palace Hotel (the name seems unnecessarily magnificent) is wonderfully good. The *salle à manger* is as fine a room as any hotel need care to have, the food was excellent, and the attendance good. In the evening after dinner I had a walk through the town. The streets are broad, and promise to be handsome when the buildings are finished. The lighting was wonderfully good. I went into several stores and talked to the storekeepers, and into a chemist's shop which would not have done discredit to Belgravia, and here enjoyed an evening in listening to a performance of Strauss's band, given through the phonograph! Strange experience! a witness to the advance of civilisation in the heart of Africa! I learnt from every one that Buluwayo was in a state of expectancy. Some men had got on well, others were struggling. It was a *beginning* time, and as yet, of course, there was not much money in the place. Still, that Buluwayo would progress in the future no one doubted. Every place must have struggles and beginnings, but if English energy is induced to act here in increasing degree, as it has already acted, there ought to be a flourishing future for Rhodesia, and especially for Buluwayo. In minerals, there are gold, lead, copper, iron. So far the gold is reef gold, and, of course, it cannot be so productive, or so quickly productive, as the *banket* beds on the Witwatersrand; but by-and-by, with capital and English energy, all this will mean much, and there will be no steady pressure of hindrance, such as the Rand must suffer from more and more under the wretched government of the Transvaal, in case civilisation permits the continuance of that blighting and corrupt oligarchy. There are within reach sandstone, granite, trachyte, quantities of wood, and soon railways will place within easy reach extensive coalfields. The country, of course, affords immense agricultural tracts. The railways before long will transform this country as they have transformed others. It is startling to think that in this so lately distant and savage place people already can feel that they are in touch with Capetown—1360 miles away. Soon the railway from Beira to Salisbury will go on to Buluwayo. About thirteen hundred miles of travelling will before many years be managed by railway, and then by the great lakes, so as to bring the place in touch with Egypt. It cannot be very long before Buluwayo will be within thirteen or fourteen days of London.

Whether the necessary energy will be forthcoming remains to be seen. Many signs point to the conclusion that the Dutch Afrikander is wanting in this quality. The English Afrikander too suffers—possibly from the enervating tendency of so warm a climate. Cape Colonists have laughingly observed to me: "The English immigrant has backbone. His children have less backbone. His grandchildren are intermittently invertebrate!" The Boer of the Transvaal is certainly a poorer creature—degenerate in every way as compared with the rough old Vortrekker. He is "gone to seed," and his race is terribly debased. Still, although climatic conditions must affect any race, there is no reason to think that they will seriously impair British energy. There is plenty of vigour in the English in India, and the conditions of climate there are much more trying for the white man than those in Africa. For, though the heat may be great, much of the country lies high and has a fresh bracing air, and even the fever and the tetze-fly must retire before civilisation and the efforts of science. Let us hope also rinderpest, horse-sickness, and the locusts will yet be conquered. "You are by nature colonists," said a distinguished German to me not long ago at the Cape; "your Government has made many mistakes, but nothing can stop you, you can't be kept back." As far as a layman in such things can judge, there is a great future for Rhodesia. What is needed is *more immigrants*, and with our overcrowded island, and this vast and splendid possession with the great stock-raising stretches and territories suitable for agriculture in Rhodesia and in Bechuanaland, which invite occupation, this is, Englishmen being Englishmen, only a question of time. What is further wanted is *capital*, and confidence will grow. The English Government has, we may hope, learnt at last from a bitter experience. The folly of granting that foolish and mischievous Convention to the Boers in 1884 was the last dying sigh of the old, backward, pusillanimous and *laisser-aller* policy.

With ever-growing confidence capital will come. Englishmen will learn to use their great heritage in a way to be a blessing to the native races and the progressive colonists. The feverish hurry for money-getting—born of sudden opportunities like the Rand goldfields and lucky speculation—with its reaction of disappointment and demoralisation, in many cases, will give way to the healthier spirit of seeking success from honest labour. Before very long, especially if the life of South Africa's great genius and statesman is spared, railways and telegraphs and intimate intercourse with Europe will have done their work, and South Africa, under the beneficent influence of English force of character, sense of duty, respect for justice and fair play, strong common sense, and reverence for high and pure affection, will, we have every reason to hope, be one of the noblest parts of our Empire and a blessing to mankind.

Buluwayo lies, as I have said, on a plain. There are no very high hills near it, but the ground rises to some extent towards the spot where once stood Lobengula's kraal. Leaving the town to walk thither one had to travel over a long and broad avenue, which goes for two or three miles in a perfectly straight direction. At either side of the broad avenue are plantations which, with the rapid growth in this favouring soil and climate, will, in not so many years, give grateful shade. At the end of the avenue the drive sweeps up to Government House. Only a little more than four years ago here was the kraal. A tree close to the house marks the spot which has gruesome association with Lobengula's inhuman tortures and butcheries. Under this tree the monster sat while he ordered to death or suffering innumerable helpless wretches at his mere whim. The place was once filthy with all the loathsome surroundings of savage life. All this is almost incredible to the visitor to Government House. The house itself is built in the old-fashioned African-Dutch style, with the rooms opening out into a broad *stoep* or verandah—a pleasant resting-place, as usual, in the shade when the sun is hot and in the early night hours. By day there is an extensive view over the surrounding country, by night the wide heaven with the glorious African moon or brilliant stars. Near the house are exceedingly picturesque "huts," which are bedrooms, dressing-rooms, or offices of one kind or another. The whole place is the creation of Mr. Cecil Rhodes's taste and liberality. It is a home of brightness, comfort, elegance, and hospitable kindness, and the present Administrator—the Hon. Arthur Lawley, supported in all things as he is by his delightful wife — is not the least of the hopeful influences in action for the future of Buluwayo. To remember that this home of grace and kindness, with natives around it in peaceful occupations, and hospitality shown ungrudgingly to numbers of young Englishmen busy at their callings in the town, is only so lately the substitute for the headquarters of savage cruelty is to open one's eyes to the energy of the English race, and the genius and indomitable strength of purpose of their great leader in South Africa. At Government House one rubbed one's eyes and wondered if one were looking at actual realities or only listening to a story in the *Arabian Nights*.

From Buluwayo, by the kindness of friends there, I spent some days in the Matoppos. The drive of some twenty miles to the outlying farm where we were hospitably received was sometimes very pretty, sometimes very wild. Before leaving the town I had lunched with officers of the police force in their extremely nice barracks. In the mess-room for the first time I saw a punkah at work in Africa. Buluwayo and the country around it stands high, and, even when the weather is hot, there is a delightful air. The weather, indeed, was very hot during my visit, and on that day in particular it was grilling. Every one was wishing for rain, and no one was sorry to see heavy clouds rising above the horizon. While we were at luncheon the storm broke. There was rolling thunder, vivid lightning, and then real African torrents of rain. There was comfort in the earthy smell, and in the sight of the baked earth and the thirsty eucalyptus-trees drinking in the refreshing rain. One of the officers kindly drove me in a Cape cart with four horses to the farm above the Matoppos. As we crossed the *spruit* below the town, the place which had been a dry bed a few hours before was a rushing torrent. Indeed, but for the excellent driving we should not have passed it in safety. However, we did get through it with no greater mishap than a splashing and bumping, and after a pleasant drive in the now cooler air we reached the farm.

The buildings stand on a plateau of some elevation, and look across the valley towards the Matoppos. There are a number of very nicely-built huts, one or two as bedrooms, one for a kitchen, one a sitting-room, and, across a sort of courtyard, others for the native servants. The garden and farm stretched away down the slopes to the bottom, and farm buildings were not far off across the little valley on one side, while beyond the valley bottom at the other side was a neat farmhouse and farm worked by an industrious German. Mr. Cecil Rhodes was, as usual, the inspiring genius of these undertakings, and indeed it is one of the most striking facts in English colonial history that Africa possesses a great Englishman, who, in startling contrast with most men who have made their money and accumulated large fortunes by labour or good luck on this continent, spends vast sums in helping on the country of his adoption and developing the vast district which bears his name. Two young Englishmen—cousins—work the farm where I stayed, and their sister, a bright young girl, has devoted herself to them, and lives as mistress and guiding spirit of this picturesque assemblage of English *kraals*. I have to thank them for great hospitality and kindness during my visit to the Matoppos.

On the following morning my wandering among the hills began. The Matoppos are interesting for more reasons than one.

The Matabele War of 1893 had been eminently successful. The Matabele tribe, a vigorous and warlike division of the Zulu race, had given no peace to their neighbours. Their cruel incursions into Mashonaland had brought misery and ruin again and again to the unfortunate and less warlike natives there. At length their continued attacks upon the white settlers made it necessary to break Lobengula's power. With a curious perversity the attempt to do so was viewed with great disfavour by "the Exeter Hall people" at home, but it was absolutely necessary that the thing should be done. Dr. Jameson and a small body of troops, after two severe engagements, completely defeated and dislodged Lobengula, and, to the great relief of many of the Matabele themselves, as well as to the great advantage of South Africa, the Matabele power was completely broken.

Some of the more warlike spirits, however, among the members of the tribe could not view with equanimity the end of their savage habits and customs, and the passing of their power into the hands of the white man. There were other grounds of disaffection. The Chartered Company seem to have been entirely free from blame, but the acts of individual settlers were, very probably, in some measure blameworthy, and there were cases of forced labour which were exceedingly distasteful to the idle and lazy Matabele, who altogether objected to work and delighted only in rapine and murder. The exercise and training to habits of diligence were probably very good indeed for the undeveloped savage, but probably there may have been some harsh acts, which were, of course, magnified by the sentimental philanthropists, ever ready to find fault with their own countrymen. In addition to this the police had been withdrawn to Pitsani in view of eventualities in the Transvaal, and there was great calamity brought upon the Matabele by the widely-spreading scourge of the rinderpest.

These various reasons for discontent placed weapons in the hands of the Matabele agitators, and the rebellion began. We all remember the sad story of atrocities and murders committed on the helpless and trusting white population in the scattered farms in Matabeleland. Of the vigorous and courageous efforts of young Englishmen who flocked to the front to assist the Matabeleland police force; of their successful struggle; of the difficult character of the war in the Matoppo Hills, where the well-armed Matabele warriors under the cover of that rocky and bush-sheltered district carried on their guerilla warfare with serious consequences to many an Englishman; of the manner in which what appears to be a permanent settlement and peace were effected by the splendid courage and address of Mr. Cecil Rhodes, who visited unarmed the Matabele *indabas* in the heart of these hills;—all know it was his extraordinary personal influence with the natives which, better than battles, settled the question.

The district is exceedingly beautiful, and unlike any district I have ever been in before. A great tract of country is covered for miles and miles with *kopjes* of the most fantastic forms. These are wrecked remnants of some great geological convulsion. They are made up of huge round or oblong boulders piled or poised on one another and making up weird rocky hills. Some of them rise to considerable height; in some places, indeed, there are wild scarped rocks and sheer precipices. They are for the most part clothed with luxuriant herbage, and gnarled low-growing trees, and beautiful tropical flowers. The highest peak to which we climbed has been called " The World's View." It does command a wonderful prospect. As far as the eye can reach in every direction, peak above peak, precipice after precipice, boulder above boulder, with the waving boughs of the trees, and the rich green crests of the large tropical plants and ferns—this strange land stretches away to the horizon. Every here and there are deep valleys, and through these wind the roads or tracks. It seemed a smiling and beautiful land under the brilliance of the African sun. Here and there was a Matabele kraal perched on some of the rocky ledges or sheltered under the groves of oak or mahogany trees or bamboo or eucalyptus, with a patch of mealies close by; but except three Matabele with whom we conversed (my companion understood their language) we saw no sign of living man. Down in the hollows and among the rocks by the track-side was a perfect wealth of arum lilies and splendid ferns. I lay down for a time to rest on a huge rock fringed with waving grasses and delicate flowers, and just over a cool, rushing, sparkling little mountain stream. I dared not sleep, for imagination haunted me, supplying plentiful unseen horrors in the shape of black mambras and puff adders. At last came a movement in the grasses on the edge of the stream, and up my rock advanced, calm and observant, that faithful defender of man against snakes, an intelligent little mongoose. I thought affectionately and admiringly of Rikki-tikki-tavi, and was delighted to see his little relative. He seemed equally delighted to see me. The mongoose is the most curious of little beings. His curiosity quite out-distances any fear. I sat up and looked at him, and inquired of him whether he knew my friend Rikki-tikki-tavi personally, and whether he had lately seen him. He did not answer, but came up closer and closer, sat up on his hind legs, and then went round me and examined me with the greatest care; and not until he had thoroughly inspected me did he say good-morning and trot off home.

Here and there in the Matoppos we came on some other deep mountain *culs-de-sac* which must have been terrible places in the rebellion, when the hills at either side had Matabele armed with rifles lying behind the stones. Fortunately, the Matabele—though splendid fellows and with a courage which awakened the admiration of the Englishmen who had to fight them— were not such good shots with rifles as they had been with assegais. To look across that wide and varied scene was to feel in an extraordinary degree the grandeur and loneliness of Nature. Beyond, and far away, our imagination pictured some great city, with stately domes and spires and towers, where in future centuries Englishmen would carry on their peaceful pursuits, and the then members of the Matabele family would take their place in assisting and adorning the arts of peace; where there would be no more possibilities of violence between the white and the coloured man, no more excuse for the injurious intervention of the ignorant or sentimental mischief-maker, where art and culture would adorn the happy homes of noble children of one mighty Empire championing the cause of human progress in the faith and fear of God, and men would look back with a sigh over the mistakes, and with thoughts of gratitude and admiration to worthy ancestors who had striven in the travail of the Past!

Dreams! all dreams! from which that gracious and weird Nature awoke one to feel what great things, after all, Englishman had done and were doing for the service of man, in spite of all mistakes, and to remember that future dreams of blessedness for others can only hope to be realised by our own faithfulness to truth and duty *now*; to feel, even for others' benefit, Goethe's advice is the best:

> "Wouldst fashion for thyself a seemly life?
> Then fret not over what is past and gone;

And spite of all thou mayest have lost behind,
Yet act as if this life were just begun.
What each day wills, enough for thee to know ;
What each day wills, the day itself will tell.
Do thine own task and be therewith content ;
What others do, that shalt thou fairly judge ;
Be sure that thou no brother-mortal hate,
Then all besides leave to the Master Power." *

The Matoppos *will* compel to dreaming—so strange, so unique! So full of Nature! So lonely of man! The Matoppos, and many another dream they created, haunt one still.

Buluwayo may take some time to develop. As it is, it is a perfect miracle of energy, considering its youth and its vicissitudes — streets, houses, stores, churches, a fine post office, a club where one saw drop in for luncheon or dinner as fine a set of young Englishmen as I ever saw. There is something marvellously thrilling in a new place grown by work and perseverance in a few short years from savagery to civilisation. There is something stirring to see the young pioneers of a new world. The dear old world has much to offer—a great inheritance. Still, there is a sentiment—stirring, unspeakable—in the *beginnings* of a new world looking forward to the future, and all through the energy of the English race. After being in the Transvaal, too—gold or no gold—there was the sense of escape from a land which reminds us of our national mistakes and disgraces, and a sense of freedom after the stifling moral atmosphere of a land whose government is founded on debasement and corruption.

From Buluwayo I went to Kimberley. The town is

* Goethe. *Sprüche*, quoted in Morley's *Studies in Literature*, p. 87.

bright and clean and pretty. The Sanatorium—which is, in fact, an extremely healthy and roomy hotel—is excellently managed, and has been of great benefit to many who have needed the strong fine air of Griqualand. The interest of Kimberley is, of course, the diamond mines. The Weselton Mine, where the whole process is plainly to be seen, is the most interesting of all. For those who understand and are interested in precious stones, the numberless beautiful diamonds which one was permitted to see must be full of interest. I was specially struck by the neatness and even beauty of the workmen's houses, with their pretty *stoeps* and flowers, built by De Beers, and the fine fruit-gardens, where the workpeople can buy fruit at the lowest possible prices. The "compounds" for the native workmen are also excellently managed, and the whole town gives an idea of prosperity and neatness.

There appears to be no neighbourhood around Kimberley, however, of any beauty. It lies close to the border of the Orange State, and the surrounding country is tame. The journey from Kimberley occupied three nights and two days. The scenery became bold and wild as we drew south. I cannot agree with those who see no beauty in the Karroo. It seemed to me bold and grand. About Beaufort West the air is specially bracing and exhilarating, and the effects of atmosphere and especially of the sundawns and sunsets in the wild weird mountains and strange desolate stretches one can never forget. The sense of extent, of silence, of solitude, and the gracious atmosphere and splendid colour—these will always dwell with one as a weird—yes, and a happy—memory when one thinks of South Africa. And here again is Capetown and its "scimitar of shining sea"! Few things anywhere in this continent, or, indeed, anywhere, can, after all, rival the beauty of this matchless peninsula.

PART II
HISTORICAL

CHAPTER I

CAPE COLONY

It is often felt that only within recent years has Africa been "discovered." Within the easy memory of men who cannot be called old, the greater part of this immense continent was believed to be uninhabitable desert, and those vast tracts of country which are now in great measure explored and even settled and utilised, were for centuries, and until quite recently, literally unknown.

Even that part of South Africa which has been explored and inhabited more or less by Europeans for about a couple of centuries, or rather more, excited but a languid interest in the European mind until these later years.

Cape Colony has the distinction of being the centre from which civilisation and political advance have spread towards the North, just as Egypt is that from which they spread towards the central and Western regions.

The first visitors, however, to whom is due the discovery of this important part of Africa, did not, from it, extend such power as they have retained on this continent.

It was towards the end of the fifteenth century, in the year 1486, that Bartolommeo Diaz, a Portuguese navigator, discovered what he named "the Cape of Storms." Those who are acquainted with the strength and strangeness of the winds on the peninsula cannot wonder at the name. This title was afterwards exchanged by John II. of Portugal for the more attractive one of "the Cape of Good Hope." Diaz seems to have explored the coast for some little distance, but, beyond the honour of being the first to discover South Africa, he made no lasting impression on the country.

Vasco da Gama, whose name is most usually associated with the discovery of this region, making his voyage to India, explored a considerable part of the coast from the Cape eastward; and on a later occasion, in 1502, he visited Delagoa Bay and Sofala. Like the Spaniards in America, and others at that time, the Portuguese were bent on prosecuting a search for gold. It is now known that far into the interior some pioneer in very remote antiquity had penetrated and worked some gold mines. It was probably from these mines that Solomon's "gold of Ophir" came. The Sabi River is believed to derive its name, which is not a native word, from the Queen of Sheba; and even in the later times of the kingdom of Judah the fleets of Uzziah, in the days of his great prosperity and able administration, sailed from a harbour on the Red Sea down the eastern coast of Africa, rounded the Cape, and returned by way of the Straits of Gibraltar and the Mediterranean—touching at the Spanish coast— to the shores of Palestine. When the Portuguese explorer visited Sofala in the early days of the sixteenth century, Arabs were found in possession as traders in ivory and gold. The Portuguese reduced them to obedience and used them for the purposes of trade, and for quite a century remained in undisputed possession of the eastern shores of Africa.

It was in 1510 that D'Almeida, the Portuguese Viceroy, perished in a fight with the Hottentots at a point not far from where Capetown now stands, and henceforth, fearing the power of the natives, which was greatly overrated in that part of the country, the Portuguese restricted their enterprises to the eastern coast. They seem to have penetrated for some distance into the interior from Sofala, and their missionaries worked with diligence and, as it appeared, with considerable success among the natives; but they, in the long run, retained small hold upon the country, and have but slightly influenced its history. The constant intermarriage of the Portuguese with Kaffir tribes, the unhealthy nature of the coast-land where they had their headquarters, the successful attacks of the natives upon them, and even—for a time in the early days of the seventeenth century—the attacks of the Dutch, the indifference of their home Government, who were more interested in their East Indian enterprises, all combined to take strength and enterprise out of the Portuguese settlers, and to lead them, as a race, to sit loosely by such possessions as they had acquired in South Africa. It is only within recent years that the possession of Delagoa Bay, and its strategic value to the nations holding the interior, have revived a languid interest in their East African possessions in the minds of the Government at Lisbon.

While the name of the great Portuguese navigators, therefore, must be for ever connected with the Cape of Storms, or Cape of Good Hope, that Cape and its surroundings, so far as it concerns Portugal, can only act as a memorial of lost opportunities and departed glory.

Very different is the history of the nations which followed the Portuguese in the settlement of South Africa. These nations were the English and the Dutch. It would be difficult to say which came first to have some connection with the Cape. Both these nations very early in the seventeenth century were in the habit of pausing in Table Bay for shelter on their voyages round the Cape. The English were the first to assert, in some informal way, English possession in the name of the King, James I., as early as 1620. It was in 1648, however, that the Dutch took the first step towards a formal occupation.

In that year some Dutchmen were shipwrecked in Table Bay. They succeeded, in some measure, for several months in cultivation of the soil. On returning to Holland they gave a favourable report of the country, and in 1652 the Dutch East India Company sent three vessels carrying a considerable number of emigrants under the leadership of Jan Van Riebeek. These came really to make arrangements for the needs of ships passing to and from India or other places in the East.

The Cape was looked upon by the Dutch as only a resting-place on their way to India. When Van Riebeek landed there, he had no idea of founding a permanent colony. A port of call for the Dutch fleets on their way to the North from the land of wealth in India was a luxury, indeed a necessity. The stormy headlands of the Cape might be filled with the terrors of the sea, and made interesting by the superstitious legends of the Flying Dutchman in vain and impious efforts to navigate his phantom ship, but above all the Dutch East India Company found it useful as a place for fresh meat for the crews of their vessels, sick with the weary struggle with an illimitable sea, and as a useful ground for the growth of vegetables needed by those crews.

Dutch colonisation — like the Dutch people — is singularly devoid of romance. The Portuguese were the great discoverers. The Dutch followed them and wrenched their possessions from them. Then they worked them on the narrowest principle, as a big commercial concern. Twice the British in turn deprived *them* of their empire; twice with Quixotic generosity gave it back, receiving in return about as much gratitude as they have received from their degenerate descendants for the retrocession of the Transvaal.

In the early days and, indeed, for several centuries, the Dutch settlement extended no farther than the peninsula. Stellenbosch, not far from Capetown, was the extreme point of settlement during the greater part of the seventeenth century. And only quite at the end of that century did the colonists advance beyond the vast range of mountains which hems in the peninsula, and separates it in a measure from the interior.

About this time (*i.e.*, the latter part of the seventeenth century) the population of the small but increasing colony was composed of the following parts. There were, in largest numbers, the Dutch who had come from Holland. They were for the most part drawn from the lower and more uncultivated classes; and having, on the whole, a very slight connection with their mother country, which was too far distant in those days to be often revisited, they soon lost any feeling for Holland and any contact with such culture as Holland might be supposed to have. Then again there came, but in only a small number, a body of French Huguenots who had fled for refuge to Holland after the revocation of the Edict of Nantes. An attempt was made by them at first to separate themselves into a distinct community. This, however, was impossible. The age was an age of religious intolerance. All sects and sections of religious bodies everywhere were inclined to be intolerant of any diversity of religious opinion, and none more narrow or conservative in all things—now so far as possible, as then—as the lower class of Dutchmen. The Huguenots were forbidden the use of their language—just as the Transvaal Government of these days endeavours, so far as may be, to be intolerant of the use of English; they were forbidden the exercise of their own form of Protestanism which was inclined to Lutheranism, and forced into the Dutch Reformed body, which represented the narrowest form of Calvanism. Gradually these Huguenots became intermixed with the older colonists. Their language and their form of religion disappeared, but—being very superior in intelligence and culture—from them have sprung some of the most enlightened, and able, and large-minded of the modern community of Dutch in and about Capetown. Unfortunately, the number of Huguenot settlers was comparatively small : had it been otherwise the modern Boers might have been a superior race, with a culture and intelligence of a much higher stamp than anything that can now be hoped for.

CAPE COLONY 113

Further, there were the native races. These were the Hottentots, the Bushmen, and the Bantu tribes of Kaffirs. These all, of course, play a conspicuous part in the history of South Africa. Besides these were the slaves. Regular slavery was introduced in the middle of the seventeenth century. West Africa contributed her quota of unhappy negroes for this purpose; and then again, a little later, the Dutch East India Company—which was still the ruling power —began to introduce convicts from Asia, of whom the greater part were Malays holding the Mohammedan faith. Such were the races who met together in South Africa in the seventeenth century.

History repeats itself, but with many variations. In the history of all countries there recurs the story of races in occupation conquered or held in check by intrusive invaders. Then the habits and character of these latter are considerably modified by circumstances, by climate, by their relations with the other races with whom they come in contact. This happened in South Africa as elsewhere.

(1) As to the immigrant Dutch, naturally after a little time they began to expand. Increase of their numbers and the narrowness of the strip of fertile land round the promontory drove them farther afield. Those who gradually spread northward became more and more, from the scanty opportunities for agricultural farming, a pastoral people. Like the mountaineer Italians from the Abruzzi, descending for some months of the year to the Campagna, they drove their flocks, at certain seasons when the rain had given vitality to the vegetation, up to the far-stretching and wild regions of the Karroo. They moved from place to

H

place with their waggons, and lived a lonely and wandering life. They became more and more rude, coarse, and uncultivated, and formed habits—some good, some bad—of sturdy hardihood, readiness for danger and difficulty, and, on the other hand, of selfish isolation, and a staunch and dogged conservatism in maintaining their own customs and looking with suspicion on *any* changes and *any* improvements. Slave labour freed them and their women from the necessity of hard work, and in their wandering life they learnt to be slatternly and untidy to a degree which even now astonishes the traveller, especially in the Transvaal, when he thinks of the neat and cleanly habits of the Dutch in Europe. The Boer farmer became—and the large mass of the more ignorant remain to this day—as remarkable for slovenly and uncleanly ways as the Dutch in Holland are for neatness, cleanliness, and tidiness almost to a fault. Probably this and their dense and suspicious conservatism and want of enterprise and progressive intelligence make them more jealous of the Hollander of to-day, with his brisk, businesslike, and tidy ways, even than they are of the vigour of the British. Their children also grew up in deeper and ever deepening ignorance from the very circumstances of their life, while their constant war, for a time with the Hottentots, and for a lengthened period with the Bushmen, as well as the habit of hunting big game, made them hardy and physically courageous and good shots. There is one important factor in human life which the historian can never forget, as it exercises so vast an influence upon men,—that is religion. They had brought with them a grave and serious character. The form of their religion was Calvinistic. That gloomy heresy has ever tended to develop a certain strength of fibre and to contract character by its narrow and repulsively selfish views of human life and destiny, and of the character and actions of God. The result on these men was more and more to give dogged determination, a self-centred selfishness, an absence of all "sweetness and light," a severance between religion, in any searching sense, and morality, and in fact that self-reliant fanaticism and narrow superstition so marked among the least cultured of them still, and of which a conspicuous example is to be found in Mr. Krüger, the President at the present time of the Transvaal Republic. Thus their form of superstition —so common in the various developments of Protestantism—became a slavish devotion to the letter of Scripture, and especially that of the Old Testament.

This form of superstition has before now produced in history characters, which, though of extreme narrowness and of reactionary tendencies, have shown doggedness and sturdiness and determination, and it accounts for the merciless contempt for the coloured race—mere Canaanites, as they consider them—the absence of a sense of justice and fair play towards others, the unscrupulous cunning brought to play in compassing ends opposed to other nations not looked upon as " chosen people "—so conspicuous in the Transvaal Government, and the more isolated and ignorant Boer farmers; for, such as it is, with all its narrow and unlovely deformities, their religion is a *real* power, not in exalting but in narrowing their lives.

(2) As to the native races—The Hottentot tribes

soon practically disappeared from the scene. A terrible outbreak of small-pox in 1755 swept them away. They were a race with some tribal organisation, and of a light-hearted, cheerful, merry temperament. They were more or less civilised and were used as domestic servants by the early Dutch settlers. They are now gone as a separate people. Remnants of their wandering tribes are said to be still found in Great Namaqualand on the borders of the Orange River, but for the most part they have been absorbed into other races. The Dutch have sometimes mingled with them. Those whom they call the Bastards, whom English call Griquas, are sprung from unions of Dutch and Hottentots, and that numerous mixed nondescript race in and about Capetown has carried on some Hottentot blood as well as that of Malays and West African slaves. Then there were the Bushmen, who constantly harrassed the Dutch settlers by secret and dangerous attacks. Continual war went on with them. The settlers showed them no mercy nor did they give any quarter to the settlers. They had no tribal organisation and were untameably fierce. Their chief power seems to have been in their unmatched dexterity in killing game, on which for the most part they lived. They were very small in stature, very fierce. They have left some traces in the races with which their blood was intermingled. Some, though not of pure Bushman blood, are still found in the colony. The few true Bushmen still surviving under the advance of civilisation are in the Kalahari desert or some outlying districts in the interior, but as a separate people they are now a *quantité négligeable*. As to the, Malays, they are distinctly represented in the colony.

In many cases they formed connections with the negro slaves brought from West Africa, and the descendants of such unions form a considerable part of the mixed population of the Cape. There are a considerable number of Malays well-to-do traders, fruit-sellers, and middle-class merchants in the colony, and their picturesque costumes, especially at their gorgeous wedding ceremonies, and the beauty of their horses in which they take a great pride, form a striking feature among the variegated sights and populations of Capetown.

(3) As to the slaves—The sin of the importation of these unhappy beings recoiled on the heads of those who traded in them, as iniquity is sure, in the long run, to work out into evil consequences. The first effect of the introduction of slave labour was to give to the white population the habit of avoiding all manual labour themselves, a habit which has fairly established itself now throughout South Africa. The early Dutch settlers who went far afield became wandering in their ways, often living in their ox waggons, and even when more or less settled in distant farms, became gradually less and less used to toil themselves. Their national characteristics were very greatly modified. Cattle farming became the order of the day, for pasture could be had over wide reaches of country, where tillage was difficult from the nature of the soil. The consequence was not only a nomad life, but habits of slatternliness, untidiness, and dirt and laziness—for they compelled first slaves, and then natives practically enslaved, to do their work—habits far removed from the ways then and now prevalent in their mother country. The lower Transvaal Boer has become espe-

cially remarkable for all these things; the Dutch people in Holland have been remarkable for their exact opposites. They still, however, resemble each other in love of money, which in the Holland Dutch shows itself in real diligence and thrift, in their colonial kinsmen of this class, in a spirit of jealous isolation, in graspingness and cunning. Perhaps because of these early tendencies, and of ways of life which made education impossible, and fostered selfishness and suspiciousness—they have remained possessed of physical courage, ready in the use of weapons of precision, dogged and determined, slow to admit habits of progress, specially harsh in their treatment of the coloured races, with very crude notions of morality, and, as we have seen, fanatical and narrow views in religion. But we are anticipating.

The year 1779 was one to be noted in the history of the colony. In that year the colonists first came into collision with the Kaffirs—as they are usually called from an Arabic word meaning unbeliever—in fact, with the Bantu tribes.

Some of these crossed the Great Fish River and raided the cattle of the settlers. This led to the first Kaffir War, in which the assaulted settlers, with some difficulty, succeeded at last in driving off the enemy.

This year, however, was still more remarkable for showing the first overt acts of disaffection towards the mother country, which now in some measure paved the way for the British ascendency. The colony had been governed by the Dutch East India Company. A Governor and Council, responsible to the heads of the Company in Amsterdam, conducted the government.

This Government became unpopular, and not unnaturally. It is instructive, in view of the present state of things in the Transvaal, to remember that one chief cause of discontent was the exclusion of the settlers from any share in the administration. Another cause was the fact—so common among all tyrannies, whether personal or oligarchical—that the colony was governed —like all Dutch colonies—for the benefit of the rulers and not the ruled. Trade monopoly was the order of the day. The settlers were not considered so long as the Dutch merchants in Holland filled their pockets.

The connection with the mother country thus became more or less unpopular, although the disaffected settlers declared the Company, not the home Government, to be the rock of offence.

Events followed one another now with considerable rapidity, and the relations of the nations of Europe with one another led to the change which took place in South Africa. The deputation sent to Holland in 1789 led to a Commission of Inquiry sent out in 1792. The reforms recommended were considered inadequate by the Cape Dutch, and thus they were all the more ready for a change. Owing to the advance of British sovereignty in India, the necessity of protecting the growing Indian Empire, and of resisting the French, had a new effect on the views of Great Britain. It was now felt that the Cape was an important military and naval possession. An abortive attempt had accordingly been made in 1781, which the Dutch, with the aid of France, were able to resist. The French and the Dutch, however, had since become enemies in Europe. The French army had overrun

Holland. The Stadtholder was a refugee in England, and residing at Hampton Court. War with France was everywhere. The Cape, which was an outpost of the Netherlands — hardly a colony — had to be protected, and the Stadtholder sent orders that it should be handed over to England as the protecting ally of Holland. Admiral Elphinstone, with a fleet of eight ships of war, accompanied by General Craig with a force of 4000 men, anchored off Simon's Town in June 1795. The Dutch East India Company had made themselves, by their oppression, most unpopular with the Dutch burghers.

The Governor, with the assistance of a Dutch Reform minister—a kind of official ecclesiastic called the "Sick Comforter"—was guilty of genuine tyranny. The arrival of the English was a real blessing to the burghers, but the death-knell to the exactions of the officers of the Company. Commissary Huysken and his staff determined accordingly to disobey their Stadtholder and resist the British. The British Admiral landed his forces at Muizenberg, and soon overcame the resistance; the Dutch population were freed from the tyranny of the Company, and the officials left the Cape in November 1795, and the British took over the government of the country.

Two things are worthy of note—(1) That the tie between the Dutch settlement at the Cape and the mother country was of the loosest. The modern attempt at *rapprochement* by Mr. Krüger with Holland is, and is felt to be, curiously absurd. The liberators of the Cape Dutch, the only people to whom any debt of gratitude was due, when they were groaning under the oppressions of the Company, were the English. The land to which, from first to last, they have owed their freedom is England. How many of them have shown their gratitude to her we know too well!

But England behaved with chivalrous loyalty to the Dutch and to Holland with regard to the Cape and the other Dutch colonial possessions.

General Craig became English Governor, and set about real and practical reforms to meet the needs of the Cape burghers who had suffered from Dutch oppression. Then came the Peace of Amiens in 1803, and England faithfully restored her empire to Holland, and, among other possessions, the Cape of Good Hope.

The settlement of Amiens, however, did not last long. England and France were again at war. One or other must hold the Cape. Holland was as helpless as the Dutch colonists themselves. In 1806, accordingly, General Sir David Baird anchored off Table Bay, landed his forces, and after one or two skirmishes inaugurated the final occupation of the British. It is almost accurate to say that it was taken from the French rather than from the Dutch. If England had not taken possession of it, France would have done so; and considering its strategical value in view of our Indian Empire, it was impossible, it would have been criminal, to run such a risk.

England had behaved with almost Quixotic generosity before in restoring the Dutch empire to Holland. It was perhaps Quixotic, for the Dutch had taken it from the Portuguese for no other reason than that they desired to have it! However, England *did* restore it.

Now, again, it was intended only to occupy the

country for a time. The greater part of the Dutch possessions, as a matter of fact, were restored; but in 1814 the Cape was ceded to Great Britain by the Dutch Government, and England paid a large sum—some six millions—for the possession. Never did one nation behave to another with such complete generosity. Men easily forget; and when in modern times it has been sometimes said by the Transvaal Government and their supporters among politicians at home that we "took their country from the Dutch," it is well to recall the facts in order to gauge the falseness of the statement. No European nation has such a right to a colony as the English have to South Africa. It is true that the Dutch took the country from its real inhabitants — the Bushmen — and without payment! The Dutch settlement England protected when it was unable to protect itself, and restored it to Dutchmen when—had they acted as the Dutch had everywhere done to the Portuguese—they need not have done so. Then the English again protected it against the French, and at last, when it was ceded to them by Holland, *paid for it a heavy price in hard cash.* It is to England the colony owes just administration of law, advancing education, material prosperity, progress of every kind. England has, as we shall see, committed in the past grave faults in her administration in South Africa, but faults not to be compared with the faults of Dutch government there, faults often springing from foolish generosity. If any nation has a just title to colonial possessions, England has that title to South Africa.

Besides, it should be remembered that the settlement

of the colony by the Dutch had not been of great antiquity. The colonists were comparatively few in number, and among them were Germans and French Huguenots. Englishmen in 1620 had, as we have seen, in an informal manner, asserted a right to the Cape. The settlers had, as we have seen also, been asserting their rights against the Dutch Company, and had no enthusiasm for their home Government, and no other government had they, so that the settlement under British rule has by no means the character of hardship which would be natural in an old and established country taken from its possessors by conquest.

At the first blush it would have seemed that things would go smoothly. The two races had affinities in race, in language, in the general tendencies of their religious feelings and their love of liberty and independence. But deeper down were causes which were soon to be fruitful in friction. In the early days of English rule things seemed to promise well. The Government was fair and just. Reforms which had been held back by the Company in the past were at once carried out, and in many respects things went well. Among the more cultivated and better educated, social fusion began. Intermarriages took place, and from these are descended some of the most intelligent and important of the colonial families. It was fated, however, that, in the long run, things would not go so smoothly as might have been reasonably hoped. In spite of all the friendly social and private relations which have, on the whole, prevailed, there appeared, and have ever since been more or less evident, powerful stimuli to political disagreement.

There were other Dutch besides the more advanced

members of the community in or near Capetown. There were the pastoral and stock-farming Boers of the more remote districts. They loved a liberty which was really a licence, for they were constantly inclined, as we find both then and afterwards, to form small rival Republics. They were wanting in education, disliked mixing with others, and were obstinately set upon selfish isolation, and a desire to have their own way which rendered their law-abiding character more than doubtful. This has often been a fruitful cause of difficulties. The incapacity of the uneducated Boer for the conduct of civil government on lines leading to a true system of colonisation is as marked as that capacity is striking in the English race. The English have naturally—with many demerits—certainly one great gift, the gift of colonising and governing. A *home Government* may—as in British policy towards the American colonies—act with stupidity and injustice; but *the people*, the *nation itself*, has the right instinct for law-protected freedom, as the English in America who revolted against the home Government show. It was the mistakes of a home Government— acting contrary to the opinion of men who knew matters on the spot and understood their bearings— which, in dealing with people so narrow-minded, ignorant, and conservative of the most undesirable customs as the early Dutch Boers, led to incalculable mischief.

It has been often said that what is called "the Slagter's Nek incident" went far to separate the Boers from the English. This is to attribute to a mere surface matter the power of causes lying much deeper. It is, in fact, to "put the cart before the horse," and the story of that incident, as often stated, is a misrepresentation and an exaggeration.

The following was the story. There was a rising in the Eastern Province of no great extent in which the two races came into conflict. A charge was made against a farmer of cruel treatment of a native. The authorities attempted to arrest him, but the Boers rose in his behalf. Of these, as the rising was soon suppressed, six were condemned to death, and of them five were hanged. No doubt this incident has, from time to time, been furbished up for political purposes, and especially has been employed more than once on the hustings * for the purpose of arousing animosity against their English fellow-subjects among the less instructed Boers. But in itself it was a slight matter. When honestly and fully told, indeed, the story redounds to the credit of the Cape Government. The convicted men did certainly deserve punishment in the interests of public order, but the Governor rightly deemed the execution of the extreme sentence unjustly harsh. He reprieved the criminals. The Field Cornet, on whom the duty of carrying out the execution devolved, for some reason of his own played the part of a Martin Relph, not from exactly the same motive, but probably from some motive of private spite. He had *in his possession* at the time of the execution the Governor's order for the pardon of the incriminated prisoners, and he suppressed it. But so sure was he that he himself would be punished for his iniquity that he committed suicide. Will it be believed that the latter part of the story has been often omitted for party purposes? Yet such is the case. It is probable

* 1898. *E.g.*, in the course of one of the recent electioneering campaigns

that it had never been known, or had ceased to be remembered, by such men as the angry and clamorous Boer mob who so bitterly referred to it at the time of the Raid and Reform excitement in Johannesburg and Pretoria. This intermittent and recurring remembrance of an unfortunate incident, long past, is a revelation of Boer character. The *cause* of the unhappy misunderstandings between the Boers and the English Government in the early days of the colony lay much deeper. It was not any mere incident like Slagter's Nek, nor the alterations in local administration, nor the use of English in law matters, in all which English Governments have been much more liberal—as we can judge by the action of the present Transvaal authorities —than Boers left to themselves have ever been. The causes of friction came from that which forms and will form *the* problem of South Africa. The relation of the conquering to the coloured races, and the opposing views on that subject taken by the Boers and by the home Government, lay at the root of it all. Both were in the right; both were in the wrong; and some form of this difference of view has been the fruitful cause of similar difficulties in South Africa ever since.

The case for the Boers is this: In their outlying farms those who had gone to the farthest limits of the colony had to face terrible difficulties from Hottentots, Bushmen, and Kaffirs. In 1809 strict arrangements had been made as to the natives. It was found to be absurd in the interests of civilisation to regard the Hottentot as belonging to a free and independent people. It was required that he should have a fixed dwelling-place, that he should be registered, and must have a "pass" or certificate when moving from place to place, and should be fined or punished as a vagrant if unable, when required, to produce this pass. In 1828 this was all swept away, and coloured persons were freed from the "pass" law, and so made on a complete equality with Europeans. This was probably imprudent. It was scarcely possible to treat these savage races wisely without some such restrictions, and in fact at this moment these are in use, to the benefit of the coloured man himself no less than of the white man. Such restrictions are evidently, indeed, open to grave abuses, and they are, in fact, at present abused very grossly in the Transvaal. The Boers, however, of those early days felt that they—a small community—could not be safe from savages without some regulations of the kind.

As to the Kaffirs, the Boers felt the policy of the home Government still more galling. The Kaffirs, they knew, were, as much as they themselves, intruders, and that is true. They were savages, and dangerous savages. There had been many Kaffir wars, but the inroad in 1834 was of the most alarming character. Men who have to defend their lives and property are not likely to be influenced too much by sentiment, or to take an idyllic view of the "gentle savages" who carry off their cattle, and murder men, women, and children with impartial barbarity. The frontier farmers, when these terrible irruptions came, were wont to have *commandos* of settlers, and punish their enemies in battle. This was changed, by what we must call the folly of the home Government, acting under what the Boer considered sinister influences. Soon it was required that Kaffirs should be protected by treaty, though it had to be acknowledged that barbarous tribes could not be trusted to observe treaties, or indeed to possess the right sentiments and sense of honour upon which the observance of treaties must depend. To the Boers, in fact, it appeared that they were not allowed to protect their property themselves, and that the Government did not protect it; that it was folly to deem that a white man if he was in Kaffirland should be subject to Kaffir "law"— *i.e.*, the victim of savage custom and hate; and that the home Government took no account of the reports of the properly constituted authorities, but always attended to the false reports of "missionaries."

The earliest instance in 1811 turned out, indeed, to be only a sample of many afterwards. Then it was stated that the settlers were guilty of inhuman cruelty to the coloured people, and that in the neighbourhood of Uitenhage alone they had murdered more than one hundred. This turned out, when really looked into, to be the grossest exaggeration; but thus it was that, one way or another, the Colonial Office mistrusted the Boer settlers, and the Boers mistrusted the Colonial Office. What fault there was on the side of the English was not the fault of those on the spot and of the English fellow-subjects of the Dutch settlers, but the fault of a distant Government not careful enough to investigate and master facts on the scene of action. The Boer farmers then had certainly a real grievance.

On the other hand, there was something to be said for the home Government. There is always a tendency—human nature being what it is—for a superior race to bear heavily upon an inferior, and all the more when the latter far outnumber the former. Their hard life, their narrow fanaticism as well as the necessity of self-defence laid upon them, made the Boers inclined to be, as they still are, harsh and even cruel masters to the coloured people. The home Government was much pressed by home opinion; and home opinion began to be, and for some time was, intensely influenced by the reports of the missionaries; and the missionaries had something to be said for them, for they were in fact the only friends the natives had.

The fact is, however, that in the days when the Colonial Office came into conflict with Boer opinion in Cape Colony the philanthropists and missionaries made great, perhaps inevitable, mistakes. That the Boers have always been in an attitude of special hostility to the native races cannot be doubted, nor can it be doubted that their treatment of them had been exceedingly harsh; but the missionaries who took the part of the natives were, to say the least, imprudent, and for a long time they were the inspirers of the action and of the policy of the home Government. As early as the beginning of the seventeenth century colonial and missionary opinion came into contact. The Boers were wrong. They acted as if a coloured man could not be considered as possessing rights as a human being, as if he were a mere animal and only born to labour. This the missionaries naturally and rightly resented. The Moravian missionaries, in the early days of the century, found themselves in an unenviable position, and for attempting to treat natives as worthy of receiving baptism one of them at least had to leave the country. As early as 1658 slaves had

I

been imported from West Africa, and with slavery came its usual consequences—degradation and misery to the slave, to the white man a worse degradation still.

The contest raged for quite a century. From 1828 and onwards the missionary party showed unflagging activity. Circumstances at home favoured them. They gained the ear of the Colonial Office, and the efforts of many governors were fruitless in trying to dispel prejudices and to encourage dispassionate judgments. It is curious to observe how a wave of philanthropic sentiment, in great measure false or exaggerated, swept over England from 1828, or earlier, which was unreasonably hostile to the colonists and especially to the Boers; just as a similar wave swept over the country from about 1880 until recently which has been as unreasonably favourable to them. The whole thing speaks better for the heart than for the head of the British people. There was in both cases much real generosity and indignation against supposed wrongdoing; there was much blind prejudice and a refusal to oppose prepossession by calm judgment based on real inquiry; there was a good deal of the kind of unhealthy, semi-religious sentiment which may be described in some such recently often-used phrases, coming from friends or foes, as "Exeter Hall sentiment," or "demands of the Nonconformist conscience," or "unctuous righteousness." There were mixed feelings and various degrees of moral rectitude. One way or another the nation was moved by a genuine and generous, if sometimes blundering, enthusiasm, and colonial secretaries and prime ministers and cabinets were often swept off their feet by the torrent.

CAPE COLONY 131

The fault of the home Government as regards the South African question was allowing itself a bias from which came its action, without examining actual facts or being guided by those who knew; and in important instances the Colonial Office seems to have had a fatal tendency to fall foul of any strong and wise governor, and to have been only amenable to the guidance of the weak and inefficient. It cannot be wondered at that the originally fair promise of complete union of mind and loyalty of the colonists, and especially the Dutch, was nipped in the bud by the Colonial Office, and that they learnt, until quite recently, not unnaturally to consider Downing Street their worst enemy.

In 1830 Lord Goderich (afterwards Lord Ripon) forbade the settlement of Boer farmers on the new frontier districts. In 1833, when Mr. E. Stanley (afterwards Lord Derby) was Secretary of State, and in 1834, when the office was held by Mr. T. Spring-Rice and then by Lord Aberdeen, the same course of conduct was pursued; but the most marked supporter of the missionary party and opponent of the colonists was the Secretary of State from 1835–1839, Mr. C. Grant, afterwards Lord Glenelg.

He seems, as far as one can judge, to have been a man of a narrow and pedantic mind, and of overweening confidence in his own supposed perfect knowledge. The Colonial Office, in fact, at the time, was in the hands of a weak politician. The philanthropic or missionary party, at the same time, had immense forces on their side in two remarkable men who greatly influenced the action of the home Government.

Mr. Fowell Buxton, a man of great zeal and generous nature, exercised a vast influence both in his endeavours to ameliorate the condition of the native races, and especially for the extinction of slavery. In both he seems to have been carried away by generous sentiment, and to have been, as regards South Africa at any rate, very much in the hands of the missionaries. Dr. John Philips was also a remarkable person. He was secretary to the London Missionary Society; he seems to have had zeal and determination, but on examining the evidence he brought forward, it is impossible to acquit him of gross exaggeration and even what look very like unscrupulous misstatements.[*] Much of the action taken by the Government was based on his book of "Researches," which is proved to be in great measure unworthy of credit. In 1827 new reforms for the administration of justice which were framed had every appearance of hostility to the Boer colonists. In 1828 Mr. Fowell Buxton moved in the House of Commons for instructions to be sent to the colony to give rights to the natives which had not been thought of before and were alarming to the Dutch mind. These were passed with general approval and forwarded with his *imprimatur* by Sir George Murray, then Secretary of State. These, as a matter of fact, were based upon Dr. Philips' statements — many now known to be false or at least inaccurate. Sir Lowry Cole, the Governor, urged strongly the dangerous trend of English opinion as unfair to the colonists,[†] but all in vain.

Sir Benjamin D'Urban became Governor in 1834,

---

[*] *Cf.* "Results of the Publication of the Cape Records," by Donald Moodie, 1841, *passim;* also "Correspondence between Donald Moodie, Esq., and Rev. John Philips, D.D." especially Appendix, *passim.*

[†] Theal. *History*, p. 377.

and was sent to carry out the policy of the home Government. He had believed entirely in that policy, and was deeply prejudiced against the colonists. When he became acquainted with facts on the spot he saw reason—as has so often been the case— to reverse his judgment. The Kaffir War of 1834 was serious. It was found necessary to extend British sovereignty as far as the Kei River. This was done by treaty on December 6, 1835, and the treaty was especially advantageous to the unfortunate Fingoes enslaved by the Kaffirs. Lord Glenelg, however, was unmoved by any knowledge of those on the spot. He answered Sir Benjamin D'Urban in his usual *doctrinaire* fashion, and the treaty was disavowed.* Sir Benjamin D'Urban pointed out that this conduct towards the colonists was wrong, that the action of the home Government was unjust and calculated to lower British prestige and diminish British authority. In vain often does history seem to teach; it only repeats itself. The sole consequence of this wise remonstrance was the recall of Sir Benjamin D'Urban, just as in late years Sir Bartle Frere was silenced and his policy thwarted when it might perhaps have saved Africa. The policy of vacillation and seesaw, the policy of treating the colony in conformity with the sentimentalism of certain parties at home, went merrily on then, as it has done since more than once, with the consequences which are well known.

Then came the abolition of the slave trade.

No one can hesitate to approve of this; but it cannot but be regretted that it was done *in the way* in which it actually was. The mother country had, in

* *Kaffir Wars, Descriptive Handbook,* p. 23. Noble.

the eighteenth century, *encouraged* the slave trade to the uttermost. As late as 1775 the Board of Trade disallowed a Jamaica Act by which additional duty was placed on imported slaves. They could not "allow the colonies to check or discourage in any degree a traffic so beneficial to the nation."* The tide of opinion opposed to this odious traffic rose higher and higher, but unhappily with it there did not rise a sense of responsibility towards the unfortunate slave-owners. The slave trade was unquestionably an abominable and odious thing, still it had been not merely tolerated, but encouraged and extended, by the Government of Great Britain. Any nation surely is guilty of a moral iniquity which does not give due compensation for injuries or loss inflicted on individuals by the abolition of practices or forfeiture of possessions which have been theirs under the approval or encouragement of that nation. Philanthropic enthusiasts or faddists are not unfrequently blinded, however, as to moral considerations with regard to opponents. They are too much given to the gratification of pleasing and even excellent sentiments, costing themselves nothing, and others much. In late years some of the advanced Temperance leaders have, as we know, advocated improvement in liquor laws which would ruin a large number of persons, without giving compensation, and have seemed to fancy that, in such cases, the demands of justice may be put aside, and that, in so doing, they are acting on high moral principles. Others have demanded the robbery and spoliation of a venerable religious society—the Church of England—

* From Bridge's *Annals of Jamaica*, quoted in Egerton's *British Colonial Policy*, p. 274.

without compensation, and have talked as if to do so was to do good service. Such was, in great measure, the state of feeling in some quarters with regard to the slave trade. In 1823 resolutions were passed in Parliament intended to mitigate the hardships of slaves. As far as the colony was concerned, these were strictly enforced, but their chief effect was to add to the discontent of the Boer farmers, without doing much good to any one. In 1833 the full measure of abolition passed both Houses. The value of the slaves was, in round numbers, £50,000,000. Parliament voted £20,000,000, and of this about £3,000,000 — far below the value required — fell to the share of the Cape Colony. This, moreover, was made payable in London. Most slave-owners, therefore, were practically obliged to sell their claims far below their value. And so it has been truly said: "Amidst loud self-laudation and congratulations the nation paid up conscience money to the extent of something less than ten shillings in the pound."* In fact, a fate seemed to dog the steps of the Colonial Office, so that either mistakes were made and wrong things were done, or if right things were done they were done in a wrong and irritating way.

Thus it was that from this and many causes, with some of which we may have to deal afterwards, "the Great Trek" began in 1836. This was that emigration on a large scale of the Boer farmers, seeking, as they seem to have viewed it, to be free from the restless and dominating English Government, so as to go on in their own way; seeking, as their opponents felt with considerable truth, to work their cruelties un-

* See Egerton's *British Colonial Policy*, p. 278.

molested on the native races, and to be undisturbed in isolated quietude in their own unprogressive stagnation. This remarkable movement, however, led to far-reaching consequences, which must be considered in a future chapter.

To turn back to Cape Colony. The colony had steadily grown, especially between the years 1817 and 1820, by the then large influx of energetic and able emigrants, who spread out in the Eastern Province. These became the nucleus of one of the most vigorous of the provincial communities, and their vigour and value had much to do, as we shall see, with future events.

While the home Government, at this time and onwards for many years, was affected by a spirit of indifference or disgust with its South African possessions—which took form, as we shall see, in various acts of what now seems to have been incredible folly—the Cape Colony, always the centre from which matters radiate, and the largest and most important of the English divisions, increased in importance and material prosperity. After the Boer emigration there was greater contentment. Indeed, afterwards, and more especially for the twelve or thirteen years following the year 1845, immigrants came in considerable numbers, both British, assisted by the Government, and some from the German Legion who had taken service with England in the Crimean War. Some thousands of Germans also came and settled in the South, seeking the freedom more and more to be found under the British flag, and these have been merged in the British element, and have added to the strength and prosperity of the colony. Ostrich-farming, sheep-farming, and cattle-farming, later also fruit-farming, developed. The usual consequence of more peaceful days followed. Churches and schools were built, roads were made. In 1859 the first railway was opened—a beginning of that system of railways now more and more spreading, and likely to spread, over the country. About 1869 began the development of mineral wealth, by the discovery of diamonds, which went further by the discovery of the gold mines, and has, in the last twenty years, so much affected the history of South Africa.

We have seen how the short-sighted policy of the home Government led to many of the sorrows of the colony and of South Africa generally. The misguided zeal of the missionaries, especially of the London Missionary Society—roused, probably enough, by harsh acts of colonists, especially of the Boers, towards the native races—was always brought to bear on the Colonial Office. The governors sent out, who had greater opportunities of knowing the truth, were constantly on the side of the colonists, and therefore as constantly removed from office by the authorities at home. On the whole, these governors, notwithstanding the arbitrary power which, if they pleased, they could wield, acted wisely and commanded respect, but this state of things led on to two evil consequences.

The first was a long series of Kaffir wars. These took place chiefly in the regions near Algoa Bay. Had the matter been dealt with boldly and strongly and consistently, it could easily have been settled once for all; but everything was done grudgingly and on a small scale, and instead of one vigorous war securing peace, there were endless petty wars causing constant discomfort. The home Government were apparently governed by party considerations, not by thoughts as to the welfare of the colony. They were ever fearing the wrath of the taxpayer in England, and consequently in the end squandered much more of his money than need have been the case. Strength and determination always tell. At last, after the series of wars extending more or less from 1846 to 1853, British Kaffraria was formed into a province and administered by British officials and had in it garrisons of British troops. This worked fairly well.

A strange calamity, however, befell the Kaffirs which helped the future peace of the colony. Under the fanatical inspiration of their wizards, those of British Kaffraria destroyed their cattle and their grain stores, with the idea that the ghosts of departed ancestors—to whom the South African savage attributes extensive powers—would come to their aid with renewed resources, and assist them in the destruction of the white men. The consequence was that in spite of every effort made by the colony to assist them, multitudes of them were swept off by famine. The Kaffirs of the Kasa tribe were so reduced that henceforth there were none of the usual wars, merely slight risings readily suppressed, and at last, in 1894, Kaffraria became part of the colony, the Pando territory was incorporated into it, and it extended henceforth to the frontier of Natal.

Another unfortunate consequence of the relations of the colony with the home Government, since 1820 at any rate, was the growing inclination at Downing Street to look askance at our South African territories as possessions of which England might well be rid. The whole history of our colonial policy in that period, especially as applied to South Africa, is an illustration of the marvellous manner in which the energy and courage and persistence of Englishmen have succeeded *in spite of* the paralyzing efforts and narrow *doctrinaire* ways of Downing Street as it then was.

No doubt much greater allowance is to be made for the home Government in those days than could, if they go wrong, be made for them now. Communication was much more difficult. South Africa was very much farther from London than it is to-day. Still, there was a good deal of pettiness and pedantic cant in the air. Men were losing the vigour and breadth of mind which comes with the Imperial idea. They were full of petty party exigencies. They were bored by the demands of distant possessions. It was a sad time for England, for nations as well as men are on the high road to decay when they are too cowardly or too lazy to accept their responsibilities.

And this was very much the case. Had the then policy continued, South Africa would have been lost to the Empire. The peculiarity of our action at the Cape was this—we found the station a necessary one for our Indian route before the opening of the Suez Canal, but, fearing expense and trouble, one Colonial Secretary after another opposed any expansion. This was absurd as well as suicidal. A great colonising people must, by the law of their being, expand, and had we not expanded in South Africa we should have entirely lost the large opportunities given us there, as—through vacillation and a petty struggle against expansion— we have partly lost them. There are opportunities given to nations as to individuals, which they can neglect only at their peril; and to England have come opportunities of using for an ever-increasing and ever-enterprising people one of the richest and fairest regions of the globe, and opportunities of carrying to these regions that freedom in action and life and trade which can be had fully only under the English flag.

The effort to resist expansion was therefore, and happily, a vain one, but it caused many evils, created much irritation, and crippled to some extent our prosperity and usefulness. There was no consistent policy. It was all vacillation; and vacillation will never found, nor preserve in prosperity, a great empire. Had the men of 1795 and 1806 been the petty, vacillating, fidgetty *doctrinaires* that those who followed them have been until lately, we should have had no South Africa at all. Had our advance depended upon our Governments instead of upon Englishmen themselves, we should have no command of such South Africa as we have; and indeed in later times the opening of the trade route upon which depends, to a large extent, South African prosperity, and the paramount influence of England, we owe not so much to our Colonial Office, as to the energy and self-denial of one great Englishman—Cecil Rhodes.

The fault, however, was not merely smallness of spirit and "shortened thought" resisting the natural laws of expansion of a great people, like a man with a shovel resisting a rising tide; it was the tendency to try to govern in all details from a distance, to govern too under the influence of "every wind of doctrine" instead of by the advice of men who knew and who were on the spot. The consequence has been that in South Africa there has been a *waste* of statesmen.

We have sent out many able governors, and then failed to use them, and worse than failed. Until quite recently no governor could long work on under the home Government unless he proved himself a mere figurehead, a helpless cypher, and contentedly and without remonstrance allowed the officials at Downing Street to perpetrate abundant and ever-varying blunders. When strong and capable men came to represent Great Britain they were not trusted, they were sure to be thwarted and then withdrawn. South African Blue-Books are a constant record of the endeavours of governors to persuade the Colonial Office to act with common sense, and to consider the interests of South Africa, rather than the exigencies of party in English elections. Among many distinguished men, three really great statesmen have been among the governors at the Cape. First, there was Sir Benjamin D'Urban— already mentioned. He had been sent out in 1834 to carry out a new policy—the policy of treating the Kaffir tribes as if they were independent civilised nations, the policy which went on the assumption that the colonists were wholly in the wrong, and the English philanthropists of "the Exeter Hall" stamp, whom the Government then delighted to honour, wholly in the right. On the spot and facing facts, D'Urban, who was a man of ability and judgment, saw the case as it was. He found it necessary to annex the country between the Keiskamma and the Kei. The answer to him was a pedagogic despatch from Lord Glenelg giving a sketch of the history of the Kaffirs and their relation to the colonists drawn from his lordship's omniscient imagination, countermanding, of course, the step that had been taken. D'Urban's answer was a plea for the colonists, and an urgent request for compensation for "faithful subjects who had been visited with calamities rarely paralleled, undeserved by any act of the sufferers." Needless to say Sir Benjamin D'Urban was dismissed, his work undone, and all had to be done again at a heavy cost of blood and money, and at the cost, worse than that, of disaffection and irritation among the colonists and evils from which we suffer still. England and South Africa have paid dearly for the ignorance and false economy of inefficient Colonial Secretaries.

Another great statesman who, had he been allowed, would have saved us endless trouble in South Africa was Sir George Grey. His far-seeing policy of confederation, which would have neutralised, at least, the folly of our Government as to the Orange Free State, was, of course, refused in 1858, when it could well have been carried out, and soon after he was insultingly dismissed. He had, however, to be again placed at the head of affairs. By his wisdom he carried out to the full Sir Benjamin D'Urban's policy, so cavalierly put aside by Lord Glenelg some twenty years before, and in fact "Sir George Grey, while as an interlude helping to save India, did more to consolidate Cape Colony than had been done since the time of the first occupation."* Years after, in a native address presented to Sir Bartle Frere, Sir George Grey is spoken of as "a good Governor, good to tie up the hands of bad men, good to plant schools, good to feed the hungry, good to have mercy." And it has been truly said, "not again until the time of Sir Bartle Frere

* Egerton. *British Colonial Policy*, p. 355.

was Cape Colony to have a really great Governor." *
The time came when Sir George Grey's services, from
misunderstanding with the home Government in
another colony, were lost to the Empire.

He also went the way of all good governors. Then
we remember Sir Bartle Frere. Of him we shall have
to speak again—he, the greatest of all our "great proconsuls," hindered, thwarted, misunderstood, misrepresented, had his really great policy checked, and, with
the blessings of South Africa following him, had to
withdraw into retirement and (so far as his opponents
could manage it) disgrace, to die at last of a broken heart
as a reward from a helpless and ungrateful Government
for long years of devoted service.

The history of these three brilliant statesmen reminds
us of the folly, for many years, of our South African
policy. All that Sir Benjamin D'Urban urged has
had to be done. All that Sir George Grey and Sir
Bartle Frere would have easily achieved, had they not
been thwarted and opposed, has now to be aimed at
by any able and useful Colonial Secretary. Much of
it has had to be carried out with great difficulty since
they were sacrificed; much, with still greater difficulty, will have to be attempted.

The history of our South African policy, or want of
policy, is a long record of mistakes. I quote a short
summary in the words of an able writer: "First there
were the methods adopted to carry through slave
emancipation; then there was Lord Glenelg's policy,
with its attendant Boer exodus; then there was the
treatment of the exiles, the hesitation between a
policy of expansion and the frank recognition of in-

* Egerton. *British Colonial Policy*, p. 355.

dependent Dutch communities. Even then, however, the fates were forgiving, and, with the assumption of the Orange River Sovereignty, England had the opportunity to wipe out past mistakes. That Sovereignty, however, was only assumed to be promptly abandoned. Even then Sir George Grey's policy of confederation offered yet another opportunity, which was at once refused. Henceforth the problem became tenfold more difficult, the time being given to the Dutch republics to cultivate an independent patriotism. In spite, however, of sentimental considerations, the material and economic forces making for the union of South Africa were so strong that it seemed, at the beginning of the seventies, that that consummation might soon come to pass. But then the annexation and the subsequent retrocession of the Transvaal intervened to make peaceful confederation more distant than ever." *

No mistakes have been wanting. Our fatuous policy of vacillation, betrayal, friction, irritation, postponing, changing, doing and undoing has been such, that it is the loyalty and effort of individual Englishmen, in the very teeth of wrongheaded administration, which have saved South Africa.

Mistakes, alas! are more easily made than corrected, but to look our mistakes full in the face is going half-way to correct them. Even if many of them have arisen from ignorance and *laisser-aller*, many have arisen from an exaggerated generosity; and, after all is said and done, South Africa has had, and yet will have, her best opportunities under the British flag.

As to Cape Colony, the Committee for Trade and

* Egerton. *British Colonial Policy*, p. 472.

CAPE COLONY 145

Plantations sent in a report on a constitution. This was adopted in 1850. It advised that only the main provisions of the constitution should be laid down, that the then existing Legislative Council should have power to pass Ordinances, subject to the Sovereign's approval, " for regulating all subordinate arrangements, of which," said the report, "we are of opinion that as large a share as possible should be thus left to be determined on the spot." This was sensible and conciliatory, and a new constitution came into action in July 1854. The colony obtained fully responsible government in 1872.

The constitution is modelled on that of Great Britain and works well. With the exception perhaps of Mr. Cecil Rhodes, there would not appear to have been as yet any statesmen of first-rate rank. There are, however, some politicians of respectable ability. There are a considerable number of able men at present on the Opposition side, and on the Government side (chiefly made up of Dutch members, from country places) there are certainly three important politicians who practically take the lead. Parties are very evenly balanced, the Government at present having only a small majority. The debates are, on the whole, ably conducted and animated, and political matters, perhaps more than any other, seem to stir into activity the otherwise somewhat lethargic and easy-going temper of the people.

There is a good prospect before the colony now. The rapid and ever-improving communication with the mother country brings Capetown closely into touch with London ; South Africa has made forward strides in later years, and with increasing knowledge of its

K

problems and needs, and deepening sympathy on both sides, and constant communication, there is good hope that the English people and a wise and energetic Colonial Office will have learnt by experience, and be henceforth in no danger of repeating the mistakes of the past.

CHAPTER II

THE ORANGE FREE STATE

WE have seen something of the misdirected zeal and general wrongheadedness of the Colonial Office, and the restiveness under any restraint of the Boer colonists which paved the way to the Boer emigration which began in 1836, and is known by the name of "the Great Trek."

The causes of the emigration have supplied food for controversy among writers on South Africa. Some have believed that it was entirely due to the abolition of the Slave Trade, and this, of course, had a good deal to do with it.

There can be no doubt that the rude and less educated Boers have always been more harsh and cruel to the natives than the English settlers have ever been. That these latter have also been guilty of unkindness and even cruelty to the coloured races is, of course, probable; but the attitude of the Boer has been and is very different from that of the English Government or the English colonist to the unfortunate native. The best excuse to be made for the Boers, even by writers of the extreme Radical or "Little England" type, who have seemed to find delight in taking sides against their own countrymen, is that New Testament morality cannot be expected from those who are chiefly students of the Old Testament. We have seen that the early missionaries (and especially the celebrated Dr. Philips) had given exaggerated and inaccurate accounts of the ill-treatment of natives at the hand of Boer farmers; still there were plenty of unpleasant matters of that kind to report which were certainly true. No one can seriously doubt, for instance, in later times, the very general testimony to the fact of the practice among the Transvaal Boers, when not interfered with by the British, of kidnapping native children and really selling them into slavery, though it has not been called by that name, but designated by the less invidious title of "apprenticeship." Boer public opinion would never condemn this. Advocates of the Boers have unblushingly contended that the children in question were fortunate in being placed under Boer care and training, rather than being left with their own people; that there were large numbers of orphan and destitute children whose parents had perished in war; that these required care, and so on. This has been the Boer pretence. It is, of course, a mere invention. The British in their wars with natives found nothing of the kind, for the simple reason that there was nothing of the kind to find. In native wars children were killed or carried off to slavery, and the invention that Boers always found (while the British never did) numerous children, abandoned and destitute, is a pretence so clumsy that it shows how strong the Boer belief is in the "gullibility" of the English people. The Transvaal Government denied that such trade was in any way tolerated by them—according to their simple method of denying everything that is to their discredit—and it was difficult to bring the charge home; and those who know most of the Transvaal Government appear to be thoroughly convinced that they are past masters in the art of managing wrongdoing in such a way as to make it difficult to trace it by legal evidence to its authors, and that denials of anything that may prove inconvenient are not difficult to offer. It is acknowledged on all hands that the Boers have ever looked upon themselves as the Elect People of God, and upon the native races as mere Canaanites to be exterminated or enslaved.* There can be little doubt then that the abolition of slavery was one cause of the discontent in 1836, whilst the really inadequate compensation given for the property in slaves was (not unnaturally) another.

Then, of course, another cause, akin to the first, is doubtless to be found in a desire for larger freedom in attacking or destroying native races than the British Government would sometimes allow. So that, generally, the movement came from a strong inclination in the people to be free from any restraints. Their independent characters and dogged perseverance cannot but be admired; but *corruptio optimi pessima*, and in this case some fine qualities degenerated into great vices. They longed for selfish isolation. They were resolved every man to be "a law unto himself." They fretted against any government. Not to be law-abiding, but to disobey all law was their delight;

* Not long ago (December 1898) Mr. Krüger is reported to have preached, as his custom is, to congregations of three United Dutch Churches on Dingaan's Day (December 16), and to have given his version of "the Great Treck," pointing out "that the Lord was always with the nation even in this last campaign against Magato." Mr. Krüger is always in the habit of assuming that he has special information as to the counsels of "the Lord."

and they were people who would not always, indeed would very seldom, tolerate even the Governments set up by themselves. They did not like the trouble of working. In labour they had become indolent and lazy, and so all the more did they hate the Government which had deprived them of the slaves whom they could force to toil.

They enjoyed the excitement of hunting and of war. Indeed it was only war which ever led them to act together. If they had physical courage they were also wanting in any steady cohesiveness, as well as in any shade of refinement or culture. In real civilisation they were, as they are, a century or more behind most other European races. Their ideal was, as it is, to disregard or crush others, and—with alternating fits of indolence and activity such as characterise wild animals—to do what they pleased themselves. To think of them as a great and simple people with a passionate love for freedom is to amuse the mind with an unsubstantial romance. The Transvaal Boer desires licence, and has neither wish nor understanding as to liberty in its true sense. At this moment he tolerates, and on the whole approves, a tyranny so long as it presses hardly upon others and not upon himself; and if our Colonial Office before and about 1836 acted with a folly that aroused the worst side of their natures, at least all who have love of just dealing between man and man must rejoice that, if they could not hinder them from robbing and raiding among the native tribes, they then and always have prevented them from the open practice of slavery.

Once away from the colony the emigrants made for the wilderness in different bands and from time to time. However impossible it may be to sympathise with their ideals or with many of their doings, we must admire their determination and courage. They travelled, as now, in covered waggons with their wives and families, and driving their herds of cattle. The country across the mountains had many wild beasts and a thin population, and beyond it were the far-stretching solitudes inhabited by the Zulu tribes.

Tshaka had been the great Zulu king. Cruel and fierce as he was, he had conquered and enslaved or murdered all around him. He himself had fallen by the hand of an assassin some years before the Trek, and had been succeeded by his brother Dingaan, who ruled the Zulus in the tract of country to the north-east of Natal.

The Government did not hinder the trekkers from going, though it in no way renounced a claim to their allegiance; but while in some quarters it was thought a thing not to be regretted that many such disaffected persons should leave the colony in peace, it was also felt that in any case it was not possible to hinder them going if they pleased. The British, however, had always been the protectors of the native races, and it was known well enough that these were not likely to fare well at the hands of the emigrants, so not with unmixed feelings these latter were allowed to go.

The first party who left the colony fared ill. They suffered severely from the attacks of the natives and from fever. Their cattle died in great numbers, and so a miserable remnant only succeeded in reaching Delagoa Bay. This party had included names not unknown in colonial history. It was led by Louis Triechard, who had been specially violent in speech against the British rule. J. Pretorius was with it, and it was joined by a contingent under Van Rensburg, with whom were De Wet, Van Wyk, Prins, and others. This contingent afterwards separated from Triechard's party, and perished, it is supposed, at the hands of natives. Triechard himself died at Delagoa Bay. Others, made up of scattered bands meeting together at Thaba Ntchu in what is now the Orange Free State, made their way to the north. The head of this movement was Andries Hendrik Potgieter, and in the band were families of the Liebenbergs and Krügers. Among the latter was Paul Krüger, now Transvaal President, then about ten years of age. A part under Potgieter went on to inspect the country, and returned to find that some of those left behind had been roughly handled by the Matabele. Accordingly they raided the territory of Mozilekatze. He had fallen into disgrace with Tshaka many years before, and had fled to Mosega, between what is now Johannesburg and Mafeking. There he ruled over the Matabele, and carried on the usual predatory wars with any other tribes, such as the Bechuanas, who were weaker than himself.

The emigrants succeeded in defeating him and driving him across the Limpopo. Mozilekatze, in his turn, attacked the tribes between the Limpopo and the Zambesi, and finally established himself in Buluwayo, for long the headquarters kraal of the Matabele kings, until it became of late the capital of Rhodesia. It was in this wide region between the Orange River and the Limpopo that the various wandering parties of Boers settled in a loose fashion, so far as these nomad groups of stock farmers could be said to settle. And then there was a further settlement, for the fact was—as became more evident in later years—that the Boer wanderers were continually dispersed owing to dissensions among themselves. The further migration was that led by Piet Retief, but the details of these adventures belong to a later part of our history.

Leaving for a moment the affairs relating to what became the colony of Natal, the results of the emigration of Boers from the Cape Colony are important in two directions. The first touches matters in connection with the territory between the Orange River and the Vaal. There were bodies of Boers scattered over the district north of Cape Colony, from its then frontier about Colesberg. There were, including these, three sets of inhabitants near that frontier continually coming into collision: (1) The Griquas (called also the Bastards), who were half-breeds, and were sprung from unions of Dutchmen and Hottentot women. These unions were very numerous, as the Dutch, with coarser natures and less refinement of character, have been much more intermingled with the native races than the English. (2) Then there were the Basutos. These were made up of remnants of tribes driven from the north by the fierce Zulus. They became a hardy race, and under the wise rule of Moshesh, their celebrated king, grew into a sort of native nation which still flourishes under British protection in the mountain district west of Natal and south of the Free State—"the Switzerland of South Africa," as it is usually called. (3) And then there were the wandering Boers.

Among these opposing forces there were continual quarrels. The state of uneasiness which then existed was a source of anxiety both at Downing Street and Capetown.

The question was, what could be done to avoid the constant unsettlement caused by the friction, and the consequent danger of fresh native wars? This exercised all minds given to think on the subject. Had a consistent policy been pursued all might have turned out well, and many of the after troubles in South Africa would have been avoided. But such was not the case. The policy of shilly-shally, which had before, and has since, done such infinite mischief, set in and became an epidemic at the Colonial Office, followed in this instance, as in others afterwards, by confusion all round, by greater irritation among the Boer emigrants, and a practical betrayal of the English colonists.

The first idea—which emanated from the missionaries, and especially from Dr. Philips—was to protect the colony from Boer disturbance by a line of native states. This would further have the advantage of keeping the natives in touch with the British, who looked upon themselves as their natural protectors. As might have been expected, however, this arrangement would not work. A treaty had already existed for a few years with Waterboer (as he was called), a Griqua captain. Another was now made with Adam Kok, another Griqua leader, and with Moshesh, the Basuto king. Still the quarrels with the natives went on. The whites would not, as might have been expected, obey Griquas; some new arrangement was necessary. From 1843 to 1846 these abortive efforts had had their trial and had failed. In 1846 Bloemfontein was made a centre for a British Resident and a small British force, and this was followed up by further sensible steps, which would have worked well for the future of South Africa had they been consistently carried out; but again there was vacillation at home.

It is, of course, proverbially easy to be wise after the fact. The home Government, doubtless, had difficulties—especially from want of more rapid communication—which would not be encountered now. Still, in great colonial, as in foreign, questions, it is not unfair to demand from British rulers careful accumulation of evidence, wisdom in following the advice of responsible Governors on the spot, and, indeed, at any rate, a steady instead of a tentative and uncertain policy. This demand, however, has not, until quite recently, been satisfied. What may be called Lord Glenelg's policy alienated Dutch subjects, as we have seen, and now the policy of those in power at home further stereotyped such alienation, and led up to the first of those shortsighted betrayals of people who depended upon our Government, of which there have been later and even more miserable examples. All along it is melancholy to see the constant shortsightedness and vacillation which has led to so many unhappy consequences in the history of South Africa.

The fact is, the English Government had got into the habit of looking upon our South African possessions as a troublesome heritage which, above all things, should not be allowed to expand, on which as little money as possible should be spent, and which—unless, perhaps, Table Bay and Capetown—should be got rid of, if that were found possible. Governor after Governor was sent to the colony to carry out a policy of this kind. Governor after Governor learnt facts on the spot, took a truer and more statesmanlike view, pressed it upon the home Government, and was each in turn consequently recalled. The only safety of a Governor became at last a servile imitation of a vacillating Government. The treatment accorded afterwards to Sir Bartle Frere, as a reward for his energy and farsightedness, may have warned Sir Hercules Robinson of the need of weakness or at least of a shrinking from responsibility. It is always more and more evident that, so far as the situation has been saved in South Africa in later times, it has been saved by the energy and dash of Englishmen, in the teeth, for the most part, of the home Government. For many years—at least as regards this immense territory which offered itself for British enterprise—the home Government of both parties was *in toto* as much made up of "Little Englanders" as the small groups of curiosities who have been subjects of quiet toleration, or have exercised a passing influence over Englishmen of our own day.

In 1847 Sir Harry Smith became Governor of the colony. He seems to have been a man of statesmanlike views and considerable capacity. He saw clearly enough the defects in the Boer character, but he had also a clear view of their strong points, and he had a real liking for the Dutch people. He had known South Africa; he believed that the misunderstandings with the Boer farmers could be dispelled, and that the true solution of the difficult problem, arising out of the disturbed relations between Boers, Griquas, and Basutos, was the formation of a self-governing colony north of the Orange, while the British had a controlling protectorate over the natives. Accordingly he went to Bloemfontein and thence to Natal. He succeeded in checking any further exodus (for an exodus after the formation of that colony had begun) of the Dutch settled there, and on February 3, 1848, the "Orange River Sovereignty," as it was called, was proclaimed.

The British Government, as was usual then, were thoroughly annoyed at African troubles — albeit in great measure induced by themselves—and only grudgingly assented to Sir Harry Smith's arrangements. Some of the details required correcting, and the British Resident, Major Warden, does not seem to have acted with prudence as to these. Many of the colonists were thankful enough for the restoration of some sort of order and good government, but the more turbulent and anarchical of the Boer farmers, as usual, stirred up opposition. Others from beyond the Vaal—where every man was "a law unto himself"—joined them; the Resident was besieged in Bloemfontein, and almost driven to capitulate. Sir Harry Smith, however, acted with promptitude, and with a small force with which he advanced from Capetown defeated the Boers under Andries Pretorius at Boomplatz on August 29, 1848, and, while leaving the Transvaal Dutch to themselves, re-established the Orange River Sovereignty on what would appear to have been a solid foundation. The Boers who were opposed to British rule moved across the Vaal; those who were more in favour of it remained, and a considerable number of colonists from Cape Colony crossed into the Sovereignty and settled there instead of those who had left.

There seemed some hope now that things would go right, but the vacillation and wrongheadedness of the home authorities, as usual, extinguished such hope. The Secretary now at the Colonial Office was no friend to expansion, and, like the rest, had little knowledge of South Africa and little care for it. There were still some difficulties with Pretorius and his party across the Vaal, and when they showed signs of willingness to come to some settled terms with Great Britain the Government seized upon the opportunity. Assistant Commissioners were appointed by Lord Grey. They held that a treaty made with Pretorius would detach the disaffected in the Orange Sovereignty from the Transvaal Boers. This was the pretext for signing what was called the Sand River Convention, and it was accordingly signed in 1852.

This guaranteed the independence of the Boers beyond the Vaal, and definitely distinguished between them and those in the Sovereignty. What is now called the South African Republic is in the habit of considering that its independence dates from that time. The Convention, however, was a serious blunder, to say the least of it. Had the Government acted firmly and sincerely towards South Africa, the after difficulties which came from it would have been avoided: (1) There was then no South African Republic. Pretorius was merely one leader among many, and the Boers across the Vaal were in a state of utter anarchy, and divided into mutually hostile "republics." If the British Government had shown them once and for all that they meant to be masters, and then treated them with justice, the Transvaal would have been a prosperous self-governing colony long ago; the natives would have been protected from the excessive harshness of the Dutch, and the causes of friction, which are still at work in South Africa, would have been removed. Then (2) even if the Convention was to be made with Pretorius and his detachment, at any rate the treatment of the Orange River Sovereignty should have been consistent and sincere. Colonists had settled in that Sovereignty trusting in the good faith of the British Government; the arrangements made by Sir Harry Smith were beginning to work well, any details which required correction could have been corrected. The Transvaal Boers were now at least pledged, and indeed seemed determined, not to settle south of the Vaal. Their hands were quite full enough with their own intestine disputes. The statesmanship of Sir Harry Smith was just beginning to bear good fruits, when everything was wrecked by the folly of Downing Street. The "Little England" spirit, with all its selfishness and huckstering pettiness, and fear of responsibility, was abroad, sheltering itself, as usual, under vague ideas of inopportune generosity and cheap philanthropy. The consequence was that betrayal of the colonists for whom Great Britain was responsible— the first of our unhappy betrayals in South Africa— which must be looked back upon by every Englishman with a deep sense of shame.

There is something really pathetic in the determined loyalty towards the Empire of the colonies again and again, when the object of the home Government— ruled by this contemptible temper—seemed only to be a desire to be rid of them. Never has that loyalty been more conspicuous than in the case of the Orange River Sovereignty; never has a betrayal of responsibility been more flagrant than in the deliberate ejection of these loyal colonists from the unity of the Empire, at a time when they were too young and too unformed to resist such selfish disregard of their loyal desires.

A statement had been drawn up by them in 1851 in these words:

"No sooner had your Excellency extended the authority of the Queen than order and subordination were established, the confidence of the peaceful and well-disposed revived . . . flourishing villages suddenly sprang up, and the apparently waste land of a year or two previous became studded with substantial homesteads."*

This, however, was altogether disregarded. Even in the February of 1852 Lord Grey had shown his bias. "The ultimate abandonment," he wrote, "of the Orange River Sovereignty should be a settled point in our policy"; and in that same spring Sir Harry Smith, having succeeded in settling that Sovereignty on a satisfactory basis, was, in accordance with the usual methods towards South Africa, recalled. His habit of judging of facts as they were, and his statesmanlike arrangements for the Orange River difficulty, had naturally given umbrage at Downing Street.

Matters now moved rapidly in favour of the policy of the Colonial Office. Sir John Pakington was Secretary for a short time, and during his tenure of office the matter was left undecided. General Cathcart, however, had been sent out as Governor, instead of Sir Harry Smith, in 1852, to see with the eyes of the Government. The Duke of Newcastle, who was now at the Colonial Office (1852–54), was inclined in the same direction as Lord Grey had been. A small Basuto war which broke out at the time helped matters on. Sir George Clerk was sent out as Special Commissioner in 1853, instructed, indeed, to consider

* *Parliamentary Papers*, 1854, quoted by Egerton; also *British Colonial Policy*, p. 346.

that the decision at home might be modified, but informed by the Duke of Newcastle of the Government's intention to carry out what in later days is known as "the policy of scuttle." The minds of statesmen and politicians were fixed upon European affairs in the East just before the Crimean War. South African matters were practically voted a nuisance. Responsibility to our colonists was not recognised. The Orange River Sovereignty was in fact doomed.

The immediate occasion for this act of folly and, indeed, of treachery, as I have said, was the outbreak of the Basuto war. Moshesh was attacked by, as usual, an apparently insufficient force under General Cathcart. The Basuto country was difficult, the force suffered a reverse from an ambush. It would have been necessary to return to the attack with increased forces or surrender (as indeed happened on a later and more serious occasion), but that Moshesh, fortunately, seemed inclined to peace. This war was unpopular in England. It was of great advantage to the Dutch settlers, and was believed to have been undertaken in their behalf. Had it been so, there is no reason to think that it was wrong to protect our own colonists, but it was thought that the Dutch should have showed their energy in defending themselves. As a matter of fact the war seems to have been due to the Governor, and carried on in opposition to the wishes of the colonists, whether Dutch or English. Some excuse may, perhaps, be made for the Colonial Office. It was probably in command of insufficient information and was now fairly out of heart with colonial wars, and when the intelligence reached England the Duke of Newcastle determined on abandoning the Orange River Sovereignty.

It is always—we cannot blind ourselves to the fact—a mark of pitiable weakness, whether in a man or in a nation, to succumb to the first pressure of difficulties. For a strong man or a strong nation difficulties are things to be overcome. Petulance may be excused in a very weak woman or a child, scarcely in the responsible government of a Great people. The cry, "I can't be bothered any more; let things go; I don't care," is an unworthy cry from the lips of an Imperial Government, but the cowardly and impatient temper which finds vent in such a cry has twice at least led to a betrayal of our trust in South Africa. On the later occasion it found some semblance of excuse in the plea put forward—and by some truly put forward—of generosity and justice; on this occasion there was not even that.

It was a fatal step, and far from being to the honour of England. Delegates were sent home to pray that the State might remain subject to the British crown. It was a moment when the Basuto power appeared most dangerous; it was certainly not the time to abandon the colonists. They refused to be thrust away. They expressed their intention of draping the English flag with crape, hanging it half-mast high, and relying upon the British Parliament to come to their aid. Alas! they leant on a broken reed. "Little Englandism'—that spirit of cowardly selfishness—was in possession; men's minds were full of other things. They would not take the trouble to attend to the agonised prayers of their distant kinsfolk and fellow-subjects and to their just demands. Alas! if it was the first time it was not the last that South Africa was destined to learn that England could betray her children.

Mr. Adderley made a gallant attempt in the House of Commons to obtain a reconsideration of the sentence of dismissal for the Orange River Sovereignty, but in vain. Parliament did do something: it voted forty-eight thousand pounds to be rid of a large and loyal dependency! It is a sad and disgraceful story, and it has never been forgotten in South Africa. General Cathcart's words to a meeting of delegates praying to be retained as a self-governing colony under the British crown show how well he fulfilled the wishes of Downing Street:

"The expression,"* he said, "of the wants and wishes of the delegates are so decidedly in favour of uncompromising self-government that it would be gracious in her Majesty to grant them even more than they ask—viz., independence."

The comment reads like a grim joke.

"I have reason to think," adds the Governor, "in that event Mr. Pretorius would become President of a United Republic, and its natural independence might then be recognised. As you justly observe, the principle is the same, whether the Vaal or the Orange River be the named boundary."

General Cathcart's "reason to think" was as baseless as his remarks were cynical; though the fault did not lie at the door of that gallant officer, but at that of those whom he loyally served. Our fellow-subjects—whether Dutch or English—although they were cast off by the mother country, when longing to be one with her, felt no inclination to put themselves under the heel of "Mr. Pretorius"!

* Parliamentary Papers, 1854.

Sir George Clerk, the Special Commissioner in 1853, was an even more thoroughgoing instrument, if possible, in carrying out the cynical policy of the Colonial Secretary. Delegates were sent again by the colonists—Dutchmen and Englishmen alike—to petition for the continual maintenance of British supremacy, but Sir George Clerk was primed with a ready-made theory. The desire was due, he said—as if he understood their feelings better than their elected representatives could—" to delusions practised on the inactive Dutch by greedy English land speculators." It was in vain that the chairman of the delegates declared that there had been " hitherto no separation of interests between the Dutch and English inhabitants." The Commissioner, who professed to read their true thoughts, seemed to feel sure that they were longing to be combined in one State with those who had gone northward, and who were " living contentedly and peaceably across the Vaal." Sir George Clerk had strange notions of peace and contentment. The Transvaal Boers were in a state of utter anarchy, and rival factions were flying at each other's throats. However, the cause was pre-judged, and no effort was spared, in spite of prayers and entreaties to the contrary, to cut the Orange River Sovereignty adrift.

The Commissioner had no name for the loyal majority but " obstructionists." Those—the minority—opposed to the British connection were the " well-disposed." They fought to the last, but the Commissioner's mind was made up—or rather the minds of those who sent him—and the loyal had to be browbeaten and wearied out, and then tranquillised by "compensation."*

* Egerton's *British Colonial Policy*, pp. 349-352.

The terms of Convention were laid before the Assembly on February 17, 1854, although the Proclamation withdrawing the Sovereignty had been signed—though the fact was concealed from those in South Africa—on the January 30 preceding. There was deception all round. Moshesh and his Basutos were led to believe one thing as to the dividing-line and the Dutch farmers another. Anything, it would seem, to get rid of valuable territory and loyal subjects! It was a bad business. On March 11, 1854, the English flag was "hoisted for the last time over the Queen's fort." It was saluted and then lowered. The flag of the new Republic—a Republic forced into existence against its will by the Downing Street blunderers—was hoisted, and the Special Commissioner, having finished this miserable work, started to leave Bloemfontein with the troops and Government officials. As if to close the dreary performance in a fitting manner, just as they were departing one of the soldiers dropped down dead. They had to pause for his burial. Then, accompanied by Moshesh and the other chiefs and the members of the new-made Government, they left the abandoned territory. They journeyed together to the end of the first stage towards Capetown. "Then, in apparent friendship, the Commissioner, the chiefs, and the members of the new Government bade each other farewell, and the farmers and Basuto"—each of them deceived —"were left to settle as they could the relation in which they were to stand to each other." *

The Commissioner on his way had an interview with Adam Kok, the Griqua leader. Here he failed

* Theal's *History*, 1834-1854, chap. xlvi. p. 547.

in his proposals and then departed, leaving the complicated and difficult question — created by this wretched policy—as a heritage of difficulty for the new Government. The delegates to England had gone, as we have seen, some time before. It was not until March 16 that they were admitted to an interview with the Duke of Newcastle, and not until May 9 that Mr. Adderley was able to make his honest but abortive effort, which has been mentioned, in the House of Commons.

So closed one of the most discreditable chapters in the history of English government. So was effected a betrayal of duty and responsibility towards loyal colonists. Scarcely if ever equalled, even in the annals of the long series of blundering at Downing Street in the treatment of South Africa, it is a chapter in history calculated to bring a blush to the cheek of any Englishman, and it illustrates the strange fact—to which we have already drawn attention—that our Empire has so often done her duty towards her colonies and dependent races by the efforts and energies of Englishmen *in spite of* officials at home. That the Colonial Office had great difficulties to encounter in the affairs of South Africa, no one, I repeat, can doubt. This, indeed, must be frankly acknowledged. But what ought "difficulties" to be to a powerful, high-spirited, and justice-loving people? No difficulties can justify any Government in constant vacillation followed by final betrayal.

But though "The Orange Free State," as it is called, was now forcibly cut adrift from Great Britain, the Colonial Office had not yet filled to the full the cup of its blunderings.

THE ORANGE FREE STATE

The state of things some few years after in the new Republic was what might have been expected. The various Transvaal "Republics" were in conflict with one another. Things in the Orange Free State were in confusion. The party of the younger Pretorius threatened to absorb it. If it had been thrust away against its will from British connection, at least it now appealed for alliance with England to protect it against the encroachment of the Transvaal Boers.

When this occurred a real statesman was in power. Sir George Grey—whose death, in an honoured old age, was not long ago* the occasion for expressions of respect and sympathy all over South Africa—saw the real causes of all the vacillations and mistakes—viz., the want of trust in the future of South Africa felt by the home Government. He boldly stated that the "independence" of the Orange Free State had been forced upon it against the wishes of "nearly all the wealthy and influential inhabitants." He explained fully, at the request of Sir E. Bulwer Lytton, his view that Federation among the South African Colonies and States was the only true policy. He criticised freely the cynical policy which had been pursued, producing as it had done alienation and dissatisfaction and pressed upon the Government the need of Federation.

The moment was propitious. The Orange Free State desired it. In time the Transvaal Boers—if only in self-defence—would have been sure to fall in with it, and the calamities which have since come upon South Africa would have been avoided. The usual blundering at the Colonial Office again ruined all.

* 1898.

Sir George Grey had spoken of the matter in the Cape Parliament. The blunderers at home were annoyed that he had done so without a direct decision from Downing Street, and at his unconcealed contempt for their folly; and—as usual—Sir George Grey was recalled in January 1859. It was indeed found necessary to reinstate him soon after, when the Duke of Newcastle became again Colonial Secretary, but the mischief was done. What was in vain attempted later might have been easily accomplished then. Strong and capable governors, such as D'Urban had been in the past, such as Sir Bartle Frere was to be in the future, were not to the mind of the Colonial Secretaries in those days; and even when Sir George Grey returned as Governor of the Cape, the lion's claws were cut. He was under engagement to leave untouched for the future the question of Federation.

What he could do, however, as a good Governor he did. The Orange Free State has gone on in peaceful relations to Great Britain, and has been in many ways in advance of its fellow Republic in the Transvaal. With the Transvaal too there was considerable hostility. When Pretorius, anxious to gain strength against his various enemies, tried to arrange a union with the Free State he completely failed. The Free State would have none of it. Thereupon the Transvaal party, led by Pretorius and numbering among its officers Commandant Paul Krüger, organised a raid into the Free State. The forces arrayed against them, however, were too strong, and after the two armies had lain opposite each other for several days, Krüger was sent to pray for a pacific settlement, and an understanding was arrived at. After some punishment of a light character to a few Free State rebels, and the departure of others into the Transvaal, things settled down, and, amid various disturbances in the Transvaal, the Free State has held its own and maintained its independence.

Probably owing to a closer connection with the British, the people of the Free State have shown much greater enlightenment than those of the Transvaal. They are less ignorant, and less jealous and narrow-minded, and less selfish and retrogressive. The English and Dutch elements are closely united. There are more enlightened views on education and religion. There are now no troubles with the natives. On the Boundary Reserve large numbers of them live, keeping their cattle and holding land. Elsewhere they must not hold land, nor have they the franchise. They appear, however, to be treated tolerably well. Nowhere, where the Dutch are in the majority, can they expect so much freedom as in an English colony. But then nowhere is freedom understood fully as it is under the British flag. The community appear now a happy and contented one. They have had wise and statesmanlike Presidents for the most part who have guided their destinies well. They welcome immigrants, and have none of the narrowness of the Pretoria Government, and are free from the corruption and blackmailing which so largely take the place of honest and just dealing among the rulers of their Northern neighbours. They are now on perfectly good terms with the English Government, though the way in which they were cast adrift is not forgotten, and they have shown their (not unnatural) contempt for England by drawing closer to the Transvaal Republic.

The only question of importance which has arisen between them and England has been the question as to the possession of the diamond fields. By a strange irony of fate, the country which had been forcibly alienated from the most selfish motives, as not worth having, seemed likely to be the possessor of vast resources in diamonds. When the diamonds were discovered in and about Kimberley, the Free State claimed that they were within their territory, and there was a counterclaim put in on the part of various owners, including the Transvaal Republic. The troubles over these diamond fields between the various claimants are too long to dwell upon here in detail. Suffice it to say a compromise was effected. In 1876 the offer for compensation to the Free State, through the intervention of Sir Donald Currie, was accepted. This long and only dispute between the British and Free State Government was brought to an end at last, and a part of the territory, once thrown away as valueless, was finally recovered by Great Britain, and incorporated into Cape Colony, by a payment of £90,000. Happy is the people that has no history! Since then the Orange Free State has practically had none. It has appeared contented, united, and happy. It has, indeed, been drawn nearer to the Republic across the Vaal since 1895, but—in spite of any feeling for past treatment—it remains, owing to its sensible government and union between English and Dutch elements, on terms of now undisturbed amity with Great Britain.

CHAPTER III

THE TRANSVAAL ANNEXATION AND AFTERWARDS

THE state of things in the Transvaal evidently pointed to some great change, and the years from 1877–1881 became some of the most interesting in the history of South Africa. It is not always possible to reconcile the various assertions which have been made on different sides. Still, putting them together, we may, on the whole, reach a *resultant* (to use the language of mathematics) which fairly represents the course of things. The history is sad enough reading for Englishmen. At the same time the miserable blunders of those years will not have been in vain if the British Government has learnt from them more firmness and consistency. We have before us in this period examples of all the characteristic faults in British action in South Africa—the effort to govern from a distance, the neglect of the guidance given by able and responsible persons, the substitution of political exigencies and party needs in the guidance of a great colonial empire for the consideration of its best interests, the sway on the minds of home statesmen of the sentimental and humanitarian gossips as against the ripe opinion of great and trusty and responsible servants of the Crown on the spot, the influence of the prepossessions, and even the generous prepossessions, of good men on their action as rulers, instead of the study of facts,—all this, which had already done so much mischief in our colonial policy, rose to high-water mark in these fateful years in South Africa, when weakness, vacillation, unsound judgment, and short-sightedness shook the great reputation of England to its very foundations.

In 1858-9 there had been, as we have seen, a grand opportunity for Confederation which, owing to "the shortness of thought" of the English Government, was thrown away. It was seen now in 1877 that Confederation was the true policy. It is to be lamented that this had not been sooner seen. For years there had been a continual seesaw between expansion and limitation, or even disintegration, between extension or restraint of Imperial authority. This vacillation has been the source of endless difficulties. Whatever views may be held as to the advisability of one course or the other, even a "Little Englander" himself cannot doubt that want of continuity in our policy, that continual change owing to the change of the temper of parties at home, that *first* doing one thing and *then* doing another, is utterly bad.

Governments had not always the wit to see that Englishmen are, in the long run, stronger than their passing Governments—that an Imperial people can never be really turned into a "parochial" clique unless decay has set in at the heart of the race itself, and that it is better to guide, not to attempt to thwart, the sense of advance and readiness to accept responsibility, natural to a great people.

Vacillation, however, unfortunately continued then to be the keynote of the policy of Downing Street.

When the Great Trek had taken place it was held that the Boers who had moved to the north-east of the colony were still British subjects, and that it was right to send troops under orders from the Governor * to put an end to the war between Zulus and Boers.† Again Sir Harry Smith fought at Boomplatz ‡ to uphold British sovereignty over the Boers. Lord Grey, however, soon after pronounced in favour of a directly opposite policy.§ Everything that had been done was undone as far as possible, and it was declared that her Majesty's dominions should in no degree, however slight, be extended in South Africa, and that no wars between natives and natives or natives and Boers would be interfered with.||

Accordingly Sir Harry Smith was recalled, and Sir George Cathcart replaced him. Then followed "the Sand River Convention" with the Boers, and the unhappy action, already described, as to "the Orange River Sovereignty." Here was a startling change. The native interests had been so strongly espoused that England had, thereby, turned the Trek Boers from loyal subjects into sullen opponents. Now the natives were to be thrown overboard! This, however, was not so easy. In fact, it was impossible. And great Governors like Sir Harry Smith and Sir George Grey had seen that the only chance for peace and progress was the steady assertion and enforcement of the sway of England as paramount Power, that so

---

* Sir George Napier. † In 1838. ‡ In 1848. § In 1851.
|| "You will distinctly understand that any wars, however sanguinary, which may afterwards occur between different tribes and communities, which will be left in a state of independence ... are to be considered as affording no ground for your interference."—Lord Grey to Sir Harry Smith. *Parliamentary Papers*, 1854.

only could there be a continuous application of wise principles in dealing with natives and others. All golden opportunities were lost, however, and the statesmanlike efforts of such men were thwarted by the distant Colonial Office; and hence the troubles coming on us in South Africa in later times.

But now there seemed more hope for a consistent policy. Lord Carnarvon became Colonial Secretary in 1874. He saw the need of Confederation such as has made the Dominion of Canada a prosperous Power. The man for the work, too, was not wanting. Sir Bartle Frere had returned with well-earned laurels from India. With difficulty he was persuaded to undertake the office of Governor of the Cape Colony and High Commissioner. He had been a capable and successful administrator. He had large and statesmanlike views. He had a winning presence, and was a man of fearless strength and fascinating gentleness. No one was possessed of a larger sympathy joined with a wise judgment and clear common sense. He was loved and respected by the native races, though he had to manage the Zulu War. He won the respect and affection of the Transvaal Boers, although he had to deal with them when disaffection was growing.* Such a man might have been trusted to work another problem of Confederation, even under the now more difficult conditions, had he been wisely and loyally supported from home. He had one fault. He could not be the mere puppet of Downing Street, the mere creature to carry out varying ignorant official whims. Lord Carnarvon followed the usual mistake of sending out the scheme for Confederation cut and dried. When

* *Cf.* Martineau's *Life of Sir Bartle Frere*, vol. ii. p. 308.

this came before the Cape Parliament, it was curtly put aside, on the plea that it should proceed from South Africa. In this the Cape Parliament was not apparently right. The matter touched the whole of South Africa, and it was right that suggestions should come from the Imperial Government. Still, the colony had just begun to try its hand at self-government, and a young colony in that position was naturally sensitive of its authority. The matter might have been managed with greater tact, and it would so have been managed had the home Government left the High Commissioner to see to details, with no further interference, for the present, from home. This difficulty would have been easily overcome, but there were far greater risks ahead, which made able steering a necessity. To the complicated causes which threw the ship of Government upon these rocks we must now look back.

The Sand River Convention—an act of extraordinary folly on the part of the English Government—had been signed in 1852. The Transvaal Republic was not more than about twelve years old when it showed unmistakable signs of "the inability of the Boer, when left to his own devices, to carry on civil government." *

For what had happened? Immediately on the acquisition of independence in 1852, confusion of every kind began its reign in the Transvaal Republic. The Government could scarcely be called a Government at all. It was hopelessly weak. It had no revenue except that arising from a tax on the farms, which was only paid when the farmers chose to pay. There was no police. Men followed the Boer ideal and did what they pleased. Legal tribunals were used to

* Egerton. *British Colonial Policy*, p. 343.

register the decrees of party feeling, and were as un-unjust, though probably not more corrupt, than at present. A Mr. Smettekamp, a friend of Potgieter's party, was fined and exiled quite unjustly, it would appear, by the influence of Pretorius' party. The relations with the natives were, as usual, unsatisfactory. Hermanus Potgieter, a man of violent temper, while on an illegal trading expedition managed to arouse the animosity of Makapan's people. He and his party were then barbarously murdered. Commandant P. Potgieter, having placed the women and children of the Potcheffstroom and Rustenberg disticts in safety, attacked the natives, and slaughtering some and blockading others in caves until they died of thirst, practically exterminated the clan. Mr. Paul Krüger served in this expedition. Mr. P. Potgieter shortly after this died, and there were then three commandants, M. W. Pretorius, W. F. Joubert, and S. Schœman, each with a party, and all quarrelling with one another. Ecclesiastical strife followed. There was fierce dissension as to whether there should be any union with the Cape Synod of the Dutch Reformed Church or not. This dissension raged for several years. Political quarrels went hand in hand with it. There were practically several little Republics. One of the contending parties wished for a single Government, subordinate courts of control in different districts, and a Church with no connection with any other Church outside the Republic. The other clung to separate legislatures only allied for purposes of defence, and also, in ecclesiastical matters, connection with the Cape Synod.

A representative assembly was called at Potcheffstroom by the influence of Pretorius and his party, and a constitution for Church and State was drafted, and under it officers were elected in 1857; but this and all connected with it was immediately disowned by the Zoutpansberg and Lydenburg communities. Schœman who had been elected Commandant-General by the Pretorius party refused to act with them. He was therefore deposed, but their acts of this kind were answered by a re-proclamation of the independence of the Republic of Lydenburg; while by the Zoutpansberg party their newly-elected President, Pretorius, was sent on a mission to the Orange Free State to invite it to union with them. The Volksraad of the Free State were friendly and even courteous. Pretorius behaved in a hectoring manner, and the end was a threat of war and the advance of a *commando* against the Free State. War, however, was averted. An agreement was drawn up, and with the timely retreat of the Transvaal Republic from its hostile position, and various punishments to some of the Free Staters who had joined them, this episode closed. Shortly afterwards the quarrel with Zoutpansberg also came to an end by the incorporation of that Republic with the Republic of Pretorius' party, and so also ended the year 1857, and the first few weeks of 1858.

It was in 1858 that the Orange Free State was in terrible troubles with Moshesh and the Basutos, and that Sir George Grey so ably came to their assistance. It was then that—as we have seen—the English Government threw away, so unfortunately, the golden opportunity for confederation, and so " put the clock back" in South Africa.

There were fierce wars again with the natives—the Batlapin—in which Commandant Krüger now begins to figure. It is a sickening story. The usual raiding of cattle and murder of white settlers on the one side; on the other, the usual breach of faith and massacre. The Free State was out of heart with Basuto difficulties. The Transvaal Government took the opportunity of proposing a union with them. Fortunately for the Free State this was averted, and so it has escaped the danger of being mixed up with the disorder and corruption of the Transvaal. Sir George Grey, when the proposal was made, reminded both States that, if so, then the conventions between them and the British Government of 1852 and 1854 came to an end.

In 1858 to 1865 there were the usual quarrels with natives, and a serious state of things in relation to Cetewayo and the Zulus. There were disturbances as to whether there were slaves or not, under the title of "Apprentices;" the thing being asserted confidently by Europeans not Boers, and as confidently denied by the Boers. Too much trust cannot be placed in such denials. It is not the habit of the Boer mind—so persons of experience aver—to have an over-scrupulous respect for truth. To be "schlimm," *i.e.* acute in deceiving and outwitting those opposed to you in any way, is—so it is said—to them the highest proof of virtue. To trust the word of a Boer absolutely is now believed by experienced Englishmen to be an act of folly.

There were also fierce ecclesiastical disputes during these years which were concerned with "the infinitely little." Out of these arose the establishment of a new sect in the general Calvinistic body, known commonly as "the Dopper Church." It seems to be as entirely faithful to the Calvinistic heresies as the other religious bodies in the Transvaal. The important *crux* was whether it was or was not right to sing hymns, or only rhymed paraphrases of Scripture. The "Dutch Reform" held to the former view, the "Doppers" have always supported the latter. An intermittent civil war was going on during part of this period, in which Pretorius, Krüger, Vilgoen, and Schœman, were the chief figures. After the usual ups and downs of turbulence and disorder this came to an end, at least for a time, leaving an empty treasury, taxes outstanding, and of course irrecoverable, salaries in arrear, and all confidence in this lawless and noisy crew beyond the Vaal gone, not only in Natal and the colony and Europe, but also in the Orange Free State.

And so things went merrily on in the path of confusion. The Government of the Republic was little else than intestine quarrels, mismanagement, and lawlessness and interference with, and provocation to, those without. Wild, restless, and lawless as they were, they had aggressive ideas. Pretorius had proclaimed the boundaries of the Republic to be Lake Ngami. This, of course, was going a little too far. Dr. Livingstone had objected to the Boers' constant interference with the native tribes beyond their borders; and the English Government had seen that the trade route to the north must not be stopped by these turbulent burghers. Pretorius was obliged to withdraw his proclamation. As to Livingstone, his noble spirit, his pioneering enterprise, his influence with the natives, made him odious to the Boers. They destroyed his station at Kolsberg, the chief town of Secheli's tribe of Bakwains, and burnt all his possessions. He behaved with his usual splendid good temper in face of this atrocity, only remarking: "The Boers resolved to shut up the interior, and I determined to open up the country; and we shall see who have been most successful in resolution—they or I." We have seen. The same effort was made by the Boers later. The Englishmen were roused by a still greater atrocity—viz., the murder in cold blood of Commander Bethel—and at this later time Sir Charles Warren settled the question. British good sense at last came to the rescue. Our action in Bechuanaland, followed by Mr. Cecil Rhodes' energy in Rhodesia, at last confined these marauders within proper limits. But we are anticipating.

In the year 1872 race feeling was aroused by "the Keate award." There had been a dispute as to boundary between the Transvaal Boers and the Free State. It had been referred for arbitration to Lieutenant-Governor Keate of Natal as an impartial judge. He adjudicated in favour of the Transvaalers, and the Free State honourably accepted the decision.

Very different was the action of the Transvaal soon after. A dispute had arisen as to their frontier in another direction. There was a long investigation in court, and again Lieutenant-Governor Keate was appointed arbitrator. His decision was against the Transvaal. At once there was a storm. President Pretorius was forced to resign, and with him many others, and the Keate award was repudiated. It has been argued that the award was, in fact, mistaken; but (whether or not this be so) every one acknowledges that it was given impartially and in accordance with the evidence. Any people pretending to be civilised and maintaining their self-respect would abide by the result of an arbitration arranged by themselves. It is impossible to expect such conduct, however, from a community such as the Transvaal Boers, to whom "sense of honour" is an unmeaning phrase, and who, amidst abundant professions of piety and religion, do not appear to have the faintest respect for justice or truth. Such a people, however, should not be permitted to attempt to govern either themselves or others, as they are incapable of understanding the first elements of good government.

And now, in 1872, they proceeded to elect a Dutch Reformed minister, Rev. Thomas Francis Burgers, as President. It was felt in the Transvaal that things were in a bad way. Mr. Burgers was a clever man, and a man of education. It was hoped that he would put things right. There were a party of agitators and genuine Doppers, with Krüger as their moving spirit, who were probably never friendly to him, if for nothing else, at any rate because of his religious opinions. He had been charged with "heresy" (*i.e.*, some divergence from the beliefs of the larger body of Calvinists —of some of the chief religious divisions). He had been condemned, and then suspended in 1864. He brought his case before the courts of the Cape Colony, and his opponents appealed to the Privy Council, and on both occasions he was successful. He belonged to an old family, and had thorough Dutch sympathies, but his religious views stood in his way. Now, indeed, they were overborne by a sense of need, but when he failed in the war with Secocœni five years later, many Boers feared to follow his lead, and Mr. Krüger, with his accustomed unctuous pietism, declared "that the President, Mr. Burgers, confessed that he went to war without the blessing of Heaven, but that he had since then" (so it suited Mr. Krüger to say) "sought the Lord." Mr. Burgers did his best, but his difficulties were great. The Treasury, as usual, was empty, resort had to be had to a paper currency. Law, education, land boundaries—all were in a hopeless condition. The President negotiated loans, but who would trust the Transvaal? It was impossible to obtain the sum of money desired.

Then came a native war with Secocœni. The Boers were unsuccessful—a fact, it is needless to say, they afterwards, in the face of facts, denied. The Zulus were threatening seriously on the south-eastern border. It needed the power of England, after serious reverses, to deliver them from this peril.

Burgers seems to have been opposed to annexation, but he urged upon the Volksraad that to accept confederation under the British flag was the only way to safety. Sir Theophilus Shepstone had been sent as Special Commissioner to the Transvaal. He found everything in confusion. On crossing the frontier an address was at once presented to him to this effect: "In our present Government we have no confidence; with danger surrounding us, and with division and anarchy threatening us, we pray you to take prompt measures to unite us to the colonies of South Africa."

The Volksraad refused annexation at the time, but there is now no doubt that far the majority of the people desired it. "If the Press is an indication of the public mind," it has been well said, " in England, in the Transvaal, in Natal, the annexation was accepted by the public as a fair and just act."* It was all very well for persons in England, for political purposes, to characterise the annexation as a "high-handed" act. England has suffered terribly by the argument so common among unscrupulous opponents which consists in nothing but ;question-begging words. Where partisans have no better resource, such words as "Highhanded," " Imperialism," " Militarism," " Jingoism," " Clericalism," " Sacerdotalism," and so on, come to their rescue. These, and such as these, opportunely used are of vast influence with the thoughtless crowd. It was all very well *afterwards* for the English people and the Government to pretend that they had been misinformed. As we shall see, this was not the case. The annexation was widely approved, and that too in the Transvaal.

The state of the country, indeed, was such that the act was inevitable, but doubtless Sir Theophilus Shepstone made mistakes in his way of doing it, though they were the mistakes of an honest, generous, and humane man. This is evident from a moment's consideration. Indeed, it is evident that there were mistakes, so to speak, all along the line. (1) Sir Theophilus Shepstone would have strategically acted more wisely had he waited. Things were so bad that, had he allowed them quietly to go worse, had he allowed the Boers to try conclusions, unaided, with Cetewayo, and to manage their own affairs with an empty treasury and a discontented people, he would have done well for final success. The whole country to a man would,

* Carter. *Boer War*, p. 32.

before long, have been praying for annexation, as far the majority already desired it. It was found impossible to keep the *commandos* together when Secocœni successfully resisted them. The Boer farmers quickly abandoned their position and went home, as their manner is when success is deferred. Had he waited for the misery and reverses that were sure to come and then taken a *plebiscite* he would have had them to a man in favour of coming under English rule. But then, Sir Theophilus felt, no doubt, that this would have been a Machiavellian policy, and so it would. It would have cost much blood and misery, but there would have been no room for the inventions and pretences which did duty afterwards against his action.

(2) And again, it would have been wisdom to have been much more suspicious of the Boer leaders. Englishmen are, broadly speaking, naturally frank and straightforward. They are inclined to trust those who profess reciprocal frankness. Even now, after long and bitter experience, many of them are duped by their " schlimm " antagonists. They forget that for a Transvaal Boer truth, frankness, straightforwardness only implies folly. Sir Theophilus Shepstone acted openly with the leaders—with Burgers and Krüger and Joubert and the rest. They saw the Proclamation of Annexation before it was published, and suggested some slight alterations, which were made. They also allowed him to see their protest, which they represented as being merely *pro formâ* to appease the discontented. He, in turn, objected to expressions which seemed to imply that they were merely biding their time. This they explained as

being only intended to satisfy a few more fiery spirits. Sir Theophilus Shepstone suffered from an undue trust in Boer integrity.

These were undoubtedly two mistakes, but they were mistakes on the side of generosity. Anyhow, the Proclamation was issued, and the British flag was hoisted in Pretoria on April 12, 1877.

At first things looked well. Finance was taken in hand, and a large sum of money spent by England relieved the necessities of the State. Almost all the officials who had held office retained appointments by the invitation of the Commissioner. Krüger is said to have asked for and received an increased salary for his services. Jorrisen retained his position as Attorney-General. Koetze "was offered the position of first Puisne Judge." There seems to have been jealousy between Judge Koetze and the Attorney-General (who, though an able man, had been really a minister of religion), and, owing to this, Jorrisen was unfortunately removed, and henceforth showed himself as bitter and implacable an enemy of the British supremacy as Krüger himself. However, they were well treated by Sir Theophilus Shepstone, and the money and position they held from the English enabled them to plot and agitate against the British connection. Indeed, we can hardly blame them for this, considering the mistakes we made, and in many respects they were more temperate in word and action than some of the more violent spirits.*

For now a long series of mistakes and confusions and doings and undoings began. One great fault in our colonial policy—as has been already noted—had

* Carter, *Boer War*, p. 44.

been the constant change of governors. At the best of times, if a governor remained for his full term of office, he had only got a thorough grip of all things, felt the pulse of various classes and races of men, and taken the bearings of different interests and influences, when he had to go elsewhere and begin the process all over again. But there was a further and injurious practice of recalling governors as soon as they differed in opinion from the Colonial Secretary, having, unluckily for themselves, gained a clearer view of things than Downing Street. Sir Theophilus Shepstone had been sent to the Transvaal with an independent commission. Sir Bartle Frere was sent out to forward the policy of Confederation. Any action of the former was sure greatly to influence the task of the latter, but the High Commissioner had no power to interfere. As a matter of fact, the action of Sir Theophilus Shepstone, followed by the *volte face* of the Liberal Government when it came into power, wrecked all hope of Confederation for many a day to come. Mr. Gladstone, evidently from a misapprehension, in one of his speeches in Midlothian accused Sir Bartle Frere of what he considered the guilt of annexation. This was not the case. Sir Bartle Frere did not know of it. He reached the Cape on March 31. The annexation took place on April 12. The High Commissioner only heard of it, and that in an informal manner and by chance, from the sub-editor of a Cape paper on April 16. He thought it premature, disliked the word "annexation," and believed if we held the Transvaal at all it should have been by cession. This does not prove that annexation was wrong. Sir Theophilus Shepstone seems to have acted wisely and well.

He was liked by the Boers; he was conciliatory. If he made any mistake it was the mistake of acting prematurely. Had he waited, annexation would certainly have been asked for, but—as we have seen—his (possibly premature) action was prompted by humane motives. What is clear, however, is that Sir Bartle Frere was in no way to blame for what in fact he knew not of. Sir Theophilus Shepstone was in a position to act without reference to Sir Bartle Frere.

Here was divided authority with a vengeance! Such is the way in which our rulers managed our South African affairs! This, of course, led to incredible confusion. How could the affairs of the Transvaal go well when we consider that no fewer than five representatives of her Majesty of one kind or another had a hand in the management of matters within less than four years, from 1876 to 1880?

Another terrible mistake was the delay in giving to the Transvaal the representative government promised. In the Proclamation of Annexation Sir Theophilus Shepstone had said:

"And I further proclaim and make known that the Transvaal will remain a separate Government, with its own Laws and Legislature, and that it is the wish of her Most Gracious Majesty that it shall enjoy the fullest legislative privileges compatible with the circumstances of the country and the intelligence of the people. That arrangement will be made by which the Dutch language will practically be as much the official language as the English. All laws, proclamations, and Government notices will be published in the Dutch language; in the Legislative Assembly Members may, as they do now, use their language; and in the Courts of Law the same may be done at the option of suitors to a cause. The laws so in force in the State will be retained until altered by competent legislative authority."

This promise was given in good faith, and in good

faith received. Sir Theophilus Shepstone tried to fulfil it. He at once submitted to the Colonial Office his views as to the necessary legislative arrangements. No action whatever was taken on it, either by Conservatives or Liberals, and his despatch is probably lying uncared for in the Colonial Office now![*]

The scheme for government was no doubt a difficult one to draw. The Boers did not seem to care very much what government they voted for, so long as they had a vote for some. The Volksraad had been, if possible, a more absurd Assembly than it is at present. It had voted a measure one day, and voted the contrary the next. It was, as it is, perfectly unfit to govern a country. Nor indeed does it govern now. Circumstances have led to this that practically, in the majority of cases, the President's will is law. Still, a representative Assembly ought to have been given, and speedily. It is said that Sir Theophilus Shepstone had recommended two Chambers, one (of Government nominees) to control the other. Possibly for the state of things at the time this might have been temporarily a necessity, but whatever details may have been suggested in the form of government, *some* representative government should have been promptly given. Sir Theophilus Shepstone has been blamed for this. No blame, it would seem, attaches to him. He had done his best. He was liked by the Boers. He understood them, liked them, and had lived with them long. Had he been allowed to remain, to arrange for a representative Assembly at once, all would, probably, have gone well. The dawdling in the fulfilment of the promise given—a dawdling, first of the Conservative, then of the Liberal

[*] See Carter, *Narrative of the Boer War*, p. 45.

Government—roused suspicion of bad faith in many Boers who had trusted us, helped to turn friends into enemies, and assisted in hurrying on revolt which ended in our disgrace. Sir Theophilus Shepstone was retired just when he was needed, and as yet no representative government given.

But mistakes went further and deeper. If Great Britain chose to take the responsibility for putting the Transvaal disorders to rights, it was bound to expect expenditure of money. The expenditure of Sir Theophilus Shepstone was looked upon as excessive. He was withdrawn, and Sir Owen (then Colonel) Lanyon was placed in the Transvaal.

This has always been considered in South Africa as a very imprudent step. Shepstone had united the Boers. He knew them well, understood them thoroughly, and was entirely a *persona grata* to them. Sir Bartle Frere, when he came among them, was exceedingly liked, and his influence was excellent; but Colonel Lanyon—so South Africans seem to agree—was—whatever were his merits—not the man for the Transvaal. The Boers abhor the British soldier, and Lanyon's stiff and somewhat imperious military ways were said to have been exceedingly distasteful to them.

But more than that. It was necessary, especially in view of an approaching general election, to justify money expenditure to the British taxpayer. A high sense of the honour and glory of our country, of her duties and responsibilities, had long—it is to be feared —been dying out. Money was really, to a great extent, at the root of the matter. Even on *that* score, low as it was, politicians calculated badly.

Mr. Gladstone at Midlothian had spoken of repudiating annexation, even if the Transvaal were "as valuable as it was valueless." The usual ignorance of South African affairs befogged the minds of English politicians of both parties, and even of the great statesman himself. They might—on this low-calculation system alone—have known better. Gold had been discovered in the country, but not yet in great quantities. Fortunately for Mr. Krüger and his party, the great discoveries on the Witwatersrand came several years later. However, money must be had for the expenses of the country, and it was Colonel Lanyon's insisting on the payment of taxes, and even of arrears from the farmers, and the somewhat harsh measures taken in consequence, which, more than anything else, probably began to dispose the Boers, who had welcomed the advent of the English as a delivery from confusion and ruin, to listen to the voices of the agitators who had known how to benefit themselves out of English money, and to bide their time.

Meantime the hopes of these that they would peaceably recover their ascendency were greatly raised by some utterances of Mr. Gladstone in Midlothian and other matters. England was soon in difficulties with the Zulus. As usual, insufficient forces were sent against them, and these were, it is probable, badly handled. The consequence was the tragedy of Isandlwana. This was a terrible blow to the Conservative party at home. Had the Zulu difficulty been thoroughly settled, had Sir Bartle Frere's masterly and statesmanlike policy been carried out by victorious generals, and Isandlwana been a success instead of a disaster, Sir Bartle Frere's great capacity would have been recognised, and the Conservative policy in South Africa would have been applauded. As it was, to point out that Isandlwana was merely an incident —an unfortunate incident—in a true line of statesmanship did not suit party politics at home : what did it matter about the interests of a colony compared with the advancement of a party ?

The Liberals, on the eve of a general election, greedily fastened on the mistakes and misadventures of their opponents. Those opponents had to find a scapegoat, and he could only be found in the great statesman who, had he been supported, would have saved South Africa. Sir Bartle Frere had attended the mass meeting called by the Boer agitators. He had on his way thither and afterwards, by private communications with the Boers, become well aware that the agitation and the Boer "Jingoes" had obtained a following by means of terrorism. He saw plainly that England had the saving of the Transvaal in her hands if she kept her promises and gave them the government which she had undertaken to give. In 1874 he had drawn up the outlines of a constitution. For this he had the assistance of such eminent men as Mr. Brand, the President of the Free State, of Sir Henry de Villiers, the Chief Justice of the Cape Colony, of the Prime Minister, Mr. (afterwards Sir Gordon) Sprigg, and of the Attorney-General, Mr. (afterwards Sir Thomas) Uppington. This was placed at the disposal of the home Government; but it was necessary for the Conservatives to "throw" Sir Bartle Frere "to the wolves," and this recommendation was never attended to, and indeed before anything more was done in the matter he had been superseded as regards all authority in the Transvaal.

Sir Garnet Wolseley came into power there as his successor. He had come too late. The Zulu power had been broken by the victory of Ulundi. With that Sir Garnet Wolseley had nothing to do. That success was achieved by Lord Chelmsford on July 5, before Sir Garnet Wolseley had time—after his arrival in Capetown on June 28—to reach Zululand, and take command of the army in the field. He had then to make arrangements for the future of Zululand, and these were on quite other lines than those of Sir Bartle Frere. Those arrangements, indeed, did not stand very long, and in after time the more statesmanlike settlement had to be resorted to. However, for the time Cetewayo had been beaten, and (on August 28) taken prisoner, and the Boers were free from all fear of Secocœni and from the Zulus; we had pulled their chestnuts out of the fire, and now, with the "gratitude" for which they have been so conspicuous ever since, they had time to turn their attention to win from the English Government freedom from any distasteful necessity of paying taxes or obeying the law. Sometimes by terror, sometimes by persuasion, the agitation went merrily on.

Messrs. Krüger and Joubert had been twice to England as a deputation, but the same answer had always been firmly returned. Sir Garnet Wolesley, finding that the agitation was continuing, made a wise disposition of his troops throughout the country. He stationed six companies of the 80th and one troop of the 1st Dragoon Guards at Pretoria. Other troops were brought to Heidelberg and others to Standerton,

THE TRANSVAAL ANNEXATION 193

others to Wakkerstroom, and others to other centres. This had the desired effect of keeping the country quiet for the time, all the more as large numbers of the Boers were anxious enough to escape from the agitators, and the towns were thoroughly loyal.

Some have thought that Sir Garnet Wolseley scarcely allowed for the dogged persistence of the Boers, and was perhaps in some manner deceived by their previous conduct. He had himself known that the war with Secocœni was supposed to be a Boer war, in which Boers were "conspicuous by their absence," and he did not perhaps allow for the fact that, now that the fear of extermination by Cetewayo and his fine forces had been removed by the victory of Ulundi, they were free to try their peculiar tactics upon our troops. Had Sir Garnet Wolesley been left in the Transvaal, he would probably, notwithstanding the constant instructions to him of the duty of "economy," have given the Boer agitators and those whom, by conversion or terror, they were moving to rebellion, the thorough beating which they needed, and (as some think) it may be added, still need if the Transvaal is ever to prosper. Needless to say, however, Sir Garnet Wolseley was withdrawn. He had succeeded in holding down rebellion, but he had—so it has been thought—further exasperated the Boers, and so, unintentionally, helped on the schemes of the agitators, while his immediate successor had not his military ability to deal with the situation. Things, however, still looked safe for the peaceable citizens of the towns and the poor farmers in the outlying districts, who would have been glad enough to be let alone, had the English Government stood firm.

There had been two assurances from the Secretary

of State that the annexation could never be reversed. These were reiterated, by the authority of the Crown. Sir Garnet Wolseley had said, in answer to Pretorius: " Whereas it is expedient that all grounds for uncertainty or misapprehension should be removed once and for all, beyond doubt or question : Now therefore I do hereby proclaim and make known, in the name and on behalf of her Majesty the Queen, that it is the will and determination of her Majesty's Government, that this Transvaal territory shall be and shall continue to be for ever an integral portion of her Majesty's dominions in South Africa." He had spoken in the same sense on several occasions and with emphasis, and he clearly saw that it was not the main body of the people who were disaffected, but that they were incited to discontent and rebellion by ambitious agitators. Colonel Lanyon again proclaimed the same determination of English statesmen on opening the Legislative Council ; and on March 9, 1880, Sir Garnet Wolseley received a telegram from Sir Michael Hicks-Beach, with a firmer assurance than ever of the same. Then there was the Speech from the Throne at the dissolution of Parliament. "My anticipations," said the Queen, "as to the early establishment of peace in South Africa have been fulfilled," and then it went on to say that, owing to the conquest of the Zulus, " my possessions in that part of the world" had been "relieved from danger," and that it was hoped that Confederation would advance, and that such "powers of self-government as had been" enjoyed by the inhabitants of Cape Colony " would be extended to my subjects in other parts of South Africa."

England, therefore, if the words of those in authority

were to be trusted, seemed, indeed, to stand firm, and the hopes of the agitators seemed to be doomed to disappointment.

However, some of the agitators, with considerable acuteness, had taken a different view of the situation.

Deputations had been sent to England, and of these Mr. Krüger was a member. He is not, perhaps, a statesman in the ordinary sense of the word, much less a very great man in any sense; but he *is* a representative Boer in the sense that he thoroughly understands the people over whom he now rules. The Transvaal Boer, speaking broadly, is extremely ignorant, extremely prejudiced, profoundly fanatical, hates government cordially, and consequently dislikes the law-abiding Englishman. The love of money, the love of being "a law unto himself," scorn of refinement or culture, are to him second nature. All this Mr. Krüger seems clearly to understand. He has himself, however, in an eminent degree, two powerful characteristics— dogged determination and extraordinary acuteness. He had, no doubt, taken the measure of Englishmen, of English parties, of the methods of forcing and swaying English (so-called) "Public Opinion." Some wise man speaks somewhere to this effect, that Stupidity is not a want of understanding, but a resolute refusal to allow understanding to act fully by reason of some fault which hinders it. In this sense we are among the most stupid of nations. Englishmen have plenty of understanding, abundance of common sense, but they frequently do not permit their understanding to act freely owing to their prejudices and prepossessions. They often allow opinions to drift into their minds from all sorts of quarters, instead of forming them by reason acting on knowledge, and then they have, it is truly said, a zeal for their opinions, not because they are true, but because they are their own.

Krüger seems to have been sufficiently acute to know this. He was ingenious enough to perceive how things swayed to and fro in England according to party exigencies. He was quick enough to notice that a large part of the great middle class whose energies were absorbed in trade, whose religion was largely a religion—like the Boer religion—of respectable phrases and fixed formulæ, were likely to be caught with catchwords of "liberty," "independence," "pious lovers of the Bible," and so on, and sure to oppose the views of Imperial statesmen. Krüger and the other agitators were *felices opportunitate*. They, if not able or cultured, were very acute men. They had watched the English free the Boers from fear of the natives on each side. They had seen them make mistake after mistake, and they knew how to utilise their mistakes for their own ends. They were probably aware of the temper of the English and Scottish Nonconformists and Presbyterians. They saw that things must go, not from a consideration of the good of South Africa, but for the benefit of an English party. They had discovered that English Governments were sure to vacillate, to oppose each other, and, if political difficulties threatened, not to back up their own people. They saw that their business was steadily to push agitation by rousing prejudice and race feeling, by appealing to Boer love of lawlessness and hatred of the English, and when necessary by intimidation; then doggedly to bide their time, and to make the most of English blunders, English stupidity, and English generosity and frank and kindly feeling and love of justice, and they did make the most of it, and their longheadedness was crowned with success. It matters not that their success has proved deeply injurious to civilisation, and especially to South African civilisation, and to the advancement of what is right; it matters not that it has proved a grievous injury to the native races, and has set back progress indefinitely: they deserve the credit due to men who were sufficiently acute to make the most of our unnumbered mistakes, and to watch and wait, and then stir up rebellion so as to lead us to spend some seven millions of money in putting the Zulu under the heel of the Boer, in making the Boers all-powerful, and raising one of their number to the position of practical Dictator of one of the finest regions of the African continent, and in setting up one of the most corrupt and injurious of all earthly Governments, as viewed from the standpoint of civilisation and progress.

Matters came to a head in this way. Mr. Gladstone and Lord Hartington spoke strongly against annexation in their electioneering speeches: spoke in a manner to imply that if they came into power the work of the previous Government would be undone. The hopes of the agitators rose. The Liberals did come into power. Then they seemed to repudiate their electioneering words. In the Queen's Speech at the opening of the new Parliament, as we have seen, and in answer after answer from responsible Ministers, it was asserted that the Transvaal would not be relinquished, and that representative government under the British Crown would be established there. No steps, however, were taken for its establishment. Sir Bartle Frere, the one man able—if supported—to deal with the whole question, was recalled in disgrace. The Boers saw their opportunity. The agitators understood the state of things in England. There must be an appeal to arms.

On December 16 certain Boers determined formally to proclaim their independence. They determined that their proclamation should be printed at Potchefstroom. They carried out their determination in spite of a small force of English soldiers. On a small party of these, some Boers who lay in ambush fired. These were the first shots fired in the war.

On December 20 Colonel Anstruther was moving the 94th from Middleburg. On the 26th at Bronkhurst Spruit a large party of Boers lay in ambush. They sent a message to Colonel Anstruther, and, while he and his men were waiting for an answer to their return message, with the grossest treachery shot down a great part of the regiment, including the colonel and most of the officers.

Sir George Pomeroy Colley was at the time in Natal. He had succeeded Sir Garnet Wolseley in command. Colonel Lanyon apprised him of the dangerous condition of things. By orders of the triumverate—Kriiger, Jorrissen, Joubert — the Boer *commandos* invaded Natal. It is a striking instance of the cloudy information at the disposal of the British Government that the Boers were described as men "only standing on the defensive," when in fact they invaded the colony of Natal.

The Boers are apparently not good soldiers to fight in the open; they are, however, excellent marksmen. They

THE TRANSVAAL ANNEXATION 199

are used to hunting wild game or "shooting down niggers," and they know well how to manage "soldier-stalking" quite as well as "deer-stalking." They can lie in ambush and shelter themselves behind rocks, and "pick off" with unerring precision any object at which they fire.

"Economy" was, as we have seen, the order of the day with the British Governments. It is needless to say that there were, in consequence, insufficient forces in Natal. What could be got together were used, including Natal mounted police and various volunteers. Sir George Colley marched for Pretoria. Then followed disaster after disaster. He received a severe check at Ingogo Heights, and then a worse at Laing's Nek. Our troops, it appears, were not sufficiently numerous, and were—so some think—badly handled (although there are very contradictory opinions on this point), and the country lent itself to the tactics of the Boers.

Sir Evelyn Wood was then hurrying up with reinforcements. It has been said, with what truth I know not, that Sir George Colley was privately urged to retrieve the first partial disasters and to act decisively before Sir Evelyn Wood arrived with fresh forces. Whether that be so or not, he resolved upon the ill-fated expedition to Majuba Hill.

On the nights of February 26 and 27 a small force was led to the top of this rocky hill. The Boers lay below. Our men were tired. Time was wanted. No entrenchments were thrown up. When a charge at the point of the bayonet would have saved the situation, and the men expected the order, no order was given. The Boers climbed the hill, and from behind the rocks shot our men down. These for a time stood their ground, but they were not led on. They turned and fled, and were killed almost to a man in their flight. Sir George Colley was a brave soldier. Whatever mistakes he had made—if he *had* made mistakes—he paid the forfeit with his life. Sir Evelyn Wood was in time, not to retrieve our damaged honour, but to carry out orders from home for our surrender. Weak and vacillating councils at home, insufficient forces and mistakes in generalship abroad, had brought about their natural consequence. Other counsels and other methods might have averted a deep disaster to South Africa and an indelible disgrace to Great Britain.

CHAPTER IV

TRANSVAAL—THE SURRENDER

THE story of the retrocession of the Transvaal is generally looked upon in South Africa as one of the blackest and most damaging in the sufficiently melancholy history of our colonial policy there. Never, probably, we are almost forced to confess, was there a clearer instance of folly and vacillation, of subordinating the interests of a great dependency to the exigencies of party strife at home, and—with some, it is to be feared—sheltering a selfish abandonment of duty under a veil of supposed high moral principles. It was not that all who were concerned in it had not often really high motives acting upon their determinations, but that, on the whole, party and party exigencies blinded their eyes; and that they were guilty of what—the most friendly towards them are driven to confess—appears to have been, at best, culpable ignorance ; and that they were led on through want of care and statesmanlike judgment into the perpetration of a grave injustice, and to a mistake "which was worse than a crime," and to the dealing of a blow to the honour, integrity, and trustworthiness of Great Britain in the eyes of South Africa, from which they are reeling still.

It has so often been taken for granted by those on

that side in politics that England, guided by the Liberal Government of 1881, performed a noble and self-denying act in the retrocession; that she fearlessly performed an act of justice, however opposed to her own interests; that she thus set an example of high and disinterested morality,—that it is necessary to examine these contentions in the light of facts. And here it is well to summarise the reasons put forward by the British Government for the serious step of retrocession. They were the following:

(1) That there had been misapprehension at home as to the state of things at the time of annexation, and later, when refusals to reconsider matters were advanced.

(2) That there was an inadequate sense of the strength, among the Boers, of a passionate desire for their own rule.

(3) That there was clear injustice, as well as impolitic folly, in retaining by force troublesome and unwilling subjects.

(4) That Great Britain was so strong and so fearless of misunderstanding that she could well afford to be magnanimous.

(5) That, therefore, the principle of desiring always to advance the cause of freedom ought to be carried out, even when detrimental to self-interest.

These, indeed—if true—seemed to be reasons enough to satisfy any noble-minded nation; and they did prevail. But were they true? There was something more to be said. The circumstances of the moment in England, it is to be feared, gave to a sentimental pseudo-morality a great power, and to what was unsound an appearance of truth.

The general policy of Lord Beaconsfield had (and in many respects most justly) been condemned by Mr. Gladstone. The Liberal party had, after the efforts of their great chief in "the Midlothian campaign," returned to power flushed with victory. The two great leaders of the day—Mr. Gladstone and Lord Beaconsfield—were fundamentally opposed to each other—an opposition in policy which almost, if not altogether, took the form of personal dislike. The Liberal party at the moment found their chief supporters among English Nonconformists, Scottish Presbyterians, and Liberal Churchmen. They were nothing if they were not broad-minded, large of view, indifferent to conventional precedents, and the professed champions of a fearless morality. The English Nonconformists and the Scottish Presbyterians, together with many of the rank and file of the working classes, had, in some respects, a natural sympathy with what they imagined to be the character of the Boers. They were presented to their minds as a simple, guileless people struggling bravely for freedom, as devout and pious Bible-reading Christians, as men nobly opposed to autocratic insolence and assertions of the superiority of any man over his fellows, and, above all, as those whom Lord Beaconsfield's greedy policy had enslaved!

Thus some of the best, noblest, and most generous feelings of Englishmen, together with some of the meanest and most bigoted, were aroused to set up under the idea of "Republicanism" one of the narrowest and most corrupt oligarchies—nay, perhaps one may say, one of the most tyrannical autocracies—that the world has ever seen.

The reasons summarised above were constantly

put before the English people at the time. Political passion was running high, and in such cases, it is to be feared, men are sometimes tempted to mistake their political desires for noble moral principles; the consequence, at any rate in this case, was what we have to confess looked very like faithlessness to solemn engagements, and certainly that fatal vacillation and submission to party exigencies at home which, as we have seen already, had been the bane of British action in South Africa. Again was to happen, in a most aggravated form, what had, alas! happened before: statesmen at home ignorant of the real situation, refusing to be guided by those who knew, confused by their own party necessities into an insufficient care for the interests of the colonies for which they acted, forming hasty conclusions, then falling into other and contradictory conclusions equally hasty, indulging generous impulses at the expense of others, failing in promises made, and pleasing themselves or their followers at the cost of shirking responsibilities, allowing their party to enjoy the pleasures of a cheap philanthropy, throwing dust in their own eyes and the eyes of the people by advancing a favourite policy of economy under the name of a high self-denial, and creating situations of lasting menace to the welfare of the Empire they were set to rule on the foundation of fallacious arguments. This certainly seems to be the view generally taken in South Africa, and we cannot but see much justice in it—however noble may have been the motives of some, at least, of the Government—by consideration of their utterances and the details of the case.

In the first place it is a damaging fact that the deep sense of duty and the moral rectitude which were said to be the moving power to retrocession seemed not to awake until British troops had received three serious checks—at Ingogo Heights, at Laing's Nek, and above all at Majuba Hill. And following from this, it is no way unnatural that the Boers have steadily and contemptuously disbelieved the moral professions put forward by our Government, as that Government did not seem troubled about "blood-guiltiness" until after disasters to British arms. That in itself went far to discredit the step taken. No Government has any right to yield—so long as it has strength to withstand—to mere force and the force of rebels that which it will not yield to representation and petition; and no one can deny that had the Boers not defeated the insufficient forces of the British, the Transvaal would now be enjoying freedom under the British flag instead of groaning under the yoke of a reactionary Oligarchy.

This is what the British Government did, and in so doing we find it difficult to deny that they seem to have been guilty of wrongdoing. We see more clearly, however, their mistakes by examining some of their utterances at the time.

After the fatal morning of February 27 at Majuba Hill, Sir Evelyn Wood took the command. Downcast as the forces were at their unexpected reverse, they would have been glad to be led at once against the Boers to retrieve the dishonour to British arms.*
On March 6 there was a meeting of leading men to arrange an armistice, and, indeed, Sir Evelyn Wood has been blamed in South Africa for thus giving

---

* See Carter, *Narrative of the Boer War*, p. 303.

time for the *volte face* of the British Government. This is scarcely fair, as of that *volte face* neither he nor any one else could then have dreamed. Preparations were, notwithstanding the armistice, going on rapidly for military operations. Sir Frederick Roberts was on his way to the Cape to take the command, and it was hoped and expected that before his arrival Sir Evelyn Wood would have settled matters with the Boers. They were impatient as to the armistice. Military men were, of course, exceedingly annoyed; there were anxieties, doubtless, in the minds of some, but no one doubted, up to that time, the good faith of the English Government, for indeed all that was said supplied grounds of confidence.

The *Times* wrote—wrote, indeed, with great unwisdom and want of foresight as we now know—but wrote, as was natural then, and as representing the supposed mind of the Government:

"We are now fairly committed to a struggle which we cannot choose but carry through. The resistance of the Boers must be overcome, and the insurrection must be put down, at whatever cost. There can be no two opinions thus far. As for any notion that we shall be dispirited at the somewhat unexpected difficulty of the task before us, and that we shall turn back from it at the first check, we need not waste words in talking about it. The danger rather is that the combative spirit of the country will be unduly roused, and that we shall fling ourselves into the miserable war with an eagerness and determination out of all proportion to the possible value of the result. The end is the great matter, and the country is thoroughly determined what the end of the Transvaal War shall be."

Again the *Times* wrote:

"The time will come when all that the Boers will have to urge will be listened to, and will have due weight attached to it. But it is idle for the present to talk of terms. There can be no terms until our military disasters have been retrieved, and until the British authority has been restored over the Transvaal. It is to this task that the country has now committed itself. We shall show by deeds as well as by words that we know what we are engaged upon, and that we are fully determined to carry it through. If the regiments already on their way to the front are not sufficient to ensure military success, more will be sent."

The *Times* had counted without its host. It had not realised the plastic character of ministerial convictions, nor yet the shrewdness of Messrs. Krüger and Joubert, who seem to have known the sort of men they were dealing with, and to have taken their measures accordingly. And yet the confidence of the *Times* was justified by the utterances of Ministers themselves. Lord Kimberley has not, perhaps, shown himself a strong man or an exceptionally great statesman, but he has been careful and prudent. He was by no means a man to speak incautiously or without the approval of his party. He was an authority, for he had become Colonial Secretary in 1880. Now, shortly after this in a speech in Manchester he says as follows, in touching on the Boer rebellion:

"As far as South Africa is concerned, the Liberal Government had forced upon them the conduct of a war which they deeply regretted, but for which they were not primarily responsible, but which was necessary in order to vindicate the authority of the Crown. Much as they deplored the necessity, *they would not flinch from the duty which had been forced upon them* by the policy of their predecessors in office, but, at the same time, they would, *as soon as the authority of the Crown had been vindicated*, take such steps as would, he hoped, lead to the creation of free institutions in Africa, and institutions of which it could not be said that they had been forced on an unwilling people."

Here, indeed, is revealed the cloven foot of party feeling—"*forced upon them by the policy of their* *predecessors.*"[*] Here the great colony has not its own interests considered, but is made a subject whereby to score a party advantage. Here, doubtless, the Government is "sitting on a rail," and listening how the wind blows in the English constituencies, but not a syllable or apparently a thought of the unhappy betrayal that was to follow! As usual, what was uppermost in the minds of the incoming Ministry was not the thoughts and feelings of Englishmen in South Africa; the important thing at the moment was popularity with English voters who had placed them in power.

However, there were distinct promises given. (1) They "would not shrink from the policy of their predecessors." (2) They would "vindicate the authority of the Crown." (3) They would then grant "free institutions."

Was it any wonder that the loyal part of the Transvaal trusted the Government? Alas for them! Every promise was broken on the ground of high morality and high policy. (1) They *did* flinch "from the policy of their predecessors. (2) They did *not* "vindicate the authority of the Crown." (3) They did *not* grant "free institutions." They might have formed a self-governing colony for all men. As a matter of fact they acted so as to create a tyrannical Oligarchy out of a section of the people, and that section the rebels. Instead of a noble, loyal policy, instead of the fulfilment of promises given—there followed—what? What has been felt in South Africa to have been a discreditable and humiliating surrender.

[*] *Cf. Times.* The italics are mine.

The loyal English, however, and the loyal Boers had even better reason for trusting the English Government; for, telegraphing to the High Commissioner in May 1880, the Colonial Secretary had said, "under *no* circumstances can the Queen's authority in the Transvaal be relinquished." And this telegram was confirmed at a later time. Mr. Gladstone himself had said, "Our judgment is that the Queen cannot be advised to relinquish the Transvaal,"* and he had said other strong things in the same direction. It was afterwards pleaded that the Government *had* so intended, but had changed their minds as they felt they had been deceived concerning the real feelings of the people; to this we may allude presently, but meantime it cannot be denied that this wore every appearance of an afterthought which it was scarcely ingenuous to put forward. For there is no concealing the fact that they *did* know of discontent among the Boers, and also of their grievances, *before* they announced their unalterable decision to hold the Transvaal, for Boer deputations had waited upon them in London and pressed their case, and Mr. Gladstone himself had already said during "the Midlothian campaign" that the annexation was "the invasion of a free people," and had denounced it accordingly. And Lord Wolseley had written as early as October 1879:

"I regret to have to inform you that the attitude of the Boers in the Transvaal appears to me to have assumed a serious aspect. . . . I am compelled most reluctantly to recognise the continuance of grave discontent. . . . The grievance has been largely a sentimental one, and it turns on the delicate and sensitive points of national dignity and injured honour. . . . I do not myself wish to imply that

* Letter to Messrs. Krüger and Joubert, June 8, 1880.

I myself apprehend the serious outbreak that is said to be threatened, but I have felt it my duty to state that there is good reason for the conclusion which is now, I think, accepted even more completely by Colonel Lanyon than by me, that the main body of Boers have a rooted dislike to English Government."*

The British Cabinet were *well* aware, therefore, of the state of feeling of the Transvaal Boers *long before* they came to their decision to undo the policy of annexation, and after being made aware of this state of feeling they authorised the effort to suppress the rebellion, and only altered their line of policy after defeat.

The case, however—and this is the damaging charge against the then Government—was not one merely of the discontented Boers, but of the *whole* community, including large numbers of loyal Boers, of loyal English, and of natives. For these England was also responsible. In the interests of a professedly high sense of morality that responsibility was, we are reluctantly driven to acknowledge, contemptuously thrown aside. Nothing, it is to be feared, can fully excuse the conduct of the Government. They knew well, as we have seen, the state of the case. They said decidedly again and again that annexation they would not undo. They led the loyal to trust to their promises, to their own undoing. They marched up troops to oppose the rebels who had advanced into Natal, and to assist the loyal towns which they had besieged. When some of those troops suffered reverses they made a *volte face;* took completely the side of the rebels, and abandoned all who had placed trust in their promises. They had said " *Vestigia nulla retrorsum,*" and then turned and

* Despatch, October 29, 1879. Quoted in Egerton, *Colonial Policy*, p. 433, *n*.

fled. Is it to be wondered at if men did not attach much importance to subtle arguments advanced in defence of such conduct? Is it to be wondered at that the Boers looked upon them with contempt as men moved by fear, and the loyal with indignation as traitors to their best friends? Is it not true, as has been said, that, however subtle arguments might be used, "to plain men it seemed as though the motto of England had become *Debellare subjectos, parcere superbis.*" *

The wrongs done to loyal subjects and the soreness caused by those wrongs may best be judged by a glance at some passages in a correspondence between Mr. Gladstone and Mr. White at the time. Mr. C. K. White was President of the Committee of Loyal Inhabitants of the Transvaal. Among other things are the following:

"The Committee desire to express the hope that you will be able to support the prayer of the petition, and thus endeavour to see justice and right done to the loyal subjects of the British Crown, who have lost friends and property in defence of the honour of their country, apparently without hope of redress or consideration."†

Along with this letter went a petition to the House of Commons which stated lucidly the whole case. It was, however, hopeless. The Government had resolved upon their change of front, the Prime Minister had certainly convinced himself that this was right, and the Liberal majority in the Commons were his submissive followers.

To the above letter Mr. Gladstone had answered, among other things:

* Egerton. *Colonial Policy.*
† Letter of May 1, 1881. Quoted by Carter, *Boer War*, p. 494.

"I desire to state with respect and sympathy as much as appears to be material.

"It is stated, as I observe, that a promise was given by me that the Transvaal never should be given back. . . . If the reference be to my letter of June 8th, 1880, to Messrs. Krüger and Joubert, I do not think the language of that letter justifies the description given. . . . The insurrection in the Transvaal proved in the most unequivocal manner that the majority of the white settlers were strongly opposed to British rule. It was thus shown that the original ground upon which the Transvaal was annexed—viz., that the white settlers were prepared, if not to welcome, at all events to acquiesce in British rule—was entirely devoid of foundation."

It will be observed that the Government after having this "proved in the most unequivocal manner," had still prosecuted warlike operations, had still remained firm to their judgment that annexation could not be reversed. Indeed, it must be remembered that when things were getting bad in the Transvaal, the Cape Government telegraphed to know if England was prepared to continue to hold the Transvaal; and the answer from the home Ministers was "Certainly."

However, the sophistries by which the British Cabinet tried to justify what has been felt in South Africa to be a shuffling policy are best exposed in Mr. White's answer to the Prime Minister from which the following remarks are extracted :

"If I should, under the influence of strong feeling, occasionally use language which may be distasteful to Her Majesty's Government, you will believe that I do not intend any disrespect either to your colleagues, or to yourself as the foremost statesman of the age ; but rather that I deeply regret you should have allowed yourselves unconsciously to be led away by the combined effects of panic, half information, and false sentimentalism into acts of wrong-doing and injustice which, if completed, will leave a stain upon the reputation of those who have been parties to them, and which will be fraught with disastrous consequences to the British race in South Africa

generally. . . . The first subject of importance with which your letter deals is the promise given by you that the Transvaal should never be given back, and which, as you conjecture, is contained in your lettter of the 8th June, 1880, to Messrs. Krüger and Joubert. You will perhaps remember that you referred the Chairman of a meeting of loyal inhabitants at Pretoria, who wrote to you for an assurance which should quieten all apprehensions of the loyalists, to the same letter as the final expression of your opinion with reference to the retrocession of the Transvaal. The letter consequently became, not only a conclusive reply to the Boer agitators, but also a guarantee and a promise to the loyal inhabitants, and a continuation of the series of guarantees which had been frequently given on previous occasions by authorised representatives of the English nation. . . . The actual words of the letter are :—
'. . . Our judgment is that the Queen cannot be advised to relinquish the Transvaal. . . .' But your letter of the 8th of June not only contained this final and absolute announcement of the policy of England, but it gave the reason for arriving at it, in words which so aptly express the case of the loyalists that I quote *in extenso :* they are as follows:—' It is undoubtedly matter for much regret that it should, since the annexation, have appeared that so large a number of the population of Dutch origin are opposed to the annexation of that territory, but it is *impossible now to consider that question as if it were presented for the first time.* We have to do with a state of things which has existed for a considerable period, *during which obligations have been contracted,* especially, though not exclusively, towards the native population, *which cannot be set aside.'*

" In your speech in the House of Commons . . . you used words of similar import. You are reported in the *Times* of January 22 as saying :

"' To disapprove the annexation of a country is one thing, to abandon that annexation is another. Whatever we do, we must not blind ourselves to the legitimate consequences of facts. By the annexation of the Transvaal we contracted new obligations. . . . I must look at the obligations entailed by the annexation, and if in my opinion, and in the opinion of many on this side of the House, wrong was done by the annexation itself, that *would not warrant us in doing fresh, distinct, and separate wrong, by a disregard of the obligation which that annexation entailed.'* "

After adverting to a statement in the letter, to the effect *that by the Boer insurrection* it was shown that annexation was wrong, Mr. White goes on as follows :

" I am at a loss to understand this statement, because in your letter of June 1880 you state that it appeared that a large number of the population of Dutch origin in the Transvaal were opposed to the annexation of that country, but, nevertheless, and in spite of the recognition of this fact *then*, you did not then consider it advisable to relinquish the Queen's sovereignty. If words are to have any value attached to them, is it not evident that Her Majesty's Government were fully conscious previously to, and independently of, the war, that the majority of the Dutch population of the Transvaal were opposed to the annexation, but that obligations since contracted did not warrant the reversal of the annexation ? And I would respectfully ask whether the obligations to the English and other settlers, and to the natives, on which you laid stress then, and which you then considered so paramount, and so binding on the Government that you could not advise Her Majesty to relinquish the Transvaal, are less binding now, when so many faithful subjects of the Crown in the Transvaal have laid down their lives, and so many more have lost their property and suffered in body and in mind in consequence of their loyalty, and their dependence on the word of yourself and other representatives of the English people ? Are not the obligations to European and other settlers intensified rather than lessened ? And are not the obligations to the natives also intensified ? If you will ask the S. N. A. of the Transvaal whether the natives were loyal during the war, he will tell you that the natives were not only loyal, but desirous, nay, even eager, of testifying their loyalty, by being allowed to fight the Boers, and the most strenuous exertions were required to make them remain quiet. If 'the wrong done by the annexation [which I do not admit] would not then warrant you in doing fresh, distinct, and separate wrong, by a disregard of those obligations,' will it warrant you now ? I would ask you, Sir, to remember that I am not citing the loose ramblings of some local politician, but the chosen and deliberately expressed opinions of the leading statesman of the country, then, as now, the Prime Minister of England, which were read at the time according to their plainly grammatical meaning, and which were acted upon accordingly. . . . I presume Her

TRANSVAAL—THE SURRENDER

Majesty's Government is not prepared to repudiate the official utterances of Lord Kimberley, Her Majesty's Secretary of State for the Colonies. I find his lordship telegraphing to the High Commissioner of South Africa, in May 1880: 'Under *no* circumstances can the Queen's authority in the Transvaal be relinquished.'

"And, further, in a despatch dated the 20th of May, Lord Kimberley confirmed his telegram and said that the sovereignty of the Queen in the Transvaal could not be relinquished.

"On the 24th of May, his lordship stated in the House of Lords that the Government would not abandon the Transvaal, and in the course of his speech he used the following expressions:

"'There was still a stronger reason than that for not receding: it was impossible to say what calamities such a step as receding might not cause: we had, at the cost of much blood and treasure, restored peace, and the effect of our now reversing our policy would be to leave the province in a state of anarchy, and possibly to cause an internecine war. For such a risk he could not make himself responsible—the number of the natives in the Transvaal was estimated at about 800,000, that of the whites less than 50,000. Difficulties with the Zulus and frontier tribes would again arise; and, looking as they must to South Africa as a whole, the Government, *after a careful consideration of the position*, came to the conclusion that we could not relinquish the Transvaal. *Nothing could have been more unfortunate than uncertainty in respect to such a matter.*'"*

After further careful and unanswerable reasoning, the writer adds :

"Some of us were deeply opposed to the autocratic system of imperial rule which prevailed in the Transvaal, and which helped, in the judgment of some of us, towards the war. I, for one, opposed the Government strenuously, though unsuccessfully, on one occasion at least, because they would not grant to the country the representative institutions which I believe necessary to ensure its proper development, and to allay the opposition of the Dutch element. But when the sword was drawn and it came to being an enemy or being loyal, we, all of us, came to the front and strove to do our duty in full dependence on the pledged and, as we hoped, the inviolate word of England; and now it is very bitter for us to find we trusted in vain;

* *Hansard*, ccliii. p. 208.

that, notwithstanding our sufferings and privations, in which our wives and children had to bear their share, and that notwithstanding our losses, including for many of us the irreparable loss of valuable lives, we are dealt with at arm's length as clamorous claimants, and told, as I was told by a member of the Government, we are 'too pronounced' in our views. If, Sir, you had seen, as I have seen, promising young citizens of Pretoria dying of wounds received for their country, and if you had the painful duty, as I have had, of bringing to their dear friends at home the last mementos of the departed; if you had seen the privations and discomforts which delicate women and children bore without murmuring for upwards of three months; if you had seen strong men crying like children at the cruel and undeserved desertion of England; if you had seen the long strings of half-desperate loyalists shaking the dust off their feet as they left the country, which I saw on my way to Newcastle; and if you yourself had invested your all on the strength of the word of England, and now saw yourself in a fair way of being beggared by the acts of the country in which you trusted, you would, Sir, I think, be 'pronounced,' and England would ring with eloquent entreaties and threats which would compel a hearing. We, Sir, are humble subjects of England, from the other side of the equator it is true, but none the less subjects, and perhaps the more entitled to consideration for that reason. We have no eloquence but the eloquence of our sufferings, of our losses, and our cruel desertion; but we urge our claims upon you as a matter of justice, of right, and of national morality; and we submit that if you do not listen to them you will incur the danger of offering a larger premium to rebellion than to loyalty; of alienating for ever the cordial respect of a number of loyal persons; of forfeiting all confidence in the national honour and justice; of utterly destroying the moral influence of England in South Africa—an influence which means more and is worth more than mere military *prestige;* and of handing down to posterity the name of your Administration as one which was guilty of one of the greatest acts of national perfidy towards faithful subjects ever perpetrated."

And then the writer ends thus:

" On all grounds, even the very lowest, we cry for justice, and we implore you, Sir, in particular, not to allow the close of an illustrious career to be sullied by the wanton abandonment of the loyal defenders

TRANSVAAL—THE SURRENDER 217

of the national honour, and an entire disregard for obligations which you yourself have acknowledged to be binding."

It will be seen from this how strong was the case of the loyalists, and how, not unnaturally, strong to a pitch of indignant anger were their feelings. The act of the Government was indeed—it is to be feared—indefensible whatever excuses may be found for it, and there are some excuses, as we shall see. Still, we are surely in danger of paltering with truth if we fail to acknowledge that it was an indefensible act, and that, since pledge after pledge had been given, it cannot well be denied that for the nation to recede from its pledged word was a terrible betrayal. We cannot wonder at a comment made upon the above letter. It is as follows :

"This letter, I believe, was unanswered; and, indeed, there could be no answer to it. The cheap half-measure of justice done to the Boers [if justice it was] was to be performed partly at the expense of that section of the inhabitants of the Transvaal who did not take up arms against Her Majesty. To use a familiar idiom, it was a robbery of Peter for the payment of Paul, and in the history of South Africa no policy of the English Government has gone farther, nay, so far, to shake the allegiance of Englishmen to the paternal Government than the issues of the Transvaal War."

Lord Cairns' words, too, in the House of Lords, are worthy to be remembered. They brought into clear light the hollowness of the reasons assigned for the *volte face* of the Government.

"I want to know," said the noble lord, "what we have been fighting about in the interval. If this arrangement is what was intended, why did you not give it at once? Why did you spend the blood and treasure of the country like water, only to give at the end what you had intended to give at the beginning? We know that there are those who have lost in the Transvaal that which was dearer to them than the light of their eyes. They have been consoled with the reflection that the brave men who died, died fighting for their Queen and country. Are the mourners now to be told that these men were fighting for a country which the Government had determined to abandon, and that they were fighting for a Queen who was no longer to be the Sovereign of that country? This has been somewhere styled the Peace of Mount Prospect, but I doubt whether it will not go down as the 'Capitulation of Downing Street.'"*

This was, of course, also unanswerable. Lord Kimberley, placed in a position as awkward as it is possible to imagine, after all these broken promises could only argue : "The object of this settlement is to preserve all that was valuable in our position when we annexed the country."†

What Lord Kimberley considered "valuable when we annexed the country" does not appear. What we have "preserved" is the indignation of our fellow countrymen in South Africa, the contempt of the Boers, the tarnishing of British honour, the loss of British *prestige*, the character of a nation the word of whose Government cannot be trusted, and the dignity of having established in power a tyrannical Oligarchy, one of the worst and most corrupt in the world, as a source of constant unrest for a long time to the whole continent.

To the loyalists the whole affair was looked upon in this way :

(1) The surrender was ignominious.

(2) It was a base betrayal, for it was a giving way to rebellion, and giving, after defeat, what had been refused repeatedly and solemnly to entreaty.

* Quoted by Carter, *Boer War*, p. 512.
† *Ibid.* p. 512.

(3) It was a flagrant violation of promises given to Englishmen, loyal Boers, and natives.

(4) It was a surrender to men from whom those natives had always received harsh and cruel treatment, and who had so mismanaged their Republic when they had it, as to bring it to bankruptcy; to men incapable of governing well and justly when left to themselves.

(5) It was the deliberate establishment of a foe in the midst of our colonies, and putting in power those who to their dislike of us now added contempt; who were incapable of understanding magnanimity, and believed us really to be cowards, actuated only by fear.

(6) It was the destruction of the high idea of English honour and strength on which the welfare of South Africa so much depended.

(7) And it was a step fraught with danger to liberty, and certain to bring endless difficulties in the future.

Such were the views of the loyalists, and it is very difficult, if not impossible, to deny that they represent a large amount of truth.

As to the motives of the British Cabinet, they were probably very various, as is, perhaps necessarily, the case with politicians. To undo the Conservative policy, and justify the strong utterances against it; to conciliate Mr. Bright and his special followers; above all, to avoid needless expenditure — were no doubt leading reasons. Probably the last was the strongest. The Treasury had some time before taken fright at the expenses of the Transvaal, and when Sir Garnet Wolseley had been sent out in 1879 as Civil Commissioner in Zululand and Natal in place of Sir Bartle Frere (who was henceforth to exercise his authority only in the Cape Colony), the home Government had, as we have seen, strongly impressed upon him the need of economy. The need of making the Transvaal less expensive had pressed upon all Governments, and the present authorities were, naturally enough, deeply influenced by it. There had been a tendency all along, as we have seen, to look upon the South African possessions of the Crown as not worth what they cost, and so questions of money, and of showing an economical Budget for the benefit of the taxpayer at home, had very much greater weight, in all probability, in bringing about the extraordinary decision of the Cabinet than any other considerations. It is curious to reflect that, as has been already pointed out, money—the severe determination with which Sir Owen Lanyon pressed the payment of taxes upon the Boers, who always object to any taxpaying—was one of the leading reasons of the Boer rebellion; and that money, the need of economy, and the idea that the Transvaal was worthless, was one of the main motives for retrocession. There is an irony in events! Five years later, had the Government held by their promises, they would have found the Transvaal—on the discovery of the more valuable goldfields—one of the wealthiest of English possessions, and under a healthy system of administration more than able to pay its expenses—as even Krüger has found, so that, instead of the chronic bankruptcy to which Boer government always led, he has been able, by oppressing the wealth-producing population of Englishmen and other Uitlanders, even with the very imperfect knowledge of

State finance possessed by the Transvaal Government, to keep the vessel of the Republic afloat, and avoid giving umbrage to the Boer farmers on their tender point—money.

There were, of course, other motives: the evils of a vacillating policy, of tergiversation, of broken promises; the wrongs done to loyal Boers and loyal Englishmen were kept well out of sight of the class who formed the backbone of the strength of the Liberal party, and to them appeals of a humanitarian and sentimental character were exceedingly telling. The idea of justice to the Boers, of undoing what was conceived to be the immoral policy of annexation, and of respecting an effort for independence made by a brave people, and of avoiding further bloodshed, undoubtedly appealed strongly to Mr. Gladstone himself. He had ever been a defender of the weak against the strong, and it is probable that he persuaded himself that this was a case in point now. He seemed to forget the dangers of a shifty policy, and the duty of standing by promises made, and intentions again and again reiterated, upon which the loyalists depended. It was an unfortunate decision; but however men may differ as to his statesmanship, no one who ever knew him as a man, could doubt the sincerity and purity of his motives, even though they may deplore what they consider a want of judgment in his conclusions in the present instance. The retrocession of the Transvaal, after all that had been said and done, was indeed a grievous mistake, and has led to grievous consequences; but behind the mistake there were certainly—especially in the case of the Prime Minister—some noble motives. But of this more anon.

We cannot, however, close our eyes to the fact that the highly humanitarian and philanthropic aspects of the matter were absurdly exaggerated. It was all very well for Mr. Krüger to talk of his "fatherland," but the Transvaal was nothing of the kind: he was a British subject, and born as such in the Cape Colony. It was all very well to talk of the disloyal section of the Boers as being the true possessors of the country, and as being there before some of the others; but the view of Krüger's own party before as to the validity of such a title to possession must not be forgotten; in 1856, when Pretorius, Krüger, and the rest opposed the then Boer Government, the historian tells us: "The community of Lydenburg (*i.e.*, the then rulers) was accused of attempting to domineer over the whole country, *without any other right to pre-eminence than that of being composed of the earliest inhabitants.*"* It was all very well to be enthusiastic for the rights of these Boers; but had the other colonists, and above all had the natives, no rights to be respected? We had saved the Boers from destruction at the hands of Secocœni, and then at the hands of the Zulus, and from bankruptcy brought on by their own maladministration. The major part of them gladly accepted annexation to save them from their troubles. Agitators had stirred them up. Many, as we have seen, had been driven by terrorism to attend malcontent meetings, and then to fight, just as, even more than, "the demands of the Irish nation" in recent times were to a large extent manufactured by means of a "Terror." It was monstrous to forget these things, and do a grave injustice in the name of high moral principle.

* Theal's *History*.

On one point the Boers and the whole community were, and had a right to be, indignant. There had been some eighteen months' delay in redeeming the promise of constitutional government. Not retrocession of the territory to a section of the community, but the establishment of constitutional government and the making of the Transvaal into a self-governing colony, was what the Government ought to have done. A mixture of good and of very noble though ill-founded motives, with some fairly defensible from expediency, and some distinctly mean, led them to do a great wrong and to make a terrible mistake.

But if the deed itself involved grave mistakes, the manner of doing it was a mass of blunders. The Government plan was carried out in a way to cause the maximum of friction with the minimum of good results.

Such extraordinary secresy was maintained as to the peace proposals that in the end, when all was known, the final settlement burst upon both parties like a sudden clap of thunder. The Boer leaders dared not for some time let their adherents know what was actually settled, as in their opinion the settlement did not go far enough. They had on May 24 sent a memorial to Sir Evelyn Wood expressing in fulsome terms their devotion to the Queen " as our future Suzerain," and their " respect " for the British nation, and for England's " noble and magnaminous love of right and justice." Their " devotion " and " respect," however, died down when they found that they were not to have everything precisely as they wished. They afterwards let it be known that their assent to the final arrangement was " wrung from them." The Volksraad when it met used the most violent language as to the settlement. It required, in fact, all the influence of Mr. Krüger and Mr. Joubert to have the Convention ratified. Mr. Krüger has all along been a most fortunate man, and one cannot but admire the dogged persistence and shrewdness which he has shown in profiting by the opportunities afforded him through the mistakes of others; and it must be owned that all along the English, whom it is said that he heartily detests, have given him abundant opportunities.

He and the other leaders saw that it was wise to accept the Convention lest the English national temper should be roused, and the people might pass out of their humanitarian and sentimental into a more practical and determined mood. There was, indeed, a threat that if the boundary question which the Government proposed was pressed, the Boers would again fly to arms, and the English Government, as usual, at once gave way; and, indeed, it is probable, in the then temper of the English Liberals, that had the Boers pressed them on the other points they would have allowed themselves to be "squeezed" to any extent whatever. No sooner, indeed, were the Boer leaders placed in power than they steadily agitated for an abolition or modification of the Convention. In 1884 such a modification was granted by Lord Derby. In the first Convention the name given was "The Transvaal State," a sensible name, corresponding to the title "Orange Free State." In 1884 this was foolishly changed into "The South African Republic," an unwise step, (1) because it is not a real Republic at all, and (2) because there is another and a much better managed Republic in South Africa, and (3) because it played into Mr. Krüger's hands in his constant and not unnatural efforts to make the Boer State, rather than Great Britain, the paramount Power, and to create a Republic at the head of Republics in South Africa, and destroy the connection with the Empire. Having gained the Convention of 1884, called "the London Convention," the Boers have since denied her Majesty's "suzerainty," which called out, as we have seen, so much *devotion* from Mr. Krüger and the other leaders in 1881. This contention, however, has no real foundation, as the "suzerainty" stands where it did. It never was in the articles, but in the introduction. Sir Bartle Frere observes : " The chief reason given for retaining a British suzerainty (whatever that may imply) over the Transvaal, was that it would be some protection to the 700,000 loyal native subjects against any aggression by the Boer Government. . . . It has not, however, been of the slightest use for that or any other visible purpose."* It has been remarked that perhaps the real use of the Convention is that it is the one sole outward and visible sign that Great Britain is the paramount Power in South Africa. To violate the Convention both in letter and spirit seems to have been a chief effort of the Boer Government ever since. That Government has intrigued with Germany, France, Portugal, and Holland. Indeed, the importation of Hollanders under the rule of the present President, for posts of importance, has been, it is commonly believed, a serious grievance to his own people. The Conservative Government had found it necessary to abrogate "The Sand River Convention," and annex the Transvaal owing to its condition of powerlessness

* *Life of Sir Bartle Frere*, vol. iv.

for anything except for mischief to the rest of South Africa. The Liberals denounced this as an intolerable wrong. If it were so, the only way to right it was to return to the terms of that Convention. This they did not do; they did neither one thing nor the other; and by the course pursued sowed deep suspicion of England in the minds of the Boers, which for many a long year, if ever, will not be eradicated.

As to the natives things were still worse. In early days an exaggerated care for the natives had, as we have seen, led the then Colonial Office, guided by the missionaries, to unfair treatment of the Dutch settlers in the colony, and induced the Great Trek, so laying the foundation of the Transvaal and all its troubles. So now, in spite of professions and promises, the natives were practically abandoned to the tender mercies of their old taskmasters. Nothing is more tragic to contemplate than the shocking effects of the surrender on the unfortunate natives. Natives, after all, are human creatures, and some of them of a most promising type. They have behind them centuries upon centuries of savage life. They cannot be lifted to the heights of civilisation all in a moment. They *can* appreciate the benefits of good government. Few men have understood them as Sir Bartle Frere or Mr. Cecil Rhodes. In spite of all our faults, the natives have believed in us. Once beaten by us, they obey. The Dutch Boer they hate. They instinctively feel the comparatively low type of his manhood, and therefore fear his cruelty. He has, perhaps, his virtues —such virtues, chiefly self-regarding, as belong to a man physically courageous, hard, ready to face danger, but unscrupulous, self-seeking, narrow. He considers the native an inferior class of animal to be treated by the Boer—an elect child of God—as a Canaanite, and to be exterminated when need be. The time is (declared to be) within the memory of living men when a man of the Boer race, now of some distinction, drove natives, as animals, in his plough. It is said to be within the memory of those who live still, when the Transvaal Boer roasted natives alive as punishment for supposed offences. To these people, not altogether so gentle, simple, and religious as some philanthropists supposed, the Government of 1881 handed over the natives of the Transvaal without appeal. Probably no more inhuman mistake has ever been committed, with not only a calm unconsciousness, but even with a flourish of trumpets as to transcendant morality, by any body of well-intentioned and misinformed men. The British colonial policy has much indeed to answer for, but we cannot wonder if many in South Africa consider that it never, probably, has had to answer for a sin of such dimensions, as—in spite, too, of being done in the name of high moral principle—the surrender after Majuba Hill.

One cannot help at any time condemning folly, cant, ignorance under great responsibilities, faithlessnes even when wearing a mask of morality; one cannot help, alas! on any sound principles, condemning the action of England. Equally it is impossible not in a certain way to admire brute strength and vigour, and narrow-minded doggedness and fanaticism, pushing on perseveringly to its goal. One cannot help, on any principles of fairness, admiring the vigour of the Boer representatives. But Great Britain *v.* Transvaal Triumvirate is a sad spectacle. The one, enthusiastic for justice and forgetting to take in things as they are; the other with little thought of justice, but with a clear "weather eye" open to facts which tell in favour of a project, right or wrong.

Among the greatest sufferers were the natives. We English are astonishing persons for deceiving ourselves when—with a profoundly egotistical instinct —we *pose* as the lovers of others. We had always been the friends, the *real* friends, at times the foolish friends, of the natives. Now our morality, not untempered by political necessities, and by the cant of the time, had reached such a pitch of splendid self-denial, that we felt we could throw the native over, and leave him to the mercies of the gentle Boer!

When the natives heard of the surrender, chief after chief, a countless number, came from all parts of the Transvaal to inquire if it was a real truth that the English meant to abandon them to the Boers. There was—of that there is no doubt—a "wholesome dread" of their former masters. If it were possible for an enthusiast in favour of surrender to meditate quietly upon this truth, he would see that the terrible fear of the unfortunate natives on hearing of it was a proof of the highest importance that, until England annexed an incapable and anarchic Republic, the Boers had been to the natives no gentle masters. One who writes with full personal knowledge of all the facts, and writes with a quite extraordinary freedom from prejudice, believes that when—unrestrained by England—the Boers ruled the natives, they "ruled them with a rod of iron, if there is no harsher term that may be applied to the matter"—all who *know*, know, alas! that there is a "harsher term."

Those who know the natives, know how difficult it is for them to be roused and to express their feelings. They *did* and they *do* trust the English. They cannot, of course, distinguish between the follies and tergiversations of Downing Street and the straight true English action with which they meet in the case of individual Englishmen. They could have no conception of the mysterious ins and outs of the Colonial Office. How could they imagine that their liberators, in the name of high principle, should hand them over tied and bound to a harsh, fanatical, even cruel set of men—their most deadly enemies? However, it happened. The irony of things is wonderful when once we pass from the straight road of truth and duty. We deliberately (*i.e.*, the Liberal Government of 1881 deliberately) handed over the natives of the Transvaal to the most doubtful taskmasters. "Piteous despairing cries" were raised to Englishmen from chief after chief. Jacobus More (Mamagalic), chief of the Bakmena, wrote in a way to bring tears to one's eyes. It is too touching to read his words.

"Are the English really defeated?

"Is it really peace? May everybody really go unmolested where he likes?

"I'm very sad, because I thought your Honour would always be my father, and foster me, but now you leave the country and us to our fate!

"Oh! may your Honour, before leaving the country, not forget to do something for the black population of the Transvaal, so that they may bless you! . . . May your Honour, who has to now been our father, do acts of a father for his children, whom he leaves."

I know nothing more pathetic, more moving, more touching than the wail of the forsaken natives at this terrible time. The above is only one example of numberless "cries of the children" to fathers who hardened their hearts. Downing Street, bent on "high morality," neglected, not only for loyal Boers, when it surrendered, but for unfortunate natives, the first principles of righteousness and duty.

Of all the details of grievous mistake in the surrender of 1881 none most surely is more saddening than the treatment of those natives. We had always, as we have seen, professed to protect them, and sometimes foolishly; our betrayal now was, therefore, all the worse.

When England was winding up this affair, which seems to many in South Africa an act of pious iniquity, about three hundred chiefs were summoned to Pretoria to be informed how the vacillating mother— Great Britain—had cared for her trustful and helpless children. "The natives," after all, as was well said, were "the real heirs to the soil." They were never truly cared for. We never considered any one but a *section* of Boer rebels who were no more "heirs to the soil" than ourselves—not so much, for we could use it and govern it, which they never could.

However, by the act of the Government of 1881 the natives were sacrificed, after having been taught to trust us.

They were summoned—three hundred chiefs—to Pretoria to hear the last utterances of the Queen of England. We need not quote them. Natives are simple: they are not fools. They listened to the long exordium. We do not quote it. In its cant, pretence, and unreality it is calculated to bring a blush to the face of every Englishman.

No opinion was permitted to be expressed by any

native. They are not fools, however; they reasoned: "England is supposed to be strong; she hands over the country to Boers, pretending that it belongs to them. They are cruel, they are stupid. England was fair and, we thought, strong. She is weak. The country really is ours. We were here long before Boers. We believed in England. After all, she betrays."

It is saddening indeed for an Englishman to think of such a moment. Fighting for the liberties of mankind, a "Liberal" Government had, under the pressure of party necessities, broken every promise given, betrayed every trust, and surrendered the helpless to stupid cruel fanatics, because those fanatics *persevered* in resistance, and because all this suited English party strife. It was, indeed, a moment of deep humiliation. Nothing ought to be so humiliating as when cant wins the day.

The surrender was a deathblow to the natives, and that too from their professing friends! Thinking of the effect of the surrender on these unfortunates, we may close with the words of Sir Bartle Frere : *

"The Convention under which the Transvaal was given up stipulated for many things to be done by the new Government of the Republic, none of which have yet been accomplished and for the most part they have not been attempted. . . . The natives scattered among the European farms have been reduced to the same condition of serfdom in which we found them before the annexation. Mapoch and other chiefs to the east and north-east, who had been loyal to the British rule, have been attacked, and great numbers of their followers slaughtered. A large 'Commando,' said to comprise two thousand Burghers, with two cannon—supplied by the Cape Government—is at present engaged in crushing the tribe, blowing up their caves with dynamite. Their greatest offence is fidelity to the British Government.

* Letter to Mr. J. M. Maclean, Feb. 23, 1883.

... To the natives of the Transvaal and its neighbourhood the surrender of the British Government has brought loss of all security for liberty, life, or property."

Then as to the loyal Boers and loyal English, and the colonists at the Cape, what of them?

It is impossible to describe the horror with which the news of the surrender by the Government was received by all loyal subjects both in the Transvaal and Cape Colony.

In the Transvaal were both English and Boer settlers who were loyal to the Imperial connection. Many English had settled—in addition to those there before—after the annexation, had acquired property, had invested their capital on the strength of repeated British promises both from Conservatives and Liberals. They knew well the impossibility of Boer government and the untrustworthy character of the Boers. They would never have dreamed of willingly settling under Boer rule, and they knew well that, whatever promises might be made, and whatever paper guarantees executed, they would be the objects of Boer malice and scorn, and justice they could never hope to have. Many, at ruinous loss, left the country after the surrender: those who remained, remained only to experience the fulfilment of their fears. Boer suspicions have been more than ever accentuated since the events of 1895. Those who find themselves in the Transvaal in outlying districts learn what it is practically to belong to a subject people, and are well aware that they have to exercise constant caution, and that "the Boers," as it has been said to me, "will get a knife into an Englishman if they can." At times, pretences to the contrary may be necessary, but a Boer—a Transvaal Boer—hates an Englishman.

The "Old Colony Boers," as they themselves like to be called, are very different. Their lot after the surrender was not so hard as that of either the native or the Englishman. They do not like the Transvaal Boers. They are in every way superior to them as are the Dutch now in the colony, but the Transvaal Boers have not the same dislike to them as they have to the English. They left the Cape, not from any desire to be in a "Dutch Republic," but purely from reasons relating to their cattle farming. They have confidence in English rule, and they move very much in their own set. Like the rest, though in a less degree, they were sufferers by the change.

So closed a successful rebellion — successful partly perhaps from the mistakes of British generals, partly from the folly of two successive British Governments; closed, by the handing over of a fine territory to agitators and rebels, to a part of the inhabitants, and that part disloyal to our Empire and hopelessly unfit to govern; closed, leaving behind it in the minds of the disloyal contempt for Great Britain, and in the minds of the loyal a bitter sense of the untrustworthiness of her promises. It will be long in South Africa before these fatal betrayals are forgotten, but we may hope that a clear view of our mistakes in the past may teach us the wisdom of firmness and faithfulness and constancy in the future.

It is constantly urged—and by thoughtful and fair-minded and calm-minded men too—in South Africa that the conduct of the English Government at the time is indefensible and inexcusable. It can, indeed, scarcely be defended; but, on looking closely at the whole matter—if we are to be quite fair—there are points to be urged in excuse. We cannot wonder that men on the spot, men in close touch with all the details of events, and men who had been bitter sufferers by the policy pursued, should feel strongly, and perhaps make fewer allowances than should in fairness be made for the action of the Government. They put their case strongly thus, and a strong case it must be allowed to be:

(1) That Government, with all the facts before it, comes to the conclusion that the action of its predecessors is wrong—that the Transvaal ought never to have been annexed. This is stated in burning language by its chief representative as the wicked "wanton invasion of a free people."

(2) None the less it is felt by that Government that whatever might have been done in the past, the *status quo* must be considered. New responsibilities to those who trusted the Imperial word have been incurred. These cannot be put aside. The retrocession of the Transvaal is impossible. This assurance is reasserted again and again. Loyalists take courage and resist rebellion.

(3) Rebellion at last begins. Promises made which, if fulfilled, might have stayed all, are not kept. None the less, loyal men trust reiterated promises and trust the Government.

(4) Rebellion is increased by terrorism, worked well by the leaders of agitation (who are still receiving pay from England)—and nothing is done to counteract this; nothing to reassure the loyal except repeated promises.

(5) When rebellion comes, insufficient troops are sent up. Loyal garrisons defending the besieged towns are not supported. Mistakes in generalship, as well as the absence of support and of sufficient forces, lead to defeats. These are represented as the "defensive operations" of a free people struggling for liberty. Really they are the results of the Transvaal rebels deliberately *invading* Natal.

(6) *After* defeat it is discovered that the act of noblest morality is to break promises, betray friends, submit to rebels, forsake unfortunate natives, give in to the dishonesty, chicanery, and steady *bullying* of many inferior and not over-scrupulous people among the rebel leaders, and then ride off on the pharisaic claim of a self-denying morality.

Such is the serious side of the question.

Such is the case for the prosecution, so to speak.

Can anything be urged in defence? Scarcely; but much can be said in palliation.

Let us examine this.

There are many blessings in popular government. It was natural enough that in our early years many of us should be carried off our feet with enthusiasm for its development. It was natural, it was generous to be impatient of what appeared the narrow and inhuman ways of the Toryism of the past, and of all unworthy bolstering up of mere privilege. Sitting at the feet of John Stuart Mill, or stirred by Kingsley's sympathetic enthusiasm, or the many voices prophesying coming glories, it would have been superhuman during the years of the rising tide of Liberalism not to expect Utopias. But there are no Utopias this side the grave either in politics or in other departments of human activity. Men expected too much, and where that is the case there is a danger of reaction, a danger of seeing nothing but defects where they had hoped for impossible virtues. The reaction has made many men jaundiced cynics before now. They are hasty, however, in their cynical conclusions; they are unreal; they are wrong. It is, of course, obviously true that "in order to love mankind one must not expect too much from them." A healthy and generous mind gaining the lessons of experience learns to make large allowances and still to rejoice. Enthusiams have carried the popular masses off their feet before now. Men have been capable of expressing in books excellent popular principles, and yet have turned out no great hands at practical politics. John Stuart Mill himself was excellent in theories, but he was a failure at Westminster. Mr. Morley, in a later generation, thinks often wisely and ably, and states matters clearly, but as a practical politician his greatest admirers would scarcely describe him as a conspicuous success. Good men have done wrong things before now, not from malice, but from mistake. Party government is, so far, the best that has been discovered. No one, however, with any justice of mind can deny that it has many defects. The time may come when the evolution of things may bring us to a more perfect way of carrying on the art of government, but that time has not come yet. And we are unwise, meantime, to be either unreasoning optimists, or morose and despairing pessimists, because the best methods we yet know are far from perfect. We ought surely to look matters fairly in the face; to see and acknowledge mistakes, and grave mistakes; to notice the causes for such mistakes, so as to avoid them again, without condemning wholesale or praising wholesale, without accusing parties of cynical contempt for duty, or leaders of unprincipled charlatanism. Such accusations may, alas! sometimes be deserved, but we must, in common fairness, be chary of advancing them until we see whether or not more charitable hypotheses may not fulfil the conditions of the problem.

With us as a nation there may have been some excuse for this. The Liberal party had had broad and generous ideals, but every party is subject to deterioration. There is no doubt that they gave the impression to their opponents and, as has ultimately been seen, to the nation, that they were too fond of tinkering the Constitution continually, instead of using it; of changing and mending the machinery instead of working it. Where men were alarmed in this way, they lost sight of the constant power of readjustment and of correcting hasty mistake which is to be found in the great fund of common sense—of wise thought coming from experience and applied to conduct public and private—which is one of the most valuable possessions of the English people. However, there are, one cannot doubt, certain crises in our history where the tendency of party government is to hurry the nation into serious errors of judgment, where common sense comes in too late to correct, and can at best only modify grave mistakes. We have all of us lived through fierce controversies with regard to Home Rule in Ireland and the position of the House of Lords. The advocates for drastic measures had a good deal to say for themselves. Many of them were able and unquestionably sincere; the weaker *laisser-aller* people had abandoned hope, and allowed themselves to drift in the stream of "the thing is inevitable," so often the resource of the sluggard or the coward. The proposed drastic and revolutionary changes were examined and put aside, and—as large numbers of sober Liberals now think—wisely put aside. The fact is the people had time to think, and common sense prevailed. Crises may come when, even amid the passions of party, time for reflection is given; but there are also crises when those very passions hurry men away from their better judgment, and then irremediable mistakes may be made.

Such a crisis was, it seems to me, in 1881. It was one of the many pieces of good luck which have fallen to the lot of Mr. Krüger, whose chief characteristic, perhaps, has been acuteness in making use of other men's mistakes, that hasty mistakes were made at that time. The action of the then Cabinet with regard to the Transvaal was, it seems probable, a serious mistake into which the nation was hurried and the *mode* of that action was entirely indefensible. But although this was so, we can see, now that we have the advantage of the foreshortening effect of time upon the picture, how easily circumstances combined to lead to the mistake; and thus, though that mistake and the manner of its making cannot be defended, they may, surely, in a measure be excused.

(1) The nation was suffering from a fever of party spirit. Whoever remembers that time will remember that with one party it was the fashion to talk as though the Liberal leader had a monopoly of "righteousness" and the Conservative leader of wickedness; and *vice*

versâ that Lord Beaconsfield's conduct was that of a noble patriot, and Mr. Gladstone's that of a charlatan. Neither view was right. Both statesmen had done great good, both had made great mistakes. Party feeling at the time amounted to a superstition. Mr. Gladstone was a very noble-minded man and a great leader, but he was not infallible any more than the rest of us. Colonial or foreign policy had never been his *forte*, and he was, like other men, under the influence of the bias of party. Before elections, leaders are apt—for they are human—to speak in a way which calmer reflection will scarcely warrant. They necessarily *put* things strongly from one point of view only, and they are in danger in a peculiar degree of over-colouring, and exaggeration, and hasty conclusion. This was in some measure the case, and inevitably the case, in the speeches of many leading men at the time. A saddening example is the accusation against Sir Bartle Frere by Mr. Gladstone of his supposed responsibility for the annexation of the Transvaal. Mr. Gladstone evidently acted on imperfect information. Had he been responsible for it, Sir Bartle Frere would, in the opinion of many, have had nothing to be ashamed of. But as a matter of fact he had nothing to do with it. However, such was the impression on the minds of Liberals, in their passionate haste at the time, and this went so far that that "Great Proconsul"—perhaps the best and wisest Governor that the Cape ever had—was soon after recalled in disgrace, not because the good of South Africa required it, but for the welfare of the Liberal party! Well might Robert Browning, himself strongly Liberal, say to the present writer at the time, and in the presence of many leading Liberals, "The conduct of the Liberal Cabinet to Bartle Frere is disgraceful."

This is an example of the way in which facts were befogged at the time from party passion. No doubt Mr. Gladstone was pressed by his party, and it is quite probable that when the rebellion broke out his generous sentiments deceived him (as they afterwards did to some extent in regard to Ireland)—deceived him into picturing the violences of agitators, and the extreme measures of the more fierce and unscrupulous, as a patriotic rising for liberty. Further, there was cleverly dangled before the eyes of the Cabinet the fear of a war of races in South Africa. This is one of the trump cards even at this moment, when "Krügerism," as it has been called, means endless intrigue to stir up Dutch feeling in the colony against English feeling, for the benefit of the Transvaal Boers. This unquestionably acted upon the minds of statesmen then, as it has acted since. Nothing of the kind would have happened then, and it is highly improbable that, to any great extent, it would happen now; many of the Cape Dutch are too intelligent, and they have had opportunities of taking the measure of the "Krügerites" and all their works.

Even had it been true, there are worse things than war and even than race war. Dishonour, injustice, faithlessness to undertakings are worse, betrayal of loyal subjects is worse. However, the clever "bogie" *did* influence the minds of the Cabinet then. A great wave of very mistaken but in the main sincere humanitarian sentiment was passing over their followers. A real enthusiasm for justice and freedom possessed the mind of the Prime Minister, and very imperfect information and the clever representations of the Boer intriguers in England and at the Cape confused his sense of where justice and freedom lay !

There were characteristic views held by the great Prime Minister which doubtless influenced him to such a mistake. We can realise those now.

Apropos of the debate in 1850 on the Don Pacifico business, when Mr. Gladstone answered Lord Palmerston's celebrated " Civis Romanus " speech, it has been well said of Mr. Gladstone's speech, that *—

"[It exemplifies] at a comparatively early period and in high perfection, two of Mr. Gladstone's most conspicuous qualities, which have grown with his growth and strengthened with his strength, and have been attended by important and opposing consequences. The first of these is his high and even austere morality. He appeals to the most august of all tribunals, to 'the law of Nature and of God.' As a test of a foreign policy he asks, not whether it is striking, or brilliant, or successful, but whether it is right. Is it consistent with moral principle and public duty; with the chivalry due from the strong to the weak, with the principles of brotherhood among nations and of their sacred independence ? It is this habit of Mr. Gladstone's mind which has done so much to secure him the enthusiastic veneration of his followers, who loathe the savage law of brute force, who recognise the operation of moral principle in international relations, and who feel it a personal pain and degradation when England is forced to figure as the swashbuckler of Europe.

" But if this element has been a main factor in Mr. Gladstone's hold over the affections of his disciples, and thereby of his public success, it is not difficult to discern . . . the operation of another element which has done much to mar his popularity, to limit his range of influence, and to set great masses of his countrymen in opposition to his policy. This is his tendency to belittle England, to dwell on the faults and defects of Englishmen, to extol and magnify the virtues and graces of other nations, and to ignore the homely prejudice of patriotism. He has frankly told us that he does not know the

* George W. E. Russell. *The Right Hon. W. E. Gladstone*, p. 243.

meaning of 'prestige,' and an English Minister who makes that confession has yet to learn one of the governing sentiments of

'An old and haughty nation proud in arms.'"

This is most true, and it explains much as to the matter in hand. "Prestige" may have an evil sense, but it has a good one. The "prestige" of a great nation is a gift and a force for which it is responsible. To ignore its true meaning, and to deliberately sully it, is to throw away national self-respect. It was this characteristic in the great Prime Minister which made his fellow countrymen feel that colonial and foreign policy was not always safe in his keeping. Mr. Gladstone, with all his real greatness, had "the defects of his qualities," and a certain want of balance of judgment in applying moral principles to national life probably led him into confusions and mistakes. It was this, and no unworthy popularity-hunting, which induced the terrible Transvaal mistake, whereby the hectoring, unworthy, and the debased were exalted, and the weak and loyal and right-minded brought low.

Then further, there was a ridiculous fallacy allowed at the time, and pleaded since to do duty for truth. That was the doctrine that the Transvaal was "the Boer's country," or, as Mr. Krüger—a British subject born in the colony—described it with astute effrontery, his "fatherland." The "right" to a new country must rest (1) upon an arrangement with those previously in possession; or (2) on might, the might of conquest and the might to hold it; and (3) joined with one or other of these, the right of just and good administration. By (1) the English hold the Cape and some other possessions, by (2) and (3) some other territories in South Africa.

The Boers held the Transvaal—in so far as they did hold it—by the right of "might," by defeating some of its previous possessors. By the right of a just and good administration they have never held it, and do not hold it now. The only "right" by which they held it they forfeited to the English. We delivered them from the Zulus, who would have annihilated them; and we acted with justice while we held it, although a speedier fulfilment of our promise of self-government would have avoided many evils. By (2) and (3) the Transvaal was justly ours. The sooner, probably, it is ours again the better for itself and for South Africa. The English Government, in handing it over to a section of the inhabitants in 1881—and that the least intelligent and least capable of governing—did infinite harm. It was a sad instance of men committing a great mistake and doing a great wrong from motives many of which were noble, though some of which, of course, were less worthy, and all of which were allowed play much too hurriedly and without sufficient consideration.

The whole thing, we may hope, has taught us wider views, truer principles, and a juster sense of our responsibilities as an Imperial Power. We can see much now that could not then be so clearly seen. We must not judge too hardly, therefore, rulers who, in difficulties, on the whole did their best. The surrender was a grievous mistake and a great wrong. We cannot, indeed, defend it, but at least we can in some measure excuse it.

CHAPTER V

THE TRANSVAAL—THE RAID AND AFTERWARDS

THE mistake of 1881 began to bring forth a fruitful crop of evils before very long. Had this mistake not been made the Transvaal might have been governed, as a self-governing colony, with equal rights to all citizens of whatever nationality, and with a strong and wise Government able to meet the altered circumstances of the country with statesmanlike prudence and a strong hand. This, however, was not to be; and the Boers of the Transvaal, with their ideals of isolation and the loose relations of a farming community, with their incapacity for governing when left to themselves, had to find themselves soon confronted with the problem of a large influx of foreigners, for whom equal rights would in time naturally be demanded under pain of a growing discontent.

For a great change had passed over the Transvaal territory. As early as 1867, and onward for some seven or eight years, gold had been discovered. This was chiefly to the east. The quantities at first were small, and it was not looked upon as being of any serious consequence. Workings of a more extensive kind began, however, about 1882, and in 1885 the valuable beds of the Witwatersrand were discovered, which so deeply affected the history of the country.

The gold beds of the Rand are in many respects the finest as yet known. Where reef gold is found there is, I believe, some uncertainty. One part may be very rich indeed; another may fail. The peculiar value of the Transvaal goldfields is the approximate certainty, from the nature of its beds (called "banket" beds), that there will be a *steady* yield owing to an immense quantity of the precious metal.

On this account the Rand became famous, and as interest was awakened European capital flowed into the country. The Boers would have found it impossible themselves to work the mines, both from lack of intelligence and knowledge, and from insufficient resources for an industry so expensive. For the process, as every one who visits the Rand may see, of separating the precious metal from the materials in which it is embedded is very costly indeed. It would have seemed, therefore, that the influx of immigrants from England, Germany, America, and other places—mostly, however, English, and for the most part men of intelligence and skill—would have been welcomed by the Government. At first, indeed, it was so. The Republic had been in a state of confusion and almost bankrupt. From the most impecunious it rose swiftly to be one of the most moneyed countries in the world. The revenues of the State mounted up as the mines were developed, and towns were built and extended, but with these revenues grew the population. Mr. Krüger and his Boer advisers took alarm. If they could not work their mines without foreign labour and foreign capital, at least they could keep the immigrants always in the position of foreigners—

always " Uitlanders" with no voice or influence in the government of the Republic.

The admirers of Mr. Krüger represent him as only doing what it is natural and just to do. Things look very different according to the point of view from which they are seen. The Boer point of view was this. They had succeeded—so they believed—in outwitting the English. They had defeated them in some skirmishes, and then, as they still believe, frightened them into better terms in their Convention than they could have at first expected. They had succeeded in " squeezing " Lord Kimberley, in preventing any severance of territory, and in getting things all their own way. They had founded a narrow Oligarchy with power in their hands, and why were they not to keep it? They had frightened a feeble British Government by the threat of stirring up Dutch feeling against them throughout South Africa ; why were they not to keep the leverage for doing so well in their own hands? If their opponents had dreamt of the establishment of a free Republic, *they* had had no intention of the realisation of such a scheme. They had wanted Boer isolation. They had it, and why not keep it? If the Convention hindered them from barring the immigration of foreigners, it had forgotten to include any terms compelling them to admit those foreigners to the franchise, or to treat them with justice. They had treated the natives as true Israel treated the Canaanites, and though the meddling English would not allow them to go to such extremes with them now, still they had "jockeyed " these English into leaving them—short of slavery—to settle that question and all internal affairs. Why were they to give others the chance of meddling in such things ? In fact, they had got the Transvaal to themselves; why should they not keep it to themselves? Why should they disturb their primitive barbarism by submitting to the ideas of modern civilisation? If Uitlanders came to work mines it was well. They might, in the process, enrich themselves, but they must be kept as Helots to serve the *dominant* Boer. In fact, they wanted to be narrow, exclusive, *dominant*. They preferred reactionary methods, and a conservatism of the stiffest type. They had faced troubles to acquire a position in which their ideal might be carried out. It might be a very low-class ideal; still, it was *theirs*, why give it up? They could not, perhaps, in the long run, defeat overwhelming British power, but they had before, and they could again, outwit the stupid English by their superior shrewdness. If they must admit the goose that laid the golden eggs, still, after all, it was a goose—it could be penned and its golden egg utilised for its owner's benefit, and in time, if need be, it could be slowly killed. In any case, in fact, why should they not use the advantage which the British Government had given them? Some hundred thousand Uitlanders had settled in the country. If this went on, and if these men were allowed political rights, they would swamp the Boer minority, and Liberal ideas would prevail; and the long struggle for comfortable ignorance, easy-going immorality, untroubled repose, narrow notions, fanatical religion, domination over natives, isolation and exclusiveness would all have been wasted. Why should they not cling to the advantages they had gained?

There was much to be said in this way. How

indeed—upon ordinary self-interested principles—can people blame Mr. Krüger for holding to the advantage he had gained? The leaders among the South African Boers have always had a secret jealousy and fear of the English. They know that they are superior in energy, in large-mindedness, in breadth of view, and far before them in culture and the arts of civilisation. In one thing, however, they are their inferiors. The English can easily be " gulled," and their philanthropic and generous instincts worked upon. They had been worked upon to some effect in the retrocession in 1881. Dutch shrewdness had not only " squeezed" Lord Kimberley, but afterwards "squeezed" Lord Derby. " Liberty," to the mind of Mr. Krüger and his advisers, meant liberty for themselves and their Boers, but not either for natives, nor—in their degree—for Englishmen or any Uitlanders. As the English had been swayed by sentiment, good nature, philanthropy in 1881, so many of them have been swayed since. Mr. Krüger's point seems to have been, "Keep them down; use them; drive them out by degrees; allow them no share in political interests." This is echoed by his defenders —professional or amateur—and with a sort of reason which appeals to English generosity. "Why disturb him? Surely the Boer community may be allowed to protect themselves in their pastoral and simple ways against mere 'money-grubbers,' who enrich themselves and then go. Self-preservation is the first law of existence; you can't blame Krüger and his Boers for preserving themselves against encroachment."

There was much to be said for this.

But then, again, there was another point of view. It had been supposed that there was to be, after the retrocession, a really free Republic. Men imagined that those who settled in the Transvaal would in a short time acquire the rights of citizens, and so cast in their lot with the State which they had made their home. They considered it to be unjust to say that they made their money there for the purpose of leaving the country and spending the money elsewhere; for that the real truth was that the policy of the Government was to force them to do so; not that *they* sat lightly by their connection with the Republic, and so compelled the Government to act as they did, but that the action of the Government compelled them to sit lightly by their connection with the place. They asked why they should not be treated with the same equal justice as was meted out to immigrants to the Cape Colony? And they slowly discovered that liberty for others was the last thing that Mr. Krüger and his Boer advisers contemplated, and that, in fact, liberty was not to be looked for except under the British flag. Had Mr. Krüger been a large-minded man or a statesman, he might — one cannot help believing — have welded together the Dutch and foreign elements, and made a strong, compact, and loyal Republic, prosperous and rich and peaceful, and both able and willing to resist encroachment or interference from without. Mr. Krüger, however, is neither one nor the other. Indeed, it is hardly to be expected of him. He is a good representative of the better Boer nature —resolute, dogged, physically courageous, narrow-minded, and ignorant, to which is, probably, to be added not the faintest gratitude for the (ill-starred) generosity of England, but rather a determined dislike of the English people.

The narrowest policy has, accordingly, all along been adopted by the Pretoria Government, and the Transvaal has displayed the extraordinary spectacle of an electoral franchise, not, as elsewhere, more and more enlarged, but more and more so restricted as to render it practically impossible for any one, not a Boer, to acquire it, and the consequently anomalous spectacle of the largest part of the more intelligent and wealth-producing of the community entirely shut out from political rights, and treated as permanent aliens. In Pretoria, a large number of both Bench and Bar—men of the greatest ability and highest culture in the State; in Johannesburg, by far the larger number of the inhabitants, the most enterprising and wealth-producing of the community, have no political share whatever in the affairs of the country.

This may be thought natural and satisfactory from the point of view of Mr. Krüger and his admirers. It is an arrangement clearly likely to produce widespread and not unnatural discontent.

There are two grounds on which this discontent appears to be justified: (1) That the attitude of the Government is out of keeping with the former claims of Mr. Krüger and those who agree with him, and (2) that the exclusion from political rights subjects those who are so excluded to galling acts of tyranny, and debars them from any means of redress.*

(1) It is fairly enough contended that on Mr. Krüger's own showing it is unfair and wrong to pursue this policy. In 1856, as we have seen, he was working under Mr. Pretorius, and they were both reformers, and the matter of their objections against

* Theal's *History*, 1854-1872, chap. ii. p. 33.

the Government which they desired to overthrow was this in the words of the historian : " The community of Lydenburg was accused of attempting to domineer over the whole country without any other right to pre-eminence than that of being composed of the earliest inhabitants, a right which it had forfeited by its opposition to the general weal."*

Under Mr. Pretorius, meetings were held to protest against the actions of the Government at Lydenburg, and finally an Assembly sat to frame a constitution. Amidst many other arrangements, it was settled that the Volksraad should be elected by the people, and two of the important qualifications for seats in the Volksraad were that members were to be " electors of three years' standing," and of European (not merely Boer) origin."† This constitution—notwithstanding traces of religious bigotry in it—was, for Boers, singularly liberal. Mr. Krüger was then a reformer. One might have expected that he would have sympathy with the Uitlanders in 1895, but it was a far cry from 1856 to 1895, and from Boer factions to English and American born immigrants. "Circumstances" are said to "alter cases." What is "sauce for the goose" is not always considered "sauce for the gander." Extremes often meet. Like Pius IX., once a reformer, at last an autocrat, Mr. Krüger had seemed to see reason for his youthful indiscretions ; but, when once placed in power by the generosity of the English people, retreated from his former principles which had the effect of giving civil rights to men of " European," not necessarily of Dutch, " blood." Against this un-

* Theal's *History*, 1854-1872, chap. ii. p. 34.
† *Cf.* Hillier's *Raid and Reform*, pp. 5, 6, quoting Theal's *History*.

just inconsistency, as they deemed it, the Uitlanders protested.

Further, (2) the exclusion from political rights subjected the Uitlanders, so they considered, to galling acts of unfairness and even of tyranny.

Among the grievances complained of was, of course, the unfairness of taxing those who had no representation in the Volksraad. It is interesting to remember that this very complaint made up the heavy part of the indictment of the Boers against the English Government after the annexation—in the words of a sympathetic historian, "the levying of taxes on the Boers by an administration in which they were totally unrepresented."* And now those who supplied four-fifths of the revenue of the Transvaal Republic, and whose capital and energy raised the State from poverty to wealth, had burdens laid upon them " by an administration in which they were totally unrepresented." It cannot be denied that there is much justice in Mr. Hillier's eloquent appeal:

"Are we not labouring," he writes, "under all these disabilities to-day? The one retort to this is we are Uitlanders. That is to say, that in a country not yet sixty years old, in which the population has been formed almost entirely by immigration, in which the President himself is an immigrant, the mining community, who have been coming in for at least fifteen years past, and have done more in developing the material resources of the country in that time than was ever conceived in the wildest dreams of the earlier inhabitants, are foreigners. What proportion of the burghers of this State were actually born in the country?—this State which owes its prosperity and its progress alike to the continuous stream of immigration. The President at least was not born here." †

This injustice to Englishmen and others was felt

---

* *Cf.* Nixon's *History of the Transvaal*, quoted by Hillier, *Raid and Reform*, p. 17. † Hillier's *Raid and Reform*, pp. 20, 21.

more bitterly considering the full liberty accorded to men of all races by the English in Cape Colony and elsewhere.

It was felt further that Uitlanders were kept from their rights from corrupt motives. Mr. Cellier, himself a Transvaal burgher, described the second Raad, as it unquestionably is, as "a mockery and a sham." Mr. Emsden, once in the Afrikander Bond in the colony, then one of the Transvaal judges, said in 1892:

"I wish to ask you whether you can give any credence to the statements of a man (President Krüger) who says he is going to unite two peoples when the whole of his acts for the last ten years show it is absolutely untrue? I do not speak without knowing what I am talking about—I say you have been kept out of your political privileges not because the people have kept you out from fear that your being granted these privileges would touch or endanger the independence of this country, but to enable a few, and a greedy few, to rule the country for their own ends."*

The grievances of the Uitlanders, briefly, were these:

(1) That the Customs tariff was excessive, making food shamefully dear, and that the charges for railway freights were unduly heavy.

(2) That the duties on machinery and chemicals were extortionate.

(3) That these and the dynamite monopoly made the expense of all mining operations excessive.

And beyond this

(4) The extreme unfairness as to the vexatious laws touching on education and on the use of language. Before the Committee of the House of Commons in

* Hillier's *Raid and Reform*, p. 38.

March 1897 Mr. Chamberlain gradually extracted from Mr. Schreiner, who appeared to be an unwilling witness, and to—what may be called—"hold a brief" for the Transvaal Government, admissions of hardships as to a sort of "crusade against the English language," and a very narrow and unenlightened policy in the Transvaal as contrasted with the Cape Colony or even the Free State as regards education.* Mr. Schreiner also himself acknowledged that "the grievances" of the Uitlanders were recognised as such in Cape Colony.†

The Uitlanders then had *their* view, as Mr. Krüger and his friends had *theirs*. They felt acutely what one of them called "the indignities put upon the British section of the community," and the not only "denial of their rights, but a taking away of their rights."‡

Indeed, no one can deny, nor does the warmest partisan on the side of the Boer Government venture to deny, that these were hardships. The Boer view on such matters, however, is the view of a half-civilised people. Whatever virtues we may credit the Boer with, he always shows himself totally incapable of governing, as civilised government is understood, and very hazy as to the meaning of liberty. But for the mistakes and follies of the British Government—who have played into the hands of the Oligarchy at Pretoria—the present anomalous state of things in the Transvaal must long ago have collapsed.

It was not probable that a large number of Englishmen—far the majority of the community—together

---

* *Blue Book.* Second Report. South Africa, pp. 244-247.
† *Ibid.* p. 249, *Qu.* 4370.   ‡ *Ibid.* p. 410, *Qu.* 7877.

with other Uitlanders, who had as much right to have *their* share in the government of the country as the Dutch have in the Cape Colony, would permanently tolerate such a state of things without any effort to bring about a change.

An effort was made which began hopefully enough. It would seem that the Uitlanders were asking to have ordinary rights respected. Simple justice was, indeed, all they asked:

" Society," it has been said, and truly,* " is impossible unless those who are associated agree to extend certain rules of conduct towards one another; its stability depends on the steadiness with which they abide by that agreement; and so far as they waver, that mutual trust which is the bond of society is weakened or destroyed."

Krügerism has steadily sowed injustice and reaped, consequently, distrust. According to the Groudwet † (to find another constitution) " the country is open for every foreigner who obeys the laws of the Republic." And further, the elective franchise could be acquired after two years' residence. The President, however, was the motive power in a steadily reactionary and vexatious legislation, by which if not in word, yet in fact, the Convention was covertly violated.

There were more enlightened members of the Raad, but they were terrorised into submission. Mr. Krüger is a man of great energy, of great strength of purpose, and of dogged determination. He is, according to our standard of judgment, narrow-minded and bigoted; dislikes the English because he fears them, notwithstanding the debt he owes them for their generous conduct in 1881. He seems to abhor all foreigners

* Huxley. *Evolution and Ethics*, p. 56.
† *I.e.*, the fundamental constitutional law.

and all foreign ways. Like all uneducated and rude men, he is not unlikely to despise England for its Quixotic act, and has—so it is said—directed, by violent and passionate threats and appeals, all the Raad legislation against the very nation to whom he owes his present position.

In 1891 the National Union was formed at Johannesburg for the purpose of pressing on questions of Reform. Everything was done in a strictly constitutional way. What the Union desired is cleverly set forth in a manifesto drawn up by Mr. Charles Leonard and published on December 26, 1898.

"(a) What do we want?
How shall we get it?
1. The establishment of this Republic as a true Republic.
2. A Government or Constitution which shall be framed by competent persons selected by representatives of the whole people, and framed on lines laid down by them, and which shall be safeguarded against hasty alteration.
3. An equitable Franchise Law and fair representation.
4. Equality of the Dutch and English languages.
5. Responsibility to the Legislature of the heads of the great departments.
6. Removal of religious disabilities.
7. Independence of the Courts of Justice, with adequate and secured remuneration of the Judges.
8. Liberal and comprehensive Education.
9. An efficient Civil Service, with adequate provision for pay and pension.
10. Free trade in South African products.
This is what we want." *

How to get it was the question.

The assertion has been made that the whole thing was a move of capitalists to capture the country and

* *Raid and Reform*, pp. 54, 55.

swell their own gains. Nothing could be more untrue. Until the crisis had almost come in 1895 the capitalists were outside the movement. The Union was made up of working men and traders.

The method employed hitherto for attaining the desired ends had been the sending of petitions to the Raad, and, though the Chief Justice saw the danger of the situation and spoke with vigour, yet in the Raad itself, by Krüger's influence, petition after petition was rejected, and a monster petition, signed by 38,500 people, was in 1895 rejected by the Raad with fun and laughter.

This sort of treatment at last proved to the reformers that they could hope for nothing unless by resort to arms. A plan for a rising was adopted and efforts were made to supply the people of Johannesburg with arms and ammunition. It was a slow process, and had to be done with the greatest caution. Mr. Rhodes had offered to help them by sending in a body of the Chartered Police under the command of Dr. Jameson when called for by the Johannesburg leaders.

Every one knows now the history of the ill-starred Raid. Never was any undertaking more dogged by misfortune. Mistake after mistake, misunderstanding after misunderstanding followed one another in quick succession. Everything played into the hands of the Krügerites. The time chosen was unfortunate. Pretoria was crammed with Boers for the Christmas festival. The supply of arms and ammunition was utterly insufficient in Johannesburg. Dr. Jameson's force was much too small. Wrong impressions were left on different minds as to promises given. While things were in no way ready, Dr. Jameson, growing impatient, and underrating apparently the difficulties, "took the bit in his teeth." In vain Mr. Rhodes attempted to check him; in vain the High Commissioner sent to order him back. He believed it was the only way to help Johannesburg, and so forced the situation.

It proved a fatal mistake. He and his men fought well, and only at length surrendered when he was deceived into believing that the reformers had thrown them over. There seem to be very varying views as to where the fault lay, and the minutely true history of the matter will probably never be ascertained.

The Reform leaders at Johannesburg believed themselves to be the real sufferers. They saw—so many of them believed—their plans thwarted by Dr. Jameson's precipitation. They were persuaded by the High Commissioner to lay down their arms under the idea that only so could the lives of Dr. Jameson and his men be saved, though the wily President and his party knew well that one of the conditions of surrender at Doornkop was that all lives would be spared.

It would be hardly fair, perhaps, to blame Sir Hercules Robinson too much, for he was in such feeble health as to be unfit to cope with the situation; but the English Government are not altogether free from blame for leaving him, when in poor health, in the position he held. Having persuaded the reformers to fall in with Mr. Krüger's views, he then left them to their fate, and they certainly believed that Sir Jacobus De Wet made them promises of impunity, which were never kept. This was denied by Sir J. De Wet, and as strongly is, to this day, asserted by more than one independent witness who declared that they heard the promise given. It was one of the many misunderstandings and mistakes which were abundant in every direction in this unhappy affair. The action of the Imperial authorities was, in the main, anything but satisfactory. The whole story of the "Afterwards" of the Raid ought to bring a blush to the cheek of Englishmen.

The Uitlanders, indeed, understood that, if they disarmed, Mr. Krüger would make these concessions:

1. (As we have seen), the lives of Jameson and his men were to be spared.

2. The Uitlanders' grievances were to be taken into favourable consideration.

3. The Reform leaders were to go unpunished or to have only a nominal punishment.

Of these, as we now know, the first was a matter of course. It was carefully kept from the knowledge of reformers that that had already been made a condition of Jameson's surrender. The other promises were immediately broken.

The leaders were thrown into prison—a prison unfit for the commonest criminals—and the Boer Government had the impudence, not only to violate their engagements, but to try them and sentence the four chief men to death.

Of course, they dared not have carried out this sentence, for, however badly the British authorities had behaved, they would scarcely have sunk so low as to permit it. The English people would certainly not have permitted it. It gave the wily President an opportunity of masquerading as the merciful ruler and remitting the sentences, while at the same time the affair was turned, by the Transvaal authorities, into a successful commercial transaction by mulcting the very men to whom had been promised impunity in immense sums of money, as well as immuring them in a vile and ill-managed gaol. The mind of one of them gave way, and he committed suicide. Of the others, all, save two, after paying enormous fines were released, while compelled to sign a promise to take no further part in Transvaal politics. Two — Messrs. Karri Davis and Sampson — courageously refused to have any dealings with the Transvaal Government, feeling naturally that rulers who had, as they believed, so grossly violated their engagements should not be dealt with by honest men. They remained in prison until, tired out by their determination, the Transvaal authorities released them at the Queen's Jubilee. The Krügerites represented this as a "graceful act" of clemency. Others looked upon it as a polite proceeding to "make capital," and get rid of the remaining reminder of a broken promise.

If the British authorities in the Transvaal were thought to have behaved badly, if the Boer President was believed to have been untrue to his word, the Cape Government did not do much better. They actually arrested and handed over to Krüger's tender mercies two of the reformers, and did their best to do the same in the case of a third. The following is a not unnatural comment by one of their number:

"The action of the Cape Government in first arresting Messrs. Joel and Bettelheim, and subsequently in endeavouring to arrest Mr. Charles Leonard, pursuing him with that end to a Portuguese port, will ever remain a stain on this page of the history of the Cape Colony. The arrest of political refugees, one of them a British

TRANSVAAL—THE RAID AND AFTERWARDS 261

subject, in a British colony, to be handed over to a foreign State, is an act the character of which might be natural in Turkey, but which surely has never before in history been perpetrated by a British Colonial Government.

"To Mr. Leonard it was left to find on the shores of England that protection which even a Portuguese port would not withhold from him, but which was denied him in the land of his birth, a British colony. Well might he exclaim in the bitterness of his heart that Cape politicians during this crisis in South Africa thought of nothing but 'crawling on their stomachs before the Boers.'" *

In England things were in some respects worse. There were those who were honestly under the hallucination that Krüger and his Government were injured innocents. There were certain sections of politicians who saw in the whole matter a grand opportunity against their political opponents. Much as they hated Mr. Rhodes, they hated Mr. Chamberlain more. The latter had been the object of their most violent invective ever since he had refused to follow Mr. Gladstone in the Home Rule policy. They fondly hoped that they would "kill two birds with one stone," ruin Mr. Rhodes, and still more ruin Mr. Chamberlain, by proving that he had a knowledge of the affair. Hence vigorous efforts were made to bring on a Committee of Inquiry. The committee sat, and in both their objects the Radical leaders were foiled. To some it appeared scandalous that such a man as Mr. Labouchere should be on the committee at all, and that after the *exposé* of him and his writings by Dr. Rutherford Harris, he was still allowed to remain a member of the committee. It was better, perhaps, that it should be so, as it was in the interests of fair play all round that the worst enemy should have his

* *Raid and Reform*, p. 74.

say. The result must have been a grave disappointment to the Radical leaders. Mr. Rhodes fairly acknowledged his share, although it was clear that he had tried his best to prevent Dr. Jameson from "going in" when he did. He has frankly admitted that he had probably been wrong in some steps taken; but men could not but feel that if the searchlight of a Committee of Inquiry had been turned on the actions of many of the leading Prime Ministers, they would show to much worse advantage; that if some of the steps taken were open to blame, he at least had acted for no self-interested end, but was fighting a duel with Krüger to decide whether South Africa should be confederated under the British flag, and with, therefore, real liberty, or should be at the feet of a reactionary Dutch Oligarchy in which justice and fair play are things unknown.

As to Mr. Chamberlain, he was entirely exonerated. Vigorous efforts had been made to represent the whole thing as a "stock-jobbing transaction." The political dissenters, and generally what would formerly have been called "the Exeter Hall party," were on the war-path in behalf of Krüger and in opposition to their own countrymen. All those who—to borrow a description lately applied to Mr. Morley—have "an impartial aversion to the British Empire," were straining every nerve against England and in behalf of "the gentle Boer." Krüger's emissaries were most assiduous, as they have been ever since, in publications and in the Press, and Mr. Rhodes was subjected to every kind of vilification and calumny. This he has borne with quiet dignity, taking his full share of blame, and ever loyal to his friends. However ungrateful "England of the lion heart" may have shown herself—as, alas! often before—to one of her greatest sons, he has calmly continued to work for her and for the country of his adoption, never stinting his labours and possessions for so great a cause.

The committee above all showed plainly to all men the injustice and tyranny of President Krüger and his Government, though they — the real criminals— remain still unpunished. The saddest memory of all, perhaps, is the trial of Dr. Jameson and his officers. Their trial is in many respects a disgrace to England. The officers were deprived of their commissions, though their only fault was obedience to the orders of their commanding officer. As time has gone on, England has been ashamed of such conduct, and their commissions have been since restored to them. As they had tried and failed, they took their punishment with dignity as honest gentlemen. This was fair. It is always difficult to draw the line and say when a movement is rebellion and when right resistance. In a matter of this sort there is, perhaps, necessarily suffering and punishment if things have not proved successful. It was scarcely necessary, however, that the Lord Chief Justice should have taken so severe a line as he did in his charge. He seemed, as many felt, to hold a brief for the prosecution. A writer well acquainted with the facts says : " While Mr. Rhodes' attitude towards Jameson's serious error of judgment had been magnanimous, and that of the Uitlanders in general has been, considering what they have suffered, not altogether lacking in consideration, it has been left to the Lord Chief Justice of England, apparently through fear of foreign opinion and a feeble anxiety to pose as perfectly impartial, to treat the English officers and their gallant leader, when they appeared before him, as though they had been common criminals, instead of honourable Englishmen who had merely erred through excess of devotion to the Empire."

It was not the attitude of Mr. Labouchere, whom he regards as at any rate an open, if virulent, enemy, but the attitude of the Lord Chief Justice, Lord Russell, that Mr. Rhodes' celebrated phrase of "unctuous rectitude" was intended to describe. As applied to Lord Russell's attitude at the trial, where he seemed at times to forget that he was not the prosecuting counsel, and appeared to use all the art of a great advocate and all the weight of the highest judicial position to procure a conviction, Mr. Rhodes' phrase is admirably true, and is not likely soon to be forgotten! It was indeed a humiliating moment for true-hearted Englishmen, and no amount of English pharisaism at the time prevented our foreign critics from holding their sides with laughter at the conduct of "perfidious Albion!"

Thus closed a sincere effort for reform of abuses and a noble effort for liberty, condemned, as such things are, by its failure. Men who had whispered before the Raid that "something ought to be done" in the Transvaal vied with one another in their cries of "Shameful!" "Disgraceful!" and so on, when failure had come. There can be no doubt it was a noble blow struck for freedom, but badly planned, badly executed, and condemned because it did not succeed.

Success, after all, is the one final justification of revolution. If it succeeds, it becomes "a faithful struggle for the rights of man;" if it fails, it becomes "rebellion." And yet there are "high failures" which are better than "low successes." The British Government at home, and especially the Colonial Office, were undoubtedly placed in a difficult position in that memorable December, and the Colonial Secretary acted with vigour and, on the whole, with fairness. Still, as through the action of the High Commissioner, acting for the Government, the unfortunate reformers were handed bound, so to speak, into the hands of their enemy, and no faith was kept with them, it would appear to be a duty laid upon the British Government that wrongs should be righted at last. When the Boers rebelled in 1881, making an effort for what they considered their liberties, we gave them more than large consideration. When our own people made their abortive effort in 1895 they were betrayed and punished.

Mr. Krüger has gone on his way, as usual, ever since. Fair speeches and pious sentiments are uttered at one time, while almost in the same breath violent language and utterances of the most insulting kind are levelled at the Uitlander population of Johannesburg and the Rand. Again, at the present moment* there is grave unrest among them. Wrongs are not righted, burdens are increased, insults are uttered. The Transvaal has become, and will continue, unless measures of Reform are granted, unless there is thorough change in the methods of administration, a centre of unrest and menace to all South Africa. It is vain, probably, to hope for any real improvement from the present Boer rulers; but it is surely equally vain to imagine that some 100,000 of

* December 1898.

the Anglo-Saxon races—English, American, German—will permanently submit to be misgoverned by men inferior in knowledge and civilisation, who may be reckoned at about one-fourth of their number.

For besides acts of injustice, such as the refusal of the franchise, the unfairness as to education, and the insecurity of the independence of the Judicature, there is felt to be a thoroughly corrupt state of things.

A brilliant writer, not by any means prejudiced in favour of the Uitlanders, to whose views my attention has just at this moment been drawn, writes:

"Meanwhile the old Boer virtues were giving way under new temptations. The new Volksraad (as is believed all over South Africa) became corrupt, though of course there have been always pure and upright men among its members. The Civil Service was not above suspicion. Rich men and powerful corporations surrounded those who had concessions to give, or the means of influencing legislation, whether directly or indirectly, and the very inexperience of the Boer ranch man who came up as a member of the Volksraad made him an easy prey."*

This is a mild and superlatively charitable way of putting it. At any rate, if once inexperienced in the arts of peculation, the Boers and the Boer Government have acquired, according to the very widespread belief in South Africa, a large experience now. The expression of a Krügerite official, who had had pretty practical experience, to me was this: "Nothing is done in Pretoria without bribery."

And there can be little doubt now that the corruption of the Transvaal is deep and far-reaching. For any desired object there, it is very generally asserted that money, administered in prescribed doses, must be

* Bryce. *Impressions of South Africa*, pp. 516, 517.

forthcoming. Corruption is a thing obviously hard to bring home. There are methods *and* methods of bribery, and the Pretoria Government are masters in these. Cases are known in which large sums of money honestly offered as a proper *quid pro quo* to indemnify the Government for the surrender of certain rights in property have been refused because the money would go, of course, into the Treasury; and smaller sums have produced the necessary effect when they have been paid in the form of *douceurs* to influential persons, so that they went into private pockets. Honest and upright men have begun their careers with the firm determination to stand firm to principle and resist the use of such means, but they have found the thing impossible. For success in carrying through schemes or causes in themselves unobjectionable, they have found it necessary to make it "worth while" for those in authority. "Concessions" of one sort or another are constantly granted, or granted and then sometimes withdrawn. Men in the country declare that the meaning of this is that equivalents for such concessions are given to the people in power, or that the withdrawal occurs because the equivalent has not been arranged so as to satisfy their requirements. It is probable that even the most corrupt of the South American Republics cannot surpass the Government of the Transvaal in wholesale corruption. There is a difference, however, and one which tells favourably for the South American States. *There* the thing is fairly open and aboveboard. In the Transvaal these things are better *managed*. Men know of these things; they are driven into being parties to them in order to succeed in legitimate objects; but they cannot be put forward, nor yet abandoned, otherwise there would be little chance for them. It is widely believed that large sums in secret service money are expended from the Pretoria Government to carry out their efforts in shaking, as far as may be, the cause of the Empire either abroad or in the colony; but these things are *managed* in a way which does credit to Boer astuteness, so that it would be difficult to bring them home in a manner necessary in law courts.* It is obvious to all that the private fortunes of individuals in the highest positions flourish side by side with the depletion of the Treasury, the needy condition of the State, and the necessity and difficulty of raising loans; but the true cause cannot well be doubted. It is obvious why men of wealth are sometimes the strong supporters of the Government, and then, again, turn unexpectedly in opposition to them. From the nature of the case, it is difficult, if not impossible, to open up these things. Men know that *money* is at the bottom of it all—that money, and a judicious use of it, gains favour; also that "the crushed worm will turn;" that too much may at times be demanded! *Hinc illæ lacrimæ!* There are ways of doing everything. Corruption in the hands of the Transvaal Government seems, from all accounts, to be carried to the height of a fine art.

* A case in point occurred while we were in South Africa. During the then recent elections, it was credibly believed, in fact, pretty well known, that large sums of money from the Transvaal had been spent in the Cape Colony to obtain a return of their supporters. Mr. Rhodes had openly stated the matter, with his usual frankness, on the hustings. He was prosecuted for libel by one of the persons through whom the money was believed to come from more influential sources. The case, of course, went against him. He was sentenced to pay a nominal fine, while he assured the Court that, though technically condemned, he and every one else knew the thing to be true. No one in the colony seemed to have any doubt on the subject.

One great evil of this is that this odious system of dishonesty and trickery is carried on under the shelter of a profession of religion. We are constantly reminded that " Mr. Krüger is such a very religious man " ; that the Boers of the Transvaal "are such a religious people;" that " every day and always they read their Bibles," and so on. There is religion *and* religion ! The American negro has a religion which permits him to sing many warm hymns and at the same time " to rob the henroosts." Grave inconsistencies are certainly human. It is not necessary in the case of Transvaal Boers and their Government to put to the credit of hypocrisy what is probably—at least in some cases— rightly to be attributed to fanaticism and a low state of civilisation. Bible reading, especially the study of the Old Testament, is unfortunately not inconsistent with selfishness, narrowness, coarseness, immorality, and the love of money. A divorce between religion and morality is the gravest disaster ; and if religion in South Africa is, as it unfortunately is, marked at the present time by a widespread indifferentism, a good deal of this may be laid to the door of a corrupt Oligarchy using and encouraging methods quite inconsistent with integrity, while encouraging a narrow fanaticism and carrying on its lips the sacred words of Scripture. Corruption soon runs down from the head to the members. A corrupt Government tends to spread corruption through the whole body politic. Men cannot always breathe miasma without suffering from infection in the blood. We expect to find when such a state of things exists in high quarters looseness of moral principle gradually affecting the atmosphere of social life, and we do find it. Can men be so bitterly blamed as some have been, even by us in England who ought to know better, for having struck a blow— even if an ill-planned one—for liberty, and for having endeavoured to sweep away so corrupt a Government? It is a serious matter which ought to furnish anxious questionings to the British people, that, as a nation, *we* are responsible for having set up, and for now quietly tolerating, such a state of things. Pecksniff or Stiggins, or at a higher altitude Machiavelli, may find consoling justification for it, but it can hardly commend itself to any fairly enlightened conscience, much less to the "straight" if somewhat slow-moving mind of John Bull. To cleanse an Augean stable is no light undertaking; but it cannot be doubted that it is the duty of those who have laid its foundations either to do what in them lies to cleanse or clear it away.

But further, corruption of this sort has a close connection with that which, in whatever degree it exists anywhere, is always demoralising—viz., the determination to govern, while depriving the governed of their just rights. At the present day in modern Greece the traveller sees well-built, noble-looking men and handsome women, and wonders why there should be, in a people which has so splendid a history, much that is wanting in straightforwardness and courage. The answer is: they were for centuries deprived of freedom. The unhealthy state of things in the Transvaal tends in the same direction. The whole *tone* of life and action gradually must tend to degenerate among those who—deprived of the rights of citizens—have to live under a Government which itself lives by injustice, falsehood, and corruption.

A very striking thing is the extraordinary caution

displayed by some Englishmen living among the Boers of the Transvaal, in speaking of the corrupt proceedings, the immoral lives, and the wrongdoings of those among whom they live. They speak like those who are afraid of being overheard! If they say anything the Boers "will get a knife into them somehow." But, worse, those who are honest and upright begin to despair of the vindication of uprightness and honesty in a State where so many acts of even approximate justice have their price.

Mr. Bryce is reported lately to have said * that the race difficulties of South Africa would give way before "tact, judgment, and justice." This is a statement which few would differ from. All things in this world would probably go on much better if "tact, judgment, and justice" were the guides of social and political action. Unhappily, they frequently are not so. When dealings have to take place between two States these eminent qualities are needed on both sides. If steady injustice is to be the guide of a government, as it has been for long in the Transvaal Autocracy, a moment may arrive when justice itself demands that injustice should be severely punished and rendered impossible.

The state of Johannesburg alone cries for interference. It is worse than futile to talk about the Suzerain being bound by the Convention not to interfere in internal affairs. The Convention—feeble and foolish as it was—has been broken, as Englishmen believe, by Krüger again and again; again and again—so Englishmen contend—he has ignored his own most binding undertakings. Johannes-

* At the dinner of the Anglo-African Writers' Club, Dec. 22, 1898.

burg has, even now, no municipal government. In that fine city the sanitation is execrable, consequently typhoid fever is rife. Educational facilities do not exist, and the police arrangements are a crying scandal. The English Government still endures these violations of pledges given. Indeed, the proceedings in the Transvaal at the present time* form a curious illustration of the character of the Government there, and of the short-sighted folly of the framers of the Convention. The Raad sat until the middle of December and was then prorogued until February. Two years ago the election took place. During the session of that Assembly which terminated at the end of the year (1898) it turned its attention with more than usual vigour to the invention of new imposts to be laid upon the wealth-producing Uitlanders of Johannesburg, who are treated as civilised Helots by the enlightened Government, and who are of course systematically excluded from any share in the legislation under which they live. A crop of new taxes was grown, and the prorogation took place, it was understood, to give time to the worthies in Pretoria to get seed sown for a fresh crop. The history of this Raad had been signalised by various railway jobberies, and one of the usual "concessions" granted, and then shortly withdrawn for the usual reasons. The most remarkable action of the Raad was the raising of a much-needed loan—needed too by a small State which, if decently administered, would be one of the richest in the world. It gave rise (not indeed to surprise, for no one who knows the habits of finance so dear to the Transvaal Government is surprised at

* January 1898.

anything) but to comment that, while Cape Three-and-a-half per cent. stands at 109, the Transvaal Four per cent. is at 90! No assertions of the innocence and purity of the Government at Pretoria can stand against this. This is "an eloquent commentary," as it has been said, "on the reputation of the Transvaal Government." When things of this kind go on public confidence must be shaken; and such is the case. No one has any idea what may happen next. The energetic Englishmen and Americans who have produced the wealth of the country and who have developed its resources in a way in which the Boers had neither the capacity nor the perseverance to do, as they are in the hands of an irresponsible Oligarchy, or rather, we may say, of an autocrat—thanks to the wisdom of the Convention—must expect anything and put up with everything. It was believed with considerable probability and foundation that the time is coming quickly when fresh taxes will be imposed, not of course on the favourite companies and corporations who have contributed, in the manner approved in the Transvaal, to the resources of persons in power, but on those of English stock, who must either submit to the worst or avoid extreme attack by the usual necessary methods.

Nothing shows more plainly how well the authorities at Pretoria have learnt to flout their Suzerain and to reckon on the immeasurable gullibility or indifference of the English people, than the report in an important London journal at that time of an interview with a Transvaal emissary. With quiet effrontery he informed his questioner—and through him the simple believers in "Krügerism," if such still exist, in Great

Britain—that things were not going from bad to worse at Johannesburg, where any man with an eye in his head could see the truth! That President Krüger—dear, pious, amiable soul—desired to see "everybody in his (!) dominions prosperous and happy"; that that good man desired progress above all things; and above all, the height of trust in British blindness was reached in the statement that "never again would Krüger trust" Mr. Rhodes! Virtuous, trustful Krüger!

There would have been something comical in the stern moral condemnation of one of the foremost of modern Englishmen by the chief of the hardly immaculate clique at Pretoria, if it were not sadly true that Englishmen had more than once before been duped by the cunning of Boer leaders into betrayal of their own faithful fellow countrymen!

At the present time Englishmen in the Transvaal have to work on quietly and submit to ever increasing injustice, while the audacity of the oppressors becomes more pronounced, finding that the modern fashion of our nation is to carry their objection to evildoers no farther than protest.

It may be hoped that the nation whose proudest characteristic has hitherto been its love for liberty may yet recover its self-respect by withstanding injustice and wrongdoing with manly energy. Nothing can be really done to bring peace and prosperity to South Africa until Great Britain wakens to her duties and wipes out that corrupt Oligarchy, and transforms it into a real and free Republic, or, still better, into a self-governing colony. Where there is freedom, *there* there will be a chance of fair dealing between man and man.

PART III
GENERAL

CHAPTER I

CONFEDERATION—THE BARTLE FRERE POLICY

IN recent years—and not unnaturally—Confederation has been, among nations, "a word to conjure with." No one can doubt that, as time goes on, there is what the scientific people call "the evolution of ideas," what Christians account for by the gradual working of "the leaven which leaveneth the whole lump"—*i.e.*, the principles of Christianity, brought home by the Spirit of God—and that men and nations have more and more assimilated the ideas which lead to unity.

All powers of Evil tend to disunion. If any one wished to see the proof — not of the *doctrine*, we need not call it that, but of the *fact* of the Fall, he need only cast his eye upon the disunion of masses of mankind. All powers of Good tend to union. To those who look with a religious eye on contemporary history it is a cheering symptom that—with whatever mistakes—there *is* a deeper desire to draw together the nations. Wherever a State is found—like the so-called Republic of South Africa—which sets its face against elementary justice and cannot endure the idea of union in any form, it is certain that *there* the governing ideas are—we need not say unchristian, that of course, but—uncivilised, and devoid of the force of progress. It is a cheering truth to those who really care for the highest interest of mankind, that as times advance there *is* more and more a desire for union.

South Africa seemed to be *the* place for English expansion. Englishmen, whatever their faults, have had certainly (1) common sense in manfully using such parts of the world as they possessed not merely with a view to their own interests, but with a real recollection of the interests of aboriginal inhabitants. (2) The common sense of giving a large welcome to members of other nations who desired to come and be sharers with them of new tracts and fresh fields of enterprise. (3) The common sense of feeling that all should have equal rights and a fair share, and that they should be bound together by the sense of the supremacy of justice, and the recognition of fair play between man and man, and the dignity—to put it in a strictly Christian form — of charity. In South Africa the English met the Dutch race. Whatever great virtues are possessed by the latter, they are not those alluded to above. This race *has* virtues, the English race *has* faults, but the faults of the latter have not included narrowness, and the virtues of the former have been injured by this very thing.

The English race *has* the gift of colonisation, to a degree—on the showing of its foes even—far beyond others. We may be accused of being wanting in a sufficient sense of bureaucracy or organisation; we may—and justly—be accused of pharisaism and a worship of respectability; we may be accused—and justly—of being the victims of catchwords, and being —what I may call " helter skelter "—*i.e.*, ready to accept indefensible anomalies; but our worst enemies cannot deny that we are good colonists, that we are glad to assimilate foreign elements, that we desire fair play, that—if we are sometimes stupid, and do foolish things—taking us as a people, we are strong, healthy, fair-minded, earnest, and desire to do right.

It is quite in accordance with the English character to leave large liberty and yet struggle for close union. There are few things nobler in our national character than this. If South Africa was—as it was—a very important sphere for Imperial expansion, it was also *the* theatre for the union of scattered communities. No alien races touched the continent; the English and Dutch had grown, more or less, to understand one another. There was community of interest. The Dutch were too harsh to the natives; the English, quite possibly, too sentimentally lenient. In face of the vast problems opened up by the contact of savage and civilised man, could anything be more obvious than the duty of making an effort to confederate scattered communities of the civilised in the common cause of progress and benefit to mankind?

The opportunity was lost, and the chance was let slip by the mistakes of 1858. The English people were, as they are, an Imperial people. Their Governments have too often been the victims of a narrow "parochialism." A golden opportunity once lost in the life of a nation or an individual never quite returns. If in any measure it does, it demands, on its second appearance, a heavier tax of sacrifice. British folly with regard to the Orange Free State may, perhaps, never be quite retrieved.

In 1871, however, the idea of Confederation came up. It was recommended by Sir H. Barkley, it was approved by Lord Kimberley.* The benefits of it were before the minds of men, certainly before the minds of the then Governor.

"Uniformity of legislature, simplification of legal procedure, facilitation of postal and telegraphic communication, as well as the construction of bridges, railways, and other public works, are too obvious," says Sir H. Barkley, "to require comment. Neither need I enlarge on those higher moral ends which would be promoted by the reunion of communities owning a common origin, and still closely connected by ties of relationship or of race. If federation tended, as it undoubtedly would, to promote a milder and less encroaching policy towards the native races on the north of the Orange River, and to put an end to the much-to-be-regretted disputes with the South African and Orange Republics . . . its accomplishment should form, independently of all other advantages, the object of the warmest aspirations of every humane and patriotic mind."†

The opportunity, for one reason or another, was let slip. It is not to be wondered at that the idea lived in men's minds, and that it came up again in 1874.

The leader of the Confederation movement at this time was Lord Carnarvon. His efforts do not seem to have been forgotten — nay, they appear to be remembered with considerable respect — in South Africa. There seemed to be much to favour the movement. Lord Carnarvon had succeeded beyond expectation in Canada. In 1867 he had carried through the British Parliament a measure for that part of the Empire which has since been confessedly productive of excellent results. He was enthusiastic in the matter. He was most conciliatory. If mistakes were made, they were not unnatural mistakes, and, had

* Parliamentary Papers, 1872.
† Parliamentary Papers, 1873, also quoted by Egerton, *British Colonial Policy*, p. 418.

there been more continuity in the policy of the Colonial Office, and less influence from mere home politics, such as they were they might have been remedied.

Mr. Froude, as every one knows, was the emissary chosen to prepare the way in some informal manner for Confederation. That he retarded it—from whatever cause—there can be little doubt. He seems to have been an accredited agent, and yet *not* an accredited agent. In some way or other he went to South Africa with the approval of the Government, and yet he disowned any official position. He certainly startled men there. He seems to have spoken with rashness against the toiling people at Kimberley, and then with enthusiasm for the Dutch farmers in the Orange Free State. One thing is certain : instead of paving the way for union, he aroused animosities and created confusion. Indeed, some credit him with *creating* by his ill-advised words a hostile *Afrikander* spirit, which has, ever since, been an enemy to union and, even at times, to loyalty. His mission—of whatever exact character it was — was undoubtedly a mistake. If a wise and thoughtful statesman had been sent out to guide the ship at that critical time ; if he had been given a very free hand ; if he had been loyally supported at home ; if the English Government had acted with consistency and there had been a faithful and continuous policy—the later history of South Africa would have been very different indeed.

A wise and strong statesman was sent out ; but there was no continuity of policy, no loyal support from home, no free hand given ; but rather, amidst the many difficulties which lay across his path, he was thwarted, hindered, cramped, defeated in his efforts by the very Government to which he had a right to look for loyal and steady support.

Sir Bartle Frere is one of those great statesmen upon whom England is obliged to look back with admiration and sorrow. He was sent out with one clear object before him—Confederation. He had that clear common sense and firmness of purpose which teach a man to make for a great end, but without forgetting the necessary difficulties, and not without realising the need of moving slowly. Had he been supported, instead of being thwarted and then betrayed, England would not now be embarrassed by the misdoings, or responsible for the existence, of a State so injurious to civilisation as the Oligarchy called the South African Republic; we should not be open to the difficulty—which may one day be serious to the Cape Colony—of German West Africa; and Confederation—instead of anxiety and disturbance—would now be within measurable distance.

The real attack upon the wise policy of Sir Bartle Frere arose from two facts: (1) the disaster of Isandlwana, and (2) the political necessities of parties at home.

He saw clearly that the Boer question and the Zulu question had to be settled. As to the latter, the Zulus were threatening the Boers; they were also threatening Natal. Life and property in that colony were in jeopardy while things remained as they did in Zululand. Cetewayo was acting with brutal cruelty. He was steadily preparing for war. He was even making an effort to effect a combination of native races against the white man. He was desirous that his young braves should "wash their spears." Natal was in imminent peril. Sir Bartle Frere saw clearly the danger of the situation. He saw that the military system of Cetewayo (depending on celibacy, for no man could marry until he had " washed his spears ") must be broken, if life and property were to be safe, and if civilisation was to advance. Indeed, the *existence* of Natal and of the colonists there depended upon it.

The sentimentalists at home afterwards objected to the *ultimatum* to Cetewayo. It was an act of wisdom and humanity both for the colonists and for the Zulus themselves. No one, indeed, would ever have blamed it but for Isandlwana. On that fatal day Lord Chelmsford failed ; the death of the Prince Imperial, deplorable as it was, was an incident ; but people at home forgot—in fixing their attention on these melancholy details—the meaning and range of a whole policy. Then came in the usual hindrance of English progress —party politics. Had parties at home been able to do without opposing cries, the great statesman would have settled Zululand, and calmed the Boers in the Transvaal with a really representative form of government ; German West Africa would not have been ; and a chain of federated colonies, free, because self-governed and owing allegiance to the British Crown, would, by now, be stretching from the Zambesi to the Cape.

Sir Bartle Frere's splendid and humane undertaking was arrested by ignorance, party feeling, and folly. Varying winds of party passion destroyed a wise and statesmanlike policy.

The whirligig of time brought its revenges. The foolish people who denounced violently all that Sir Bartle Frere had done, the men who were loud in the usual cries of "Imperialism" and "Jingoism" while a wise and steady policy was pursued, were driven to send Sir Charles Warren with a large force to preserve British territory. Those who were shocked with sentimental sorrow over the deaths of Zulus in the war with Cetewayo had to close their eyes to the oceans of blood which deluged Zululand since Sir Garnet Wolseley made his well meant but utterly useless "settlement"; and Cetewayo, by an insane philanthrophy, was "restored."

The story is one of deep humiliation. Thwarted and betrayed, Sir Bartle Frere left the Cape amidst the acclaim and with the tears and love of thousands. Much of his policy has had, since, to be carried out perforce; but great mistakes are more easily made than mended, and some of the evil done is irremediable, while what he would have carried through, if supported, must now be done in a form less complete and at heavier cost and under circumstances of graver difficulty.

What can be done for Confederation now? The faults committed in the past are serious warnings. The first effort was thwarted by a failure to realise responsibilities and to read the omens of the future. The second was wrecked by party spirit, blind sentimentalism, mistaken philanthropy, and a terrible indifference to obligations incurred. We may hope that these dangers are now diminished. The cry against "Imperialism," we may hope, is dying down. Good men, when they opposed it, meant to oppose a mere wild swashbuckler interference with the rights of others. But this is not Imperialism. In its true sense it is a recognition of responsibility. It is not necessary for

Englishmen to think themselves perfect and all other nations bad; but it is a duty to realise that if they have the gift of government they should use that gift; that it is the duty of an Imperial people to stand by their kin beyond the seas; that if, under the flag of England, they can carry justice and good government and fair play, they are *bound* to carry it. Mr. Morley, indeed, and "Little Englanders" of his type may be aghast at patriotism; still—though cosmopolitanism is good in its place—patriotism is a real virtue. We have been led, as a nation, to undertake great responsibilities in the world; these responsibilities we ought to recognise and what they entail we are bound to do. Hiding a talent in a napkin may be a convenient form of laziness, but it cannot command a final reward.

There is, surely, a unity to be recognised in mankind, but we do not realise and act upon great principles by dreaming over vague ideas. A nation has a kind of personality, it is a sort of living being; it must act with the sense of other nations having a life like its own, but not so as to forget its duties. A nation must assert itself, but justly while strongly, and if it comes in collision with injustice and narrowness in the fulfilment of its duties—well, it must prepare for collision and be true to its sense of right.

Some men long for peace, and so allow injustice to triumph and evil to go on. Is it peace in the true sense to join loving hands with Russia without using any influence we have in order that the unspeakable sufferings of Siberia may no longer be ignored, or with Turkey while the horrors of Armenia are condoned? England may not be able to cure these horrors. But England *can* cure evils for which she is responsible. Is it peace to sit down quietly and acquiesce in division and injustice where our voices and our deeds tell? To vigorously oppose the effects of injustice which are within our reach *is* to make for peace. Mankind being what fallen mankind is, it makes for peace not to talk or vote while sentimentally closing our eyes to facts, but to insist on justice being done, to build ships so as to preserve a peaceful and justice-loving Empire, to live and work—not talk and vote merely—so that our country—where she *has* an influence and a responsibility—should dare even to fight, if need be, to win honest and just and well-founded peace.

Confederation in South Africa may come slowly, probably it will, but it can only come if England does her duty in ways lying plain enough before her after the experiences of her mistakes in the past.

In South Africa England has one great duty. In the cause of freedom and fair dealing she must, at all costs, be the paramount Power. There is a splendid future for the Cape Colony. There is no reason why the two white races there should not grow more and more as one—in the enjoyment of the free institutions which are the inner meaning of the British Flag, if England does her duty. In Natal the fine English feeling for freedom and self-government is pronounced. Basutoland is a protected Switzerland: where would it be but for the spirit of British fair play? The vast territories of Bechuanaland, and now of Rhodesia (thanks to the great statesman of modern South Africa), are in a fair way for true development under the rule of Great Britain. German South Africa East and West we may have been unwise to create, but these are in the hands of a kindred race, and our true colonising and just spirit may make them friends, and—if we are true to ourselves—they will feel their identity of interest and of spirit more and more. The Orange Free State, thanks to wise Presidents, has imbibed some of the British temper of toleration and equity. If we are true to ourselves—just, sympathetic, strong—if we resist the selfish and narrow spirit of " Little Englandism," this Republic even more and more will feel the benefit of our just and strong spirit. There is one remaining State in South Africa. The Transvaal—thanks to our mistakes—is the disturbing element and the centre of unrest. Our duty there is clear. We cannot permit an ill-governed and corrupt State—unfortunately, of our making—to hinder the progress and the peace of the whole.

Incident after incident has helped on its baneful influence. England ought now to be awake to the meaning of things. No one can desire the subversion of the Transvaal Republic, if a *real* Republic it become. The time, however, has surely come, when, in the interest of South Africa, one of two things should be insisted upon by England. Either the Transvaal Government must be radically reformed; " Krügerism" —meaning thereby injustice, maladministration, corruption, and all the consequent crops of evil—should be rooted up by *genuine* reform; the long story of inequitable narrowness, and retrogressive action, and suppression of just and fair dealing, should cease; there should be real and thorough change; every citizen should be a true citizen and no longer should the minority, ignorant and impervious to just ideas, seek to lord it over the majority of the intellectual and hard working—and this by a decisive abandonment by the present Oligarchy or Autocracy of its evil traditions; or England must do its duty, must see to it—at whatever cost—that a handful of selfseeking and retrograde men shall no longer be permitted to stop the path of civilisation. England must reform the Transvaal Republic, and make it a real and free Republic, or it must sweep it away, and in its place establish a free and self-governing colony to help in the advance and prosperity of South Africa, instead of hindering all that is of value for human progress.

Once the Transvaal clique is abolished or reformed, the Confederation of South Africa, under the guiding ideas of peace and freedom and progress, will be only a question of time. Incident after incident has come for some years before the world, in the Transvaal, and one or another has blinded the eyes of men in England, but in South Africa they have not blinded many eyes. The main issues remain. Tricksters seeking to maintain a corrupt Government may "draw red herrings" across the track; still the great points are clear. Day by day, and probably more and more as time goes on, it must be felt by fair-minded men that things ought not to be permitted to rest where they are. At last it is becoming clear to the most sceptical mind that the working men of the Transvaal will no longer endure the present state of things. Now at last it is more clear to the most unwilling minds in England that things there are far from healthy and sound. Many in South Africa have for long known this; but England has been hard to convince, and a wily Government has traded too long on the fact. There still lingers in the mind of Englishmen at home a rosy picture of Bible-reading, Puritan, God-fearing, simple farmers in the Transvaal—about as far from the truth, probably, as anything can be. Englishmen are waking up from their delusive dream, and discovering the real character of the people who have deluded them so long. When once they are wide awake justice will be done. If remonstrance and expostulation and warning fail, then there must be compulsion; and—however great the heresy appears in an increasingly invertebrate age— there are worse things than war.

No one can say what lies in the womb of the future for so wonderful and promising a territory as South Africa; but there can be little reason to doubt that if Great Britain abandons the vacillating and *laisser-aller* policy of the past, and learns the duties of consistency and strength, there will be a happy future for such a country, when the various States, having the blessing of peace and justice and freedom, will be at last confederated and in a union as close and as fruitful of advantage to mankind as that of our other colonies with the motherland. This will, indeed, require time. The first requirement for such a happy consummation in the future is justice and reasonableness in the internal government and external relations of the several States, and, therefore, such honest and thorough reforms, where reforms are needed, as may secure a lasting peace.

CHAPTER II

SOUTH AFRICA NOW

To the English mind the South Africa of to-day has a real and vivid interest which it had not in the past. Even recent years have aroused a stronger sense of its importance than men had any idea of when the older amongst us were boys. The time for neglecting it and disregarding it has passed. In our strange English fashion the energy of the race has compelled its Governments—often against their will—to give to it honest and earnest attention. It is a great country, practically—in great measure—a new country. It has vast possibilities, it presents interesting problems the solution of which lies in the womb of the future. It is now known that it has a fine climate, where the white man can well, with the exercise of ordinary prudence, live and work. Our children or our children's children will be those who will see it, probably, developed into something of a fuller civilisation, but *we* are responsible for the preparation for that. There have been wrong things done and abundant mistakes made in the past. From these we may learn to do better in the future. Nations as well as men

"May rise on stepping-stones
Of their dead selves to higher things."

There is a clearer view of the position and needs of South Africa than once there was. There is a more intelligent and affectionate drawing together of the various parts of the Empire. In South Africa now we have, in spite of all our mistakes, a great and responsible position, and we may at this moment by wisdom and sympathy lay foundations for progress and wellbeing there in years to come.

The economic conditions of the South Africa of to-day seem favourable. For some years to come the country must depend largely on imports from abroad. The cessation of native wars and the general subsidence of disturbance and unrest (except in one quarter) make development by railways more and more hopeful, and the more this is done not only will intercommunication and its civilising influence be more easy, but the needs of life will be met at a less severe cost.

There seems now to be a very hopeful prospect, from all accounts, for the mines of Rhodesia and the mineral wealth there will be a help at least to start the country.* For agricultural and pasture purposes there are, of course, needed capital and immigrants. There is a vast supply of labour which may be more and more wisely used from the native races. No one, it seems to me, can look on the torrent beds of Bechuanaland and Matabeleland without feeling sure that intelligence and capital will, with no great difficulty, manage the irrigation which will be needed; and as the network of railways develops there will be easy access to the sea.

---

* Independently of the British South African Company, £2,000,000 has been raised recently "by various mining companies for expenditure in Rhodesia, affording striking proof of the confidence of investors in its future," *Times*, June 8, 1899, from correspondence of Mr. C. Rhodes (with Government) as to proposed extension of railway.

Every country needs capital and energy, and there are many countries that have repaid the toil of man which cannot boast so grateful a soil or so fine a climate as South Africa. The time may yet come when corn may be grown for exportation and the needs of the world. It may never pay, indeed, to irrigate the Karroo, but it will probably pay to irrigate Rhodesia and Bechuanaland, and as capital and enterprise develop this region, certainly the mineral wealth of the country will be of great importance in its development. There can be little doubt that grazing will be carried on more and more, and that the exports now arising out of this industry will increase.

The Native question, again, is one of interest as deep in South Africa now as the problems it raises are perplexing. The mysterious "Curse of Cainan" seems ever to hang over the coloured races everywhere. Do what kindly people may, there is still a strong tendency in the white man to look upon the coloured man everywhere as an inferior animal. In many respects this is true. It must be remembered also, there are native populations—as among the Maoris of New Zealand and the Indians of North America—which seem, whatever effort is honestly made to prevent it, gradually to diminish until they appear by some mysterious process likely to die out altogether, before civilisation. Sad as in many ways this is, it certainly simplifies some problems.

The African races appear to be governed by quite another law. In the Southern States of America one of the most anxious questions for statesmen and sociologists is the steady and rapid increase of the "darkies." It is the same in South Africa. Many causes which tended to keep the coloured population within reasonable limits have been removed. Internecine wars have been checked; wholesale murder such as was perpetrated commonly by Tchaka, Cetewayo, Lobengula, has been put a stop to; the administration of "justice," by means of the witch doctors "smelling out" supposed criminals, has ceased; sanitary arrangements have been improved; human life, in fact, has been protected. These apparently naturally prolific races are becoming, under altered conditions, more prolific than ever. There is said to be a white population of some 800,000, and the coloured population is estimated at about eight or nine millions. The white population increases by immigration, but so far in no very great degree, and in no way in proportion to the natural increase of the coloured races. Clearly one of the first necessities for such a state of things continuing, with safety to life and civilisation, is that there should be some sort of unity of action, and vigour and wisdom, and justice and intelligence in government among the European races. Of this there is no prospect so long as the present anomalous state of affairs is permitted to continue in the Transvaal.

Again, there is need of a sensible, formed public opinion as to the treatment of the natives.

Several methods have been *en evidence*.

(1) There has been the method of "petting" the native. This has been the method of sentimentalists who have not realised that kindness does not mean weakness—quite the reverse. It cannot be wondered at if missionaries have at times gone too far in this. In early days or in outlying districts they were the only protectors of the natives. They were doubtless

witnesses of barbarities and cruel treatment on the part of the white man, and they sometimes went to the opposite extreme. Some of the nobler and wiser men among them have done, and do, great good, but there have been follies of the direst kind leading to real evil. Besides the mischievous influence of Bishop Colenso on the Church in South Africa, his sentimental and absurd views as to the Zulus did great harm and are crucial examples of this kind of tone. When Cetewayo was preparing for a war which, had it not been dealt with by Sir Bartle Frere, would probably have led to the destruction of the Europeans in Natal, Sir Bartle Frere corresponded with Colenso, who had espoused the cause of the Zulus with enthusiastic folly. Colenso, says the biographer of Sir Bartle Frere,* "printed and circulated" this correspondence, "not at the Cape or in Natal, where it would have been promptly criticised, but in England, where the facts were little known." This helped to form that unhappy tone of opinion in England which, believing itself to be friendly to the natives, proved their worst enemy. From this came our fatal policy in Zululand which led to such misery afterwards to the Zulus.

The opinion of one not ignorant of Missions as to this tone of mind towards natives is as follows:

"Colenso and Chesson (secretary of the Aborigines Protection Society) are the greatest burdens under which South Africa labours. To me it is always one of the saddest signs of the times to witness how the Press can be turned to incalculable mischief in the hands of an unscrupulous fellow like Chesson, who is able to insert, and get inserted, all sorts of decoy paragraphs in newspapers to catch public opinion, which, aided by ignorance on the subject, is easily entrapped. When the whole history of the troubles of Africa comes to be written,

* Martineau. *Life of Sir Bartle Frere*, vol. ii. p. 246.

Colenso and Chesson ought to be credited with the loss of thousands of lives and millions of money."*

This is a severe judgment by a missionary, of the folly of the "petting" system. Colenso's attitude towards the Zulus is a vivid example of it. He seemed to think the Zulu race a glorious race destined to guide the white men and "absorb and assimilate" them. The absurd extent to which this was carried in his case is amusingly illustrated in Miss North's "Recollections," thus :

"We came in sight of Bishopstowe, with its many-gabled house and gum-trees, like an oasis in the desert. It stood on the top of a hill. . . . Dr. Colenso's conversation was delightful, but he gave me the impression of being both weak and vain and very susceptible to flattery. His two elder daughters . . . were perfectly devoted to him and to Zuluism ! which governed everything. The dear natives were incapable of harm, the whites incapable of good. They would, I believe, have heard cheerfully that all the whites had been 'eaten up' and Cetewayo proclaimed King of Natal. His portrait was all over the house, and they mentioned him in a hushed voice, as a kind of holy martyr, and had hardly a good word to say for any white man except Colonel Durnford. . . . I was taken to see the printing-press which was continually contradicting every fact stated by the Government and officials, who in their turn contradicted every fact published by it. Messengers were continually arriving with fresh lies (I believe) from 'the King,' over which the Bishop and his daughters passed all their time. It would have driven me mad to have stayed long in such a strained atmosphere !" †

This is an extreme example of that unhappy temper which has been one way of treating the natives in South Africa and which has led to incalculable evils, and is best summarised in Miss North's words, " the

---

* Letter of Rev. H. Waller (Bishop Mackenzie's companion in Central Africa), quoted in *Life of Sir Bartle Frere*. Martineau, vol. ii. p. 430, *n*.
† Miss North. *Recollections of a Happy Life*, vol. ii. p. 279.

dear natives were incapable of harm, the whites incapable of good."

(2) Then, there has been a method precisely the opposite. All labour in South Africa is done by the coloured men; white men are needed to govern and direct them, but *they* are the workers. This arose, in the first instance, from slavery, and it has lived on. From this, doubtless, in part has come the contempt and sometimes dislike for coloured people. Hence there has been harshness in the past, and no doubt there are instances of harshness and extreme severity in the present.

Among the Dutch, but especially the Boers of the Transvaal, there have been most instances of severity and even cruelty. In the Transvaal one constantly heard of natives being tricked about their "passes," and so their fines becoming a productive source of revenue, and of their being kept in the dark as to fresh regulations until they had broken them, and were accordingly fined and punished. The labour on the mines attracts the natives because of the pay, but they are obliged by a paternal Government to serve first on the farms before being allowed to go to the Rand, so as to ensure sufficient labour for the Boer farmers. One heard also, in well-informed quarters, of employers there cheating their coloured people, either by simply treating them with violence when they demanded their wages, or giving them all kinds of provocation and ill usage so as to induce them to run away before the time when wages were due. In both the Dutch States natives have no political rights whatever, and practically no rights at all. Their condition, however, in the Orange Free State is said to be satisfactory on the whole. There are doubtless humane and good men in the Transvaal, but it is to be feared that the natives there have a very poor time. Slavery is forbidden by our Convention, but our Convention has been treated, to a great extent, as a sham, and the game of "bluff" has been steadily played, and we have kindly permitted it, and, of course, it is always possible to treat men much like slaves without using the odious name.

In Rhodesia I could not find that the natives were treated otherwise than well; I saw constant instances of great kindness towards them. It is impossible, of course, to say—speaking of so wide an area—that no harsh acts are committed or have been; but, speaking broadly, their welfare is certainly considered, and they are now wisely and kindly governed. I was greatly struck in visiting native kraals in Rhodesia with their apparently contented and happy condition. In talking to them, their evident confidence in the English impressed me, and, most of all—although he was hundreds of miles away at the time—the trustful and affectionate manner in which they spoke of Mr. Rhodes. *This*, more than anything—even more than personal intercourse — because it furnished such unimpeachable testimony, convinced me of the mistaken estimate formed, unfortunately, by some of my countrymen of that great man, of whom we may all well be proud. If they had anxieties on any subject they seemed quite confident that all would be put right when *he* had time to visit them. And eye-witnesses have related to me the patient and careful manner in which, when in Rhodesia, he has given attention to their wants, and helped them out of little difficulties, dealing, with the loving care which we country parsons spend upon our country people, with their most tiny needs and sorrows. I saw two of Lobengula's sons, whom he educates, at Groote Schurr, where they spent their holidays. There can be little doubt there have been harshness and severity, and even cruelty, in the past. I do not believe that it is so now, speaking generally, among English-speaking people. Natives will, probably, *always* be in a very inferior position in the Transvaal, and generally among the Dutch. If we are determined to maintain that ill-governed State which we call the South African Republic—well and good; we must take the responsibility of this feature in regard to natives. Still I do not believe that anywhere in South Africa there is such hatred and contempt felt by the white to the coloured population as I have heard expressed by Southerners of the United States after the war, and even by Northerners by whom slavery had been abolished. One could find nothing approaching the violence arising from this feeling which took place in America immediately after the great struggle, or even the dislike towards these races which cultivated Americans have expressed in quite recent times. We must not, however, forget that the brutal contempt of the Transvaal Boer for a native wants the restraining Christianity, or—shall we say?—civilisation, of a cultured, kind American.

(3) There is *a wise way* of treating the native races which forms a happy medium between the above methods, and which one hopes may more and more prevail. In Cape Colony the coloured races have full political rights. The same qualifications as for a white man apply to them as to serving on juries and exercising the franchise. Many wise and humane men

consider that in this matter the Cape has moved too fast, and that such privileges are not unmitigated blessings to the native races. However, that is done.

In the less settled and newer British possessions, the remnant at least of tribal organisation still continues, and while this is so the natives are, of course, not fit subjects for the franchise. In Rhodesia the Government seemed to me very sensible. There, the Matabele have a high respect for law and a clear view of the dignity of authority. It seems certain that the native tribes, once thoroughly defeated, accept their defeat, and desire to be *governed*. Our great mistake in Zululand was breaking their power and then leaving them without proper *government*. This mistake we are not repeating in Rhodesia, and the present arrangement seems to work well, and to educate the inhabitants of that vast and valuable territory for further exercise of constitutional liberty.

There is no need for harshness, much less for cruelty; and I do not believe that these are shown to the natives by the English—of course, speaking broadly. There *is* need that they should be governed. They are in the position of children—but children who may, if not educated properly, do incalculable mischief. Mr. Rhodes, who has the kindest feeling for the natives, constantly speaks of them as "those poor children." As they have generations of savagery behind them, they can only slowly be educated to better things. Like unruly children, they require discipline, but they must be treated with justice and kindness. It takes time to teach people to work who have inherited habits of laziness varied by the enthusiasms of hunting and war. They have to be taught to work, and to be shown that work must be done. They have many good points, but mere " petting " is ruinous. Exaggerated kindness they consider weakness and folly. The sentimentalists seemed to think that natives should be left alone, and that they would " evolve civilisation and liberty from among themselves." Sir Bartle Frere has some wise words on that subject. He writes :

"I have always regarded that view as a mischievous dream, the folly of which is proved by history everywhere, but especially by four thousand years of negro existence without one single step of spontaneous advance throughout this vast continent, every step out of their general animal existence being clearly traceable to some external impulse or impression." *

With the natives we must move slowly. They must be governed, disciplined, taught to work, treated with justice and wise kindness. As far as I could judge, this seemed to be the case in Rhodesia, and in the compounds at Kimberley.

One instance of this is worth noticing. We have plenty of evidence at home of the evils of excess in intoxicating drinks. This is bad enough in the case of the white man ; to the coloured man it is absolute ruin. The Chartered Company acted wisely in this. In Rhodesia the regulations are stringent, and the punishment rightly severe, for selling drink to the natives. There are native liquor laws also in the Transvaal. These are often eluded by syndicates for the illicit sale of drink, with, it is said, the connivance by the Government for financial reasons.† Restrictive

---

* Martineau. *Life of Sir Bartle Frere*, vol. ii. p. 330.

† After regular connivance, I was told by men knowing the place well, now and again a wretched native was caught, tried, and punished to show the uprightness of a paternal Government.

laws of this kind are absolutely necessary, and should be stringently enforced. It may be doubted whether the larger franchise at the Cape is not in some ways a disadvantage, as politicians must necessarily hesitate as to needful restrictions in view of the coloured vote.

A very humane and sensible man said to me that in dealing with native workmen it was necessary for their sakes to be determined, strict, and even severe at first. If so, they respected authority and felt there was no weakness, and *then* it was safe to soften into much greater kindness.

What the future of a country with such a vastly preponderating population of native races may be, who dare prophesy? But Englishmen have learnt experience from the mistakes of the past, and with the natural gift of government which they so largely possess, there seems no reason why things should not work out well, so that the natives, gradually educated and disciplined, with steady justice and kindness, should become bound by the best ties to the superior race, and useful members of the body politic. These races are much finer specimens of humanity than the American negro, and seem to promise much better in future development. That there should be a considerable social separation is probably, at present at any rate, inevitable, though here again it seemed to be less emphasised than I had seen it in America. I have seen civilised coloured people and Europeans in the same church, and receiving Communion at the same altar; and in one school, managed by some excellent "religious" women, white children and coloured children of the very poor learning together. Some English clergy do excellent work, as I know, among natives, and are able to guide them into Christian character and conduct. Too often, indeed, even good men have said that they prefer the Heathen to the Christian Kaffir, and that the latter learns the white man's vices without his virtues. Doubtless there is some truth in this. Mistakes, and serious mistakes, have been made, still the missionaries —with all their mistakes—have been, in many cases, and are, the true friends of the natives, and mistakes in the past may teach wiser ways — whether to missionaries or Governments—in the future.

It cannot well be doubted that there may be a great future for races with so many fine characteristics as the various divisions of the Zulu family. Englishmen, though in a great minority, have managed to govern coloured races in India, and to improve them and raise them in the scale of humanity. In South Africa there are none of the hindrances and difficulties of *caste*. If we act wisely and justly there seems no reason why we should not train, improve, and use, and make happier and better men of, the South African natives. Religious men cannot doubt that this possibility and duty lies before us, acting all the better from our past experience, and even our past mistakes.

Socially South Africa is interesting. A social chasm must of necessity yawn—as I have admitted—at least until things are greatly changed in this world, between the white and native races. With the white races themselves it is altogether different. There was a steady *rapprochement* for some time at the Cape between the Dutch and English races, and such there is now. Recent events, carefully used by clever wirepullers for political ends, may have caused some feeling of estrangement. This, however, is merely temporary. The Cape is as loyal as any other part of the Empire, even though efforts are made from time to time by designing politicians to rouse Dutch feeling against the English connection. It is well known and thoroughly felt that it is under the British flag that fullest liberty can be found.* Socially the races become more and more one, and will continue to do so in greater degree when the plague-spot of Transvaal misgovernment is healed.

It would be unfair to expect, in a young country, all the culture and refinement of the old world. The long centuries have given to Europe a richness of life which of course cannot be found all at once in South Africa. What *does* strike the visitor is the abundant heartiness and kindness, and the most complete absence of anything like "tuft-hunting" or "toadying" or snobbishness. There is a hearty goodwill and genuine friendliness and kindness at the Cape, and among all whom we met, whether in Rhodesia or in the Transvaal and Natal. As yet, of course, there is no wealth of indigenous writers, although there have been one or two useful historians and one novelist who has commanded some attention. There is still room for improvement in education. In time, probably, schools more like our public schools and universities will grow up. It is too soon to expect these things yet. The Good Hope College, however, is doing good work. We could not but feel a certain freshness—

* It is interesting to remember—just now when Krüger is refusing elementary justice to Uitlanders, and when there are those who think we can, without moral turpitude, permit him to persevere in his contempt for right—that at the Cape the Prime Minister is of German extraction, and the Government is carried on by a Dutch majority.—June 1899.

like that of America—as of people of a young world, and, as I have said, ready sociability and kindness. Depth and breadth of life will follow upon brightness and human geniality.

The state of religion in South Africa was naturally a subject of interest. The chief divisions of Christians were, besides the Anglican Church, the Roman Church and the Dutch Reformed community. As far as I could understand, the latter had three divisions: "the Dutch Reform," then (what may be called) "the Dutch Re-Reform," and what is known as "the Dopper." This was most clear in the Transvaal. The exact differences between the latter bodies it is difficult for an outsider to grasp. They appear all to be Calvinistic; and the chief difference between "the Dopper" and the others appeared to me to be that the latter used hymns in public worship, while "the Dopper" will use nothing but scriptural paraphrases. There is, however, a considerable feeling of hostility between them—so I understood—and I was assured that the religious differences then were such that they might in the long run, not improbably, lead to serious disagreements, if not civil war, among the Transvaal Boers. There are, of course, considerable bodies representing the Baptist, Wesleyan, and other like forms of Christianity.

As to the Anglican Church, it seemed to be doing steady work. In some places it struck me as being vigorous and effective. It possesses theologians like Dr. Wirgman; vigorous bishops like the Bishops of Mashonaland, Natal, Bloemfontein, and others; a venerable Archbishop; devoted workers, like Mr. Darragh in Johannesburg, the Cowley Fathers in

Capetown, and numberless others who could be named. There is, however, so I thought, a great need of more men for the ministry. Our Church has not been so powerful in mission work, until perhaps quite recent years, as might be desired. In anything merely falling under the arrangement of the parochial system she has done well. But it may be doubted whether that system can be anything but a very small part of the work in a young country. Regular and respectable Christians may have means of going to church and receiving the Sacraments by this system, but there are further needs. In such places as Buluwayo, for instance, one sees a vast mass of splendid young Englishmen, with all the freshness and vigour of men working hard under new conditions of life, where the old conventional lines have been to a great degree obliterated. Two things follow : (1) Moral dangers are greater ; (2) there is a wider opening for real, hearty work with souls for Christ, *if* men, real *men*, could be found to utilise such vast opportunities. What one longed to see was strong bodies of young men, as keen in the cause of Christ as these young fellow countrymen were in that of the Empire or of their various callings.

The Church at home should not lose sight of the needs of South Africa. A layman of some distinction observed to me, "The curse of the Church of England is her 'Moderation.'" He did not, of course, mean "Moderation" in the true sense, but a deficiency of enthusiasm, and a constant tendency—the real bane of true work—in some in authority to pass silently over cases of laziness and neglect, and to spend energy in restraining zeal and holding back the energetic efforts of earnestness. There is, unquestionably, too much cause to feel that whereas our Lord said He came " to send fire upon the earth," some of the Church's modern rulers seem to think that *their* vocation is to work the pumps of the fire engines. We felt this the more, because the silly hubbub called the " Crisis in the Church" was going on while we were in South Africa, and, viewing it from a distance, we realised its pettiness and unfortunate features.

In a new country, if wise and diligent missionaries are needed for native races, able and self-denying missioners are needed to work for our colonists. The bishops in South Africa have not nearly men enough or able men enough for the work that needs to be done. The Mother Church of the Motherland should exert herself. Funds are needed to make the necessary help possible. Why should not pains be taken to find able and zealous men to offer themselves? In places like Buluwayo there is need of clergy-houses where five or six strong and vigorous men might cheer each other on to so great a work. Whether or not Kaffir Missions are going on well, one thing is certain, our own young Englishmen are not sufficiently cared for in religious matters. South Africa does not need clergy who go out because their health is bad, or because they have been failures at home, nor bishops who go out for a time and will not give their lives to the work because they yearn for " promotion " in the old country. She needs apostles, men who will spend and be spent, who will live and die for their work, and not consider it a "call" to manage some little diocese at home, long organised, which any one could deal with, rather than a vast, new, difficult, and gradually forming, Church in the colonies. Much has been nobly done by servants of God at home in the great cities and in the slums of London. Two things, however, have been somewhat forgotten. Nowhere so much as in our own *country* parishes at home, and in our colonies, are strong and able men needed. South Africa needs preachers, and men who hold the faith strongly and intelligently, and can throw real enthusiasm into the cause of Christ.

Seeing, as I did, a great deal of the laity wherever I was, I was sadly struck with the apparently widespread *indifferentism*. I met many who professed themselves Agnostics—some, of course, assumed the title as the easy "label" for those who would give way to general religious slothfulness and a lazy Reason. Many, however, were good men who had never had an opportunity of learning the Faith, or who, having in some measure learnt it, had drifted away, from the absence of religious influences. There are, of course, good men and true, but our Young England in South Africa needs more clergy, and clergy of the right sort. Pious platitudes are of no use there. In the fresh life of a new country there is needed real work and devotion. Many things—the climate among others, and press of work in those carving out a new life—tend to make men "slack." To meet this is needed an increasing body of men to whom "slackness" is an unknown thing, who have been trained to mission work and can speak earnestly and convincingly to men's souls—men with "cool heads and warm hearts and a zeal that does not count the cost."

There are two dangers specially likely to assail young men far from home, in a freshly opened up land. The one is the danger of slipping out of the habit of religious observances, and so gradually losing hold of religion. The other is the danger which assails a pure moral life. The Church should be " to the front" to help them. There remains a vast deal for the Church at home to do in coming to the aid of the Church in South Africa for such purposes both with men and money. I cannot but hope that more will be done in this way.

" Preach to us," said a distinguished man in South Africa to me, "preach to us Christian dogma *and* Marcus Aurelius." It put the matter neatly in a nutshell, *i.e.*, doctrine *and* morality. Hard-working men, facing life in new lands, need above all no "vague platitudes of empty dreams," but definite teaching of the definite facts of the Faith, and clear and loving enforcement of the moral duties which depend on these.

There certainly seemed to be greater kindliness and fewer controversies among the various religious bodies than at home, but one could not avoid a suspicion that indifferentism rather than divine charity was at the root of this. Men do not quarrel over that about which they do not care in the smallest degree. In the centres of population, like Capetown and the neighbourhood, and Johannesburg, the churches seemed to be well attended, and good work going on ; but there is much more to be done—there, of course, as everywhere —but above all in outlying districts and younger places.

South Africa, then, is still in many respects a new country with needs such as one should expect and with vast possibilities. It needs for political quiet a radical change in the Transvaal, the centre and source of all unrest. It needs an increase of colonists, and capital to open up a most hopeful country; it needs advance in railway systems, and that—through the energy of Mr. Rhodes chiefly—it is likely to have; and it needs all the efforts of the Church at home to assist the Church there, in lifting up moral life, in teaching revealed religion, in spreading and maintaining the Kingdom of Christ.

CHAPTER III

HOMEWARD BOUND

WE are out on a glorious sea. The evening is as beautiful as well can be imagined. The Table Mountain and all the jagged peaks are growing hazy in the distance. South Africa will soon be a dream to us, and little more; still, a very pleasant dream.

Our last morning on the peninsula had been unusually grey and cloudy, but the afternoon turned out beautiful. Capetown and its neighbourhood smiled upon us their farewells. It was pleasant to think of home, but sad to leave dear friends, and a place which had made itself our home, none the less. There is always something solemn and moving in doing anything for the last time—perhaps from the whisper in it of the pathos of human life, of the mystery of change, of the pangs of parting, of everlasting farewells. We had met many pleasant acquaintances, we had formed some true friendships, and we were leaving some whom we love.

> Good-bye, dear friends, good-bye, then, be attended
> By loving prayers as on the swift years fly:
> May we meet yet on earth, or—this life ended—
> In that dear home where none need say good-bye.

Such were our thoughts. Our cabins have been made sweet with the breath of flowers arranged there by loving hands. Time will pass, the flowers will fade, but not the memories of happy intercourse and abundant kindness.

As the *Arundel Castle* beats her way through the waves, and the shores of South Africa fade in the oncoming of a Southern night, we find ourselves dreaming of what is over.

There are some vivid impressions on our minds. The first and chiefest is of the heartiness and kindness of our kith and kin in our Colonial Empire. We are inclined to be angry with old England, because so many of her fine young sons can find no field of energy or way of livelihood at home, and are forced to go so far. And yet, it is by this that the Empire is what it is, and—to judge by the kindness and hospitality of our South African fellow subjects—"absence makes the heart grow fonder," and—however unwisely, at times, England has behaved—the tie to the motherland is strong still.

Then we are able, on the dreaming sea, to recall the strange grandeur of South Africa—its bold mountains, its mysterious solitudes—for nothing so much touches the imagination there as just that—a dreamy land!— its delightful climate, with startling vicissitudes of sunshine and storm, its splendid flora, above all the wealth of atmospheric colour which makes all objects beautiful. Of its future we can dream; who can tell? Already possibilities of federation rise above the horizon for Australia. For South Africa they are possibilities, but they seem still—now that so many chances have been thrown away—a great way off. We are thinking of the interesting people we have met or have known there; and the whole circumstances of the case, the whole condition of things from the Zambesi to Capetown, make the meeting with interesting people a thing of course. Of these the most remarkable were certainly Mr. Krüger and Mr. Rhodes. The former is indeed, from circumstances, interesting. The latter is so in himself. No one can fail to be interested in a man of wide knowledge, deep and serious thought, unflinching courage, large schemes for the benefit of his adopted country and for the good of others; a man possessed of the frank simplicity of character of a boy, together with great capacity and a statesmanlike grip of things; a man—with whatever faults, and having made whatever mistakes (if, as in the case of all of us, it is so with him)—whom you might be with for weeks and months and yet never hear him provoked into saying an unkind word of any one—not of his worst enemy—in spite of all the malignant abuse and misunderstanding to which he has been subjected—an ἄναξ ἀνδρῶν, a king of men—a remarkable man.

Nothing, thinking it over in the dreamy silence of the sympathetic sea, seems so striking to me in South Africa as this man. Here is a man who is generous to a fault, whom his countrymen have believed to be sordid; whom they have thought selfish, who lives for others and for his country; who has made mistakes and frankly admits them; who has had unwise friends, but has ever been faithful to them. A man with a large, kind heart, with great intellectual capacity, most human, most serious, most deep-thinking—large, strong, kind in all ways—a man never to forget, to love for his faults as well as his virtues. Yes, a remarkable man, as I have said, a giant among the pigmies of the age, but, above all, a *real* man, simple, kindly, faithful, sincere.

To expect the convinced English Radical or even Liberal, or even the best specimen—the philosophical Radical—to believe me would be absurd. Nevertheless, if a man, with prepossessions in some respects opposed, sees and hears and thinks for himself, his testimony may be worth something. My country, I feel more and more, is the victim of Shibboleths and make-believes. Englishmen have so high a sense of goodness, that—only dress some one up in a dress that may *look* good—they believe in him; dress some one up in a dress to *look* evil, him they condemn. For many Englishmen Krüger is (*mirabile dictu!*) the simple-hearted, the sincere! Rhodes is the sordid and base!

One thing, as I think back, was evident to me, how thoroughly Rhodes is *loved*, by good men and men of culture whom I knew at the Cape, and—that is the striking thing—among the weak, or helpless, or struggling, of whatever colour, in Rhodesia. Another interesting point is this. Men who had never known him, who had fallen in with the English estimate and the misrepresentations of the enemies of England (which England loves to swallow), have told me, with regret, how they felt they had maligned him when once they came to know him. When once I came to *know* him for myself—after having been indoctrinated with the opposing "liberal" views at home, though I never quite believed them—I saw how it must be. A man of utter fearlessness, ready to expose himself calmly, as he did, to terrible danger in the rebellion, of large and generous views for the extension of England's dominion as the guarantee of freedom, of open-handed generosity, not only to forward his far-sighted efforts, but to help case after case of individual need to an extent incredible, and of which no one, as far as he could help it, knew—that man *must* be loved, and his influence felt, even in a *blasé* age like our own, where belief in goodness is hard to find.

No, this is not necessary where a man is measured by the modern, conventional standards. Nowadays, even men who care nothing for morality will bring up a moral text. All sorts of "old saws," without any real application, have been levelled against Mr. Rhodes. I have often heard that his view was "Might made Right." Nothing, as one found, could be more wide of the truth. I never met a man with a sterner sense of the value of Right, only with a *hatred* of the canting manner in which the moral view is used. Also it is the custom to assign to Mr. Rhodes all the faults of the Chartered Company. Those faults have, I believe, been grossly exaggerated. I am certain that, in spite of all the talk of Syndicates and Amalgamations, and so on—talk always brought up about a new country—the Chartered Company has done good work. Doubtless it has had faults, and grave faults. Critics at home, who do nothing but write " to fill the weekly page," have learnt that they must criticise the men who *act* under grave difficulty; and these home critics seem to have one or two important canons to guide them in their hurried judgments week by week : (1) Assail your own countrymen, (2) attribute the basest motives, (3) hear no word against those whom your political mistakes have placed in position.

So it has been that *any* mistake of the Chartered Company has been laid to the doors of Mr. Rhodes; that Mr. Rhodes must be supposed to act always from personal ambition—in spite of his *real* acts quite subversive of such a theory—and then that England, having committed a moral fault of the most serious character, in violating pledges and setting up the cruel and corrupt Transvaal Oligarchy—any one who calls *that* other than good is wrong—therefore Rhodes. The fact is *we* have lowered the moral standard in South Africa steadily by our mistakes and iniquities, and as—at whatever cost—appearances must be kept up, it has been found well to blame a great man of whom—were our political and moral atmosphere not so much vitiated—we should have learnt to be proud. Mr. Rhodes has been, and is, the hope of South Africa, notwithstanding the faithlessness and folly of England. Of course, this will not be believed by those who spin theories out of foregone conclusions. Still — from observing, questioning, thinking—without any prepossession whatever, or rather prepossessions in the opposite direction—(except, indeed, the conclusion formed on evidence, of the true type of the Krügerite character)—*this* is the conviction which I have formed and record, as I think of the South Africa fading away across the waves.

Our happy times in South Africa are over. We are looking back upon it already as a dream, though a happy dream, but it has left behind it impressions, new and deep and strong.

In our modern days the conditions which have to do with the civilisation with which we are concerned are very different from those of the past. Those conditions, too, vary much more rapidly than they did fifty years ago; but under these, such as they are, character and conduct are tried as much as ever they were. One interest of a new country is observing this, becoming aware of conditions very dissimilar to those at home, but which always do the same work for other men—viz., form a school of character. Certainly, among other things, the energy of our race never comes home to one more vividly than in South Africa. Even in the comparatively less important matter of games and athletic exercises, for instance, one is struck by the vigour and persistence of healthy English effort, although in a climate which would seem to invite to repose.

There is plenty of food for anxiety there for those who hold the moral and religious principles belonging to Christianity, plenty of room for labour whether in religious or social or political matters, but there is a hope that with the predominating force of English principles and character—seriousness, a sense of duty, a deep religious sense, a love of justice and fair play, a respect for the dignity of woman and the sanctities of home—there is a healthy and hopeful future before this people. In politics we must be on our guard against the secret intriguers who would injure the best hopes of South Africa by undermining the paramount power of Great Britain. We must learn larger views of things; consign "Little Englandism" and all its works to the limbo of discarded mischiefs and follies; break away from vacillation and inconsistency in our Imperial policy, and be steadily just and strong. In religion, the Church at home must rouse herself more to help the Church in South Africa; we must have done with the narrowness which makes our most able young men in the ministry imagine that because "charity begins at home" it is to end there; we must throw away platitudes, dreamy vagueness, mere "goody" respectability, and help the young and strong of a new land to hold and live the practical common sense of the Catholic Faith, and find in that a helper to teach the science of goodness and conquer the works of sin. We are leaving a land of many unsolved problems, rich in beauty, rich in possibilities, rich in hopes and fears. Foreign travel in a new land is a break in the ordinary tenour of life. It leaves us full of many thoughts and many dreams.

Our homeward-bound voyage in the *Arundel Castle* was in some ways unusual. It happened that our fellow passengers were fewer in number than would generally be the case. We had a fine boat, the steadiest I have ever known, and plenty of room; pleasant officers, pleasant companions, a holiday from the "entertainments" which sometimes, at sea, become a burden, and, as far as the Canaries, glorious weather, with all the most splendid nights and loveliest days of the tropics; and, in perfection, that sense of repose and time for thinking and dreaming, never, perhaps, fully known except at sea.

We had a tedious day at Las Palmas. The authorities had heard that there had once been a case of plague at Delagoa Bay, so, as we came from Capetown, Spanish fears and logic condemned us to four and twenty hours' inaction under the yellow flag!

From Las Palmas we became more and more conscious of the changeful temper of the North Atlantic.

In "the Bay" it at first was rough, and then blew a tremendous gale. But our good ship behaved splendidly, and about eighteen days from Capetown we found ourselves one chilly midnight in Plymouth Sound. We carried with us many memories of interest and pleasure from South Africa, yet, after all, we realised once again that "there is no place like home."

POSTSCRIPT

JUST as the last sheets of what I have written are in the press, an event is occurring which is, one must believe, of the highest consequence to South Africa — the meeting of the High Commissioner and the President of the Transvaal State at Bloemfontein. The Colonial Secretary has said that this Conference will be held "with a view of arriving at such an arrangement as her Majesty's Government could accept and recommend to the Uitlander population as a reasonable concession to their just demands"; and, he added, "a settlement of the difficulties which have threatened the good relations which her Majesty's Government desire should constantly exist between themselves and the South African Republic."

Those who have the interests of South Africa at heart may be pardoned if they are somewhat slow to believe in Mr. Krüger's protestations or promises, and if they are still haunted with a lingering fear lest the Imperial authorities be not yet sufficiently wide awake in their dealings with the Boer rulers. Still there is a ray of hope. At last England seems to have wakened up to the mistakes of the past and to her duties now. Mistakes are more easily made than unmade, but much may be done to right the wrong if the reign of hollow sentiment and vacillation is ended, and if, instead, there is right feeling, a clear view of duty, and an unbending determination that justice shall be done. The Boer President has professed a willingness to discuss all questions, if the independence of the Transvaal Republic is not threatened. Such independence as it enjoys under the suzerainty of the Queen no one can wish to threaten. It must, however, be a real independence, not, as hitherto, a tyranny; it must become, if England is to permit it to remain a separate State, a real Republic, not a narrow Oligarchy. It is to be hoped that England will be content with nothing short of this. At last our Government seems awake to its duties. At last it has considered the grievous wrongs done to the Uitlanders. If the President's professions at last mean anything, it is to be hoped that actual practical results may follow from this Conference. The letter of the State Secretary to Mr. Chamberlain lately, in answer to his remonstrance on the dynamite monopoly, is not reassuring; but if Mr. Krüger is once fully aware that England is awake and determined, all may end well. The Uitlanders have been informed that "her Majesty's Government cannot but express their general sympathy with the memorialists," and that they are earnestly desirous of seeing a speedy and substantial change effected in their condition.

There are some matters in the Transvaal which may help to convince Mr. Krüger of the folly of further resistance to what is right and just. Some of the younger and more enlightened Boers, especially those who have had the advantage of education at the Cape, are apparently not satisfied with the paternal tyranny of Pretoria. There is some disquiet as to the attitude of the religious bodies in the Dutch community towards one another. Expediency may convince even the Boer Government of the advantage of justice.

The whole administration of the Transvaal requires reform. For the State to flourish men must gain an assurance that the reign of corruption has passed away. These things, however, will come in due time, if the great and indispensable change is made—*i.e.*, if there is a wise and just franchise, at least for all men of European extraction; in fact, if the Republic becomes a true Republic instead of a sham.

The *Times* has justly remarked that "the proposals which Mr. Krüger is understood to have laid before the Volksraad for reducing the present monstrous period of qualification from fourteen years to nine are obviously a mockery. Yet these terms," adds the *Times*, "were debated in the Raad in the spirit of narrow and bitter hostility to the Uitlanders." We may still hope that better counsels will prevail. The English Government, however, must be firm. The time for paltering with these matters, and making promises not intended to be kept, ought to have passed. We ought to have learnt by the way in which we have allowed ourselves to be deluded formerly, that firmness and straightforwardness are needed, and that justice must at last be done. To quote the *Times* again, "this Conference will either result in a thorough agreement, or it will convince England and the world that the Boers have no real intention of keeping their promises, and of granting a substantial redress of grievances to the overwhelming majority of the white inhabitants of the Republic." The Transvaal is the centre of unrest in South Africa. While it is so seriously misgoverned as at present it will continue so to be. England's

x

mistakes and a well-intentioned unwisdom set up this cause of disturbance. It is the duty of England to see that this cause be removed, that justice be done, that just demands be attended to; and at the present moment there appears some hope—which all must welcome—that this may be effected if our Government shows wisdom and firmness, without any disturbance of the blessings of peace.

Is that possible? Will England do her duty? The last intelligence, as these sheets pass out of my hands, is the news of Mr. Krüger's proposals and the complete failure of the Conference. Already one respectable newspaper seems to advise that we should add another chapter to our many chapters of dishonour in South Africa, and retire and let things go! Shall we do it? Who knows? If we do, then indeed we deserve the contempt so largely given to us by the Boers, but —worse—we shall earn our own.

INDEX

A

ABERDEEN, Lord, 131
Adderley, Mr., gallant attempt of, 163, 166
Afrikander, Dutch and English, 92
spirit of, 281
Agnosticism, 307
Agriculture, difficulties of, 33, 43, 44
Albany, Settlement of, 30
Algoa Bay, 31, 137
Anstruther, Colonel, 198
Artisans, openings for, 33
Atmosphere, effect of, 18, 19 20
cold and heat of, 80

B

BARKLEY, Sir H., 279, 280
Basutos, 153, 156, 160, 162, 165, 177, 178, 286
Beaconsfield, Lord, 203, 239
Beaufort West, 103
Bochuanaland, 82, 91, 180, 292
Bethel, Commander, murder of, 87, 180
Bloemfontein, 154, 157, 165, 319
Boer Republics, confusions of, 175-183
Boers, Transvaal, compared with Cape Dutch, 28
retrogressive character of, 57
character of, 61, 62, 175, 176, 178, 181, 184, 188, 195, 197, 198, 199
contempt for English, 63

Boers, Hinterland threatened by, 84
—— 124, 125, 148, 149, 150, 164; "Old Colony," 233; Plea for Transvaal, 246-248
Boksburg, visit to, 68, 69
Kaffir dance at, 70, 71
Boomplatz, victory of, 157, 173
Bright, Mr., 219
British Flag, 136, 144, 165, 169, 185, 205
British Government, policy of, 31
Browning, Robert, 239, 240
Buluwayo, 80, 81, 82
Burgers, President, 181, 182
Buxton, Mr. Fowell, 131, 132

C

CAIRNS, Lord, 217
Cape Colony, 82, 85, 107, 136-146
discovery of, 108
Capetown, the town itself, 15; its neighbourhood, 16-29, 104
Carnarvon, Lord, 174, 280
Catchwords, power of, 183
Cathcart, General, 160, 161, 163, 173
Cellier, Mr., testimony of, 253
Cetewayo, 178, 183, 193, 282, 283, 284, 293
Chamberlain, Mr., 254, 261, 262, 263, 320
Chartered Company, 98, 314, 315
Chelmsford, Lord, 192, 283
Claremont, 27
Clerk, Sir George, 160, 164

INDEX

Climate, variations of, 41, 42
  of Johannesburg, 52, 53
Coach, drive on, 72-79
Cole, Sir Lowrie, 132
Colenso, Bishop, 294, 295
Colley, Sir George Pomeroy, 198, 199, 200
Colonial Office, 128, 129, 131, 137, 140, 141, 146, 147, 150, 154, 158, 160, 161, 164, 166, 168, 174, 188, 209
Compensation, duty of, 134, 135
Constantia, 27
  Groot, 27
Convention, 93, 158, 159, 165, 173, 175, 178, 224, 225, 226, 246, 265, 286, 297, 319

D

D'ALMEIDA, 109
De Beers, 102
Delagoa Bay, 84, 108, 109, 151, 152
Derby, Lord, 131, 224
Diamond mines, 103, 170
Diaz, Bartolommeo, 107
Difficulties, how to treat, 162
Downing Street, 138, 141, 154, 163, 166, 168, 172, 174, 186
Drakenberg, 34
Durban, description of, 34, 35, 38, 39
  character of, 36
  rickshaws of, 37
D'Urban, Sir Benjamin, 40, 132, 133, 141, 142, 143, 168
Dust, prevalence of, 28
  in Johannesburg, 52
  in Krügersdorp, 71, 72
Dutch families, of the Cape, 27
  character of colonisation, 111, 112
  character of, 113-115
  condition of, in Cape Colony, 66
  East India Company, 118, 119, 120, 121

Dutch families, religion of, 112, 114, 115, 176, 179, 181, 196
  settlement of, 110

E

EAST London, 31
Emsdon, Mr., testimony of, 253
England, responsibility of, 285-289
English, treatment of Dutch, 66
  character of, 278, 290, 291
  energy of, 80, 81, 88, 89, 139
  first settlers, 110; generous treatment of Dutch, 121, 122
  language in Transvaal, 67
  opinion easily deceived, 59, 60
  power of colonisation, 278, 279
  residency in Transvaal, 67, 68
  title to South Africa, 122; to Transvaal, 242, 243; early policy towards Boers, 126–135; settlers in Transvaal, 232; right to Transvaal, 242, 243, 248-252
  treatment of, by Dutch, 67, 273, 274
Estcourt, 41, 42
  description of, 42, 43

F

FEDERATION, 167, 168, 172, 174, 186, 194, 277-289
Forster, Mr., support of forward policy, 86
French concerns in South Africa, 119-121
Frere, Sir Bartle, 133, 142, 143, 156, 168, 174, 186, 187, 190, 191, 192, 198, 220, 226, 239, 282, 284, 285, 294, 300
Froude, Mr., effect on Federation, 281

G

GAMA, Vasco da, 108
German West Africa, 282, 283, (and East) 286

INDEX

Gladstone, feeling towards, 64
—— 186, 190, 197, 203, 209, 211, 221, 239, 261
Glenelg, Lord, 131, 133, 141, 142, 143, 155
Good Hope Hall, 15
Goderich, Lord, 131
Governors, treatment of, 141, 155, 156, 157, 185, 186
Grahamstown, site of, 31
Grey, Lord, 155, 158, 160, 173
Grey, Sir George, 142, 143, 144, 167, 168, 177, 178
Griqualand, 103, 153, 154, 156, 165
Groote Shuur, 19
  description of, 21-27

H

HEPBURN, Rev. Mr., 83
Huguenots, 112, 123

I

IMPERIAL Ideas, 139, 172; true meaning of, 284, 285
Indian Ocean, 30
Indifferentism, 307, 308
Ingogo Heights, 199, 205
Irrigation, possibility of, 89, 291
Isandhlwana, 190, 191, 282, 283
Italy, comparison with, 28

J

JAMESON, Dr., 21, 87, 97, 257, 258, 262, 263
Johannesburg, approach to, 49
  climate of, 51, 52
  description of, 53, 54
  educational difficulties in, 272
  effect of gold in, 56
  sanitary conditions of, 57
  reform leaders of, 258, 260, 272
—— 152
Joubert, General, 87, 176, 184, 192, 198, 207, 224

K

KAFFIRS, raids of, 31
  Wars of, 118'
—— 126, 127, 133, 137, 138, 141
Karroo, 103, 292
Koate, award, 180
Kimberley, description of, 102, 103, 170
—— Lord, 207, 218, 246, 280
King William's Town, 31
Khama, 83, 84
Khama's country, 82
Kowie, site of Grahamstown, 31
Krüger, policy towards Hollanders, 48, 49
  description of, 59-61
  Mr. Bryce's view of, 60, n
  success of, 62
  exaggerations about, 64, 65
  policy unmasked, 86, 87
—— 115, 152, 168, 176, 179, 181, 182, 184, 185, 188, 190, 192, 195, 196, 198, 207, 220, 222, 224, 225, 238, 245, 246, 248, 249, 250, 251, 255, 257, 262, 263, 320
—— Mrs., 65
"Krügerism," 240, 255, 257, 260, 287, 315
Krügersdorp, visit to, 71, 72
  coach from, 72, 73

L

LADISMITH, 46
Laing's Nek, 46, 199, 205
Lanyon, Sir Owen, 189, 190, 194, 220
Lawley, Hon. Arthur, 95
"Lead mines," beauty of, 78
Leonard, Mr. C., manifesto of, 256, 261
Liquor Question with Natives, 300, 301
Little Englandism, 139, 140, 147, 156, 159, 162, 172, 285, 316
Livingstone, Dr., 82, 179

Lobengula, 94, 98, 293
Lytton, Sir H. B., 167

M

MACKENZIE, Rev. John, 86, 87
Mafeking, 72, 79, 80, 81, 82, 152
Majuba heights, 46, 199, 205
Manda Valley, 46
Mankaroane, 85
Maritzburg, 39, 40
Mashonaland, 97
Matabele, 97, 98, 99, 100, 101, 152,
  respect for law, 299
Matabeleland, 82
Matoppos, 93, 96, 97, 100, 102
Mill, John Stuart, 235, 236
Mines of Transvaal, 54, 88, 244, 245
—— of Rhodesia, 88, 90, 291
Missionaries, 82, 83, 86, 129, 130, 132, 137, 148, 302
Moffat, Dr., 83
  son of, 83
Money, its effect in politics, 189, 190, 199, 219, 220; power of in Transvaal, 266-273
Morley, Mr., 236, 262, 285
Moshesh, 153, 154, 161, 165, 177
Mowbray, 17
  its character, 19
Mozilekatze, 84, 152
Mpefu, campaign against, 48
Murray, Sir George, 132
Muizenburg, 17, 120

N

NATAL, 151, 153, 157, 179, 198, 199, 219, 286
  climate of, 39, 44
  coal-fields of, 46
  coast of, 33, 34
  produce of, 39, 40, 43, 44
Natives' belief in ghosts, 47
  effect of surrender on, 226-232
  leaving Transvaal, 48

Natives, races, 115–117
  treatment by Boers, 48, 147, 148, 169
  treatment of, 83, 84, 151, 293-301
Newcastle, Duke of, 155, 160, 161, 162, 166, 168
Newlands, 17
Ngami Lake, 81

O

ORANGE Free State, 103, 147-170, 177, 178, 224, 287, 296
Orange River sovereignty, 144, 157, 159, 160-164, 173

P

PACKINGTON, Sir John, 160
Party Government, weakness of, 235-240
Philips, Dr., 132, 148, 154
Pines, stone, 18
  avenues of, 19
  woods of, 28
Pitsani, 98
Port Elizabeth, Settlement of, 31, 32, 34
  description of, 32, 33
Portuguese, 107-111
Prestige, 218, 242
Pretoria, description of, 57, 58, 169, 199
Pretorius, 84, 85

Q

QUATHLAMBA, 18, 30
  description of, 34
Queenstown, 31

R

RAID, route of, 79
  raids, Boer, 84, 85, 87
Railways in Natal, 46
  to Buluwayo, 81, 82

INDEX

Religion in South Africa, 304-309
Republic, South African, 158, 170, 175, 179
—— New, 167, 168
Retrocession, professed reasons for, 202; reasons to condemn, 234, 235; excuses for, 235-243
Rhodes, Rt. Hon. Cecil J., 19, 20, 21, 85, 86, 87, 95, 97, 99, 140, 145, 180, 226, 257, 258, 261, 262, 263
  anecdotes of, 21, 25
  as capitalist, 56
  character of, 312-315
  influence on natives, 297, 299
Rhodesia, 82, 180, 286
  description of, 91, 94, 95
  hopes for, 92-94
  needs of, 93
Rickshaws, 37
Roberts, Sir F., 206
Robin Island, 15
Robinson, Sir Hercules, 87, 156, 258
Rondebosch, 17

S

Sabi River, 108
Salisbury, 82
Schreiner, Mr., 254
Sea Point, 17
Secocœni, 181, 182, 184, 192
Shashi River, 82
Shepstone, Sir Theophilus, 182-189
Silver Trees, 28
Simon's Bay, 28, 29
Slagter's Nek, 124, 125, 126
Slaves, 117, 118, 148, 178
Slave trade, 133, 135, 147
Smith, Sir Harry, 156, 157, 159, 160, 173
Snakes, 44
  dangers from, 45
Sofala, 108
South Africa, 15
  character of central part, 34
  hospitality in, 38

South Africa, social aspect of, 302, 304
South African College, 15
Spring-Rice, Mr. T., 131
Spruits, 77, 96 (Bronkhurst), 198
St. James, 17
St. John's River, description of, 31
Storms in South Africa, 74-77
Stupidity, English, character of, 195, 196

T

Table Bay, 110, 121, 155
Table Mountain, 15
  its form, 16-17
  its range, 17
Tanganyika, 82
Team driving, 73, 78, 79
Times, testimony of, 206, 207, 291
  on Krüger's proposals, 321
Transvaal, change on entering, 48
  condition of English in, 66,
  encroachments of, 84-87
  high prices in, 49, 81
  mode of finance, 57, 266-275
Transvaal, 98, 102, 112, 114, 115, 158
Trek, Great, 135, 136, 143, 147, 150-153, 173
Tshaka, 151, 293

U

Uitlanders, grievances of, 55, 57, 88, 246; plea for, 250-256, 258, 266
Ulundi, 192, 193
Umzimvoobu, gates of, 31

V

Van der Byl, family of, 27
Veldt, idea of, 69
  effect on imagination, 73, 74
Vitteboomen, 27
Volksraad, description of, 67
Vryburg, 82

W

WARREN, Sir Charles, 87, 180
Wet, De, Sir J., 258
White, Mr. C. K., letters of, 211-217
Willows, great size of, 41, 58
Witwatersrand, appearance of, 49, 55
   characteristics of, 54
—— 190
Wolseley, Sir Garnet, 192, 193, 194, 198, 209, 219, 284

Wood, Sir Evelyn, 199, 200, 205, 223
Wodehouse, Sir P., 85
Woodstock, 17
   its Hospital, 18
Wynberg, 17

Z

ZAMBESI, 152, 283, 312
Zulus, appearance of, 37
—— 84, 151, 153, 173, 178, 182, 190, 192, 194, 219, 282, 283, 284, 294, 295

www.ingramcontent.com/pod-product-compliance
Lightning Source LLC
Chambersburg PA
CBHW030742230426
43667CB00007B/808